The
Star Herbal

The
Star Herbal

previously published as
The Herbal Dinner
(A Renaissance of Cooking)

Robert H. Menzies

Celestial Arts
Millbrae, California

For my grandfather and mother,
each our father and mother,
the spirit of Nicholas Culpeper,
and Nicholas Copernicus, and Darwin.
Especially to all those who have through
ups and downs discovered the recipes
ahead. Within this work a special thanks
to those alchemists and their alcoves
who have shared their kitchens with nature
as we prepared our meals.

Please feel free to embellish and/or color the illustrations in this book to make it *your* Star Herbal!

It is not the intention of the author or the publisher to assume responsibility for claims made about the usefulness of wild plants, whether for food or medicine. Substantiation of those claims too often depends on your ability to identify and properly prepare the plants. This book is a groundwork. It is not meant to replace the advice of your doctor and in no way do either publisher or author attempt to make claims; we merely record historical teachings.

Cover and interior design by Betsy Bruneau

Illustrations by Gale Mathews
Copyright © 1977 by Celestial Arts

CELESTIAL ARTS
231 Adrian Road
Millbrae, California 94030

First Printing, December 1977
Revised edition, June 1981
Made in the United States of America

Library of Congress Cataloging in Publication Data

Menzies, Rob, 1947-
    The Star Herbal.

    1. Cookery (Herbs) 2. Herbs. I. Title.
TX819.H4M46   641.6'5'7   76-53334
ISBN 0-89087-136-1

1 2 3 4 5 6 7 - 86 85 84 83 82 81

Contents

Herbalist's Charter of Henry the VIII

One   It's All Spirit   1

Two   The Planting, Picking, Gathering, Drying and Storing of Roots, Barks, Berries, Flowers, Leaves and Fruit   11

Three   Simples: Medicines which Consist in Their Own Nature   29

Four   Teas   57

Five   Soups   75

Six   Salads and Their Dressings   83

Seven   Grains, Rices, Cereals, Beans, and Nuts   103

Eight   Breads, Their Heads, and the Pleasures of Kneading   119

Nine   Mushrooms and Soma   129

Ten   Meats, Fish, and Fowl   137

Eleven   Brews and Other Yeastly Waters   141

Twelve   Other Extracts   149

Explanation of Medical Properties and Abbreviations   163

Utensils and Measurements   168

Seed Procurement/Stores/Retail and Wholesale   170

Botanical List of Plants   175

Bibliography   195

Index   197

We invoke and address the magical plants; plants that are red, those that are white, and those black and brown herbs, all these do we invoke! Verily the spirits are in control of the infirmities. Herbs, rooted in the seas, mothered by the lands, fathered by the sky!

Plants and herbs of the heavens! Illness and maladies coming from sinfulness do you exorcise! I call upon the creepers, upon those plants that bear the luxurious foliages. These are the herbs that give us life: they multiply by division, they are vigorous, they have strong roots.

O plants and herbs! You have the power to rescue this sufferer!
I call upon and adjure you to make the remedy I shall prepare powerful and effective.

Atharva Veda, Hindu Manual of Magic
Sacred Books of the East
Broomfield, England. 1882

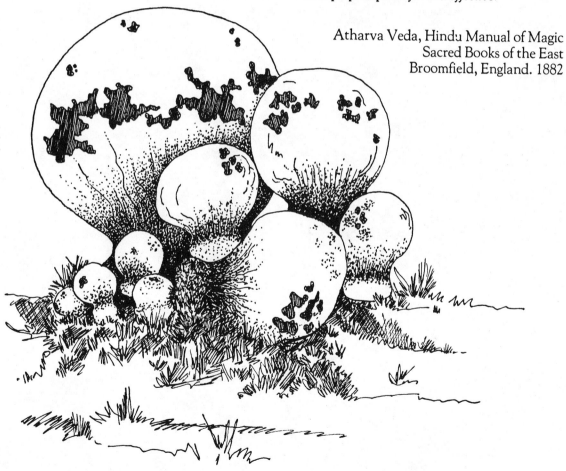

Herbalist's Charter
of Henry the viii
Annis Tircesimo Quarto and Tricesimo Quinto. Henric viii Regis. Cap. viii. An Act That Persons, Being No Common Surgeons, May Administer Outward Medicines

WHERE in the Parliament holden at Westminister in the third Year of the King's most gracious Reign, amongst other Things, for the avoiding of Sorceries, Witchcrafts, and other Inconveniences, it was enacted, that no Person within the I ity of London, nor within Seven Miles of the same, should take upon him to exercise and occupy as Physician or Surgeon, except he be first examined approved, and admitted by the Bishop of London and other, under and upon certain Pains and Penalties in the same Act mentioned: Sithence the making of which said Act, the Company and Fellowship of Surgeons of London, minding only their own Lucres, and nothing, the Profit or ease of the Diseased or Patient, have sued, troubled, and vexed divers honest Persons, as well Men as Women, whom God hath endued with the Knowledge of the Nature, Kind and Operation of certain Herbs, Roots, and Waters, and the using and ministering of them to such as been pained and customable Diseases, as Women's Breasts being sore, a Pin and the Web in the Eye, Uncomes of Hands, Burnings, Scaldings, Sore Mouths, the Stone, Stangury, Saucelim, and Morphew, and such other like Diseases; and yet the said Persons have not taken anything for their Pains or Cunning, but have ministered the same to poor People only for Neighbourhood and God's sake, and of Pity and Charity; And it is now well known that the Surgeons admitted will do no Cure to any Person but where they shall be rewarded with a greater Sum or Reward that the Cure extendeth unto; for in case they would minister their Cunning unto sore People unrewarded, there should not so many rot and perish to death for Lack of Help of Surgery as daily do; but the greatest part of Surgeons admitted been much more to be blamed than those Persons that they troubled, for although the most Part of the Persons of the said Craft of Surgeons have small Cunning yet they will take great sums of Money, and do little therefore, and by Reason thereof they do oftentimes impair and hurt their Patients, rather than do them good. In consideration whereof, and for the Ease, Comfort, Succor, Help, Relief, and Health of the King's poor Subjects, Inhabitants of this Realm, now pained or diseased: Be it ordained, established, and enacted, by Authority of this present Parliament, That at all Time for henceforth it shall be lawful to every Person being the King's subject, having Knowledge and Experience of the Nature of Herbs, Roots, and Waters, or of the Operation of the same, by Speculation or Practice, within any part of the Realm of England, or within any other the King's Dominions, to practice, use, and minister in and to any outward Sore, Uncome Wound, Apostemations, outward Swelling or Disease, any Herb or Herbs, Ointments, Baths, Pultess, and Emplaisters, according to their Cunning, Experience, and Knowledge in any of the Diseases, Sores, and Maladies beforesaid, and all other like to the same, or Drinks for the Stone, Strangury, or Agues, without suit, Vexation, trouble, penalty, or loss of their goods; the foresaid Statute in the foresaid Third Year of the King's most gracious Reign, or any other Act, Ordinance, or Statutes to the contrary heretofore made in anywise, notwithstanding.

The
Star Herbal

*Tis said you've
never met a
Scottish Gardner
till you've been
pricked by
the thistle —*

Amanita

Soma

It's All Spirit

I remember, as if the day were yesterday, walking, listening to those old grandfather tunes about plants and trees, and seeing the earth's bountiful yield through the eyes of a gentle man called Daddy Rob.

The familiar first-remembered scenes of standing with Mums (my grandmother) in her garden by the rhubarb, are clear as the day outside. Aired with life. Simple. Her pies of rhubarb and quince were incredible. Often she would say, in her own polite way, how rhubarb was cleansing.

She would step lightly to pick the stalks for her pie. Once baked it was always sort of redly runny, a delight for the mouth. Crust from scratch, with nutmeg and a touch of cinnamon, possibly sassafras.

All about their home were living friends. The rosebush had hummingbird nests and young within. I can still feel the branches and brambles of fig, quince, apple, grape, and wild berries. The vegetables, half of which I can only guess at today, appeared on the table as daily food.

Other memories arise — how Daddy Rob passed the thought to his son, then to me, that if you add anything to the soil other than what is grown from the weeds, leaves, and local composting of the soil, you'll always have to add other things, and that only becomes technologically confused. Go forage for humus. Or better, make compost by using naturally decomposed material; look for the way nature farms, and follow her plan.

I remember once Daddy Rob stopped by an outcropped rock on this magical mountainside, paused a long moment, and said, "These rocks are the evening warmth for their plant neighbors. They charge the water received from their body, store it within the mosses and lichens, and then feed the air — purifying ferns and plant life about."

Plantain Daddy Rob called Indian buckwheat. He did so because of the Indian's way of taking the seeds, crushing and mixing them with water, and letting the sun soak into the mixture like a buckwheat cake (but harder). Good.

Not long ago a group of friends and I stepped out to gather the seed, and along with the Indian buckwheat we found an abundance of fennel seed. Gathering both we made it into bread. I share these stories hoping you will receive a bit of the spirit as I have, passed from elder to younger and still going onward.

The feeling comes through me of all our pasts, the lessons we learn as forest children, old oak folk song of green. I look toward Mt. Tamalpais, the Sleeping Lady, named for the Princess Tamalpa of the Miwok, a spirit mountain truly. There, hidden meadows receive the daily dews, and the crystalled waters become a vibrant part of the power of this place. If you have not walked about such wonders, treat yourself sometime. You'll find the trees and herbs, growing in masses, springs by their feet, creeks and all wildlife abundant.

The many trails I have walked have shown me, the son and grandson who writes these words, a world within and without that has only extended the paths once walked and dreamed of by my elders. For in their visions I have learned to know the many living friends called plants.

There are so many plants, yet each walk yields a new friend. Possibly a mushroom of edible splendor. The day's salad picked clean—watercress, green, its watered breath touched, warming. And ah! some lamb's-quarters, dandelion, and fresh dock. Like the wilderness areas of the world, our bodies represent such wilderness, remaining as mysterious to scientists as did the new-found forests of our ancestors. To fear the body is to fear yourself. Listen and see; walk with reverence.

"What is an herb?" the scholar Alcuin is said to have asked his pupil Charlemagne. The reply was, "The friend of physicians and the praise of cooks."

Man's earliest cave writing tells of gathering honey (Spider Cave, Valencia). Much of man's basic effort has been in foraging, identifying as best he could, and preparing almost everything in nature as food.

Whether for survival or ritual, taste or smell, man's roots run deep into the instinctual peat of evolution. There were certainly many trials with nature and some errors in instinct—sometimes painful, many times enlightening.

Plantain, dandelion, rose hips, clover, alfalfa, and garlic have been in the fields as weeds for centuries. When our ancestors were unable to seek out the advice of a physician, they turned to nature's pharmacy. Though they could not say a plant had this vitamin or that mineral, they laid the groundwork for a greater understanding of plants as food and medicine. Many of these early contributors could only rely on past experience and instinctual awareness. The elders cared for the young and those in between cared ritually for both. Learning and giving.

The herbs of the field were sacred to early man. Many believed the gods had a great plan for the plants to cure the human ill- or dis-ease. When properly prepared and applied, each plant part could alleviate suffering or develop the spiritual, mental, moral, or physical powers.

In Turkey, as well as here in the U.S, the plant Hermodactyl (literally, "Hermes' finger") a species of colchicum, known also as meadow saffron or autumn crocus, has long been used as a cathartic. Is it at all difficult to imagine that those people who gave the name Hermodactyl to a flower with curative properties recognized the frequencies coming through the crocus as coming from our Source of Creation?

Pythagoras, the father of philosophy, often proclaimed the virtue of foods. Once

he declared that mental and reasoning faculties became clouded by eating meat. He did not condemn its use or abstain totally himself, for moderation seemed to rule his philosophy, as it should ours. In his condemnation, however, he went so far as to declare that judges should refrain from eating meat before a trial, in order that those who came before them might receive the most honest and clear decision.

Often when Pythagoras decided to retire into the temple of God for unlimited periods of meditation and prayer, he took with him supplies of specially prepared food and drink. His food consisted of equal parts of poppy and seeds, the skin of a sea onion from which he extracted the juice, flowers of daffodil, leaves of mallow, and a paste of barley and peas, as well as wild honey. For a beverage he gathered and prepared the seeds of cucumber, wild grapes, mallow, and plantain, the flowers of coriander, scraped cheese, meal, and cream, and sweetened the mixture with wild honey. This he claimed to be the diet of Hercules, which he had learned during his meditations.

Many of the ancients' recipes, now lost, would be of incredible value in rebalancing disharmony today. Yet many remain only dusty tales on a shelf awaiting our discovery. In Sri Lanka, the orchid Dendrobium has long been recognized as having properties that heal. In Buddhist mythology about the mountain known as Adam's Peak, each roof and terraced garden has this orchid growing in profusion. Its flowers are at their most beautiful during Wesak, the Buddhist festival in May. The blooms are worn in the hair of children and women, and they are supposed to possess special virtues at that time. The frequencies coming through the blossoms are reputed to make one feel better. Just what our foods should do.

Great Britain has long had a tradition of healing with herbs and flowers. Agrimony was considered useful for liver troubles. Peppermint helped deal with putrefaction and flatulence. Violets reduced headache and inflammations of the lungs. Wormwood cured wasp stings and flushed worms from the body, while yarrow (named after Achilles) was good for wounds, stomach pains, toothache, and blisters. In other parts of the world, the Hawaiian Kahuna, the shaman of Indian tribes, the brujo, and others have all employed natural entities in curing. Many of these natural substances have been refined and synthesized into staples of modern pharmacology. For example, a tea of willow bark was once used to relieve aches and pains. In the early 1800s salicin was extracted from willow bark and leaves and later was synthesized into acetylsalicylic acid, or aspirin.

What of man several centuries ago? What were his foods? His tastes? His awareness of the frequencies within these plants? Over time the Doctrine of Signatures was developed. It holds that each plant part relates to a body part, and that each plant is good for a corresponding organ or member of the body. When we apply this practically we find how to apply the plant parts for our use.

Those who would enter the world of herbs can follow this doctrine in learning not only the qualities, but also the forms of *simples*. (Simples here are defined as medicines which consist in their own nature.) Correctly used, plants have consistently cured disease, resisted poison, borne and yielded food, and helped heal sores—all at no cost but the personal interaction.

The Tree of Life I'm sure is nothing more than knowledge disguised as nature. Living in the wilds will show us this. There we can discover that instinct is an incredible teacher. Let us pause to catalog the plant's part by the Doctrine of Signatures and then take a paper walk of some of the habitats and see what's to be found.

ROOTS—as our feet are nourishers to our bodies.

STALKS—transmitters of nourishment through our bodies.

LEAVES—the body's organs and tissue.

FLOWERS—earthy matter that has become refined in vibration by color and form: brain stimulus.

SEED—the vital germ for life's procreation.

As we set off on our paper walk, we leave the fences and hedges heading toward the road and passing the familiar mugwort, cinquefoil, hounds tongue, shepherd's purse, and flaxweed. We pass chickweed, dock, groundsels, nettles, bindweed, poppy, hemlock, and horehound on the slope. Knotweed, yarrow, doggrass, trefoil, and ladies' bedstraw gather on a sunny slope with iris, larkspur, narcissus, snapdragons, and tulips; a few of the physics angelica, fennel, saffron, and masterwort; and then the real space takers, vetch, lupin, and wild pea. (Though these last three contribute neither food nor medicine, they take in our pollution and give us back fresher air.) In a boggy area we see horsemint, horsetail, and small valerian; a meadow abounds with burnet, cockscomb, and saxifrage. We climb a plantain-covered bank and plunge into the woods among tormentil, agrimony, wild strawberry, St. John's wort, wood betony, wood sorrel, and fiddleheads. Truly if we were to continue on this walk, the list of plants would be endless. These are the more common in their habitats. Once we begin to recognize the habitats we can go anywhere and find at least half of these plants and many more of local origin. Having observed these plants on our walk in nature we find no random makeup of the plants for our use.

The following list of herbs is by no means complete, but it will allow the beginning of insight, another step toward better understanding of our natural surroundings in relation to our bodies.

ginger viola tricolor godu kola heart trefoil	heart
comfrey borage mullein	hairs on the leaf like the hairs about the tongue, in lungs as alveolae, and through the stomach and intestines as cilia
sage rosemary	lungs
goldenrod	intestines
chamomile	eyes
adder's tongue snakeroot	poisonous snake bite wounds
hound's tongue	cleans poison like a dog's tongue
Solomon's seal	a sealing plant for wounds
walnuts	shaped like our skull, environed in a shell, wrapped in tissue covering, as is our brain.
kidney beans mugwort	liver, kidney
peppermint	stomach, lungs
St. John's wort	very thick leaves with small holes, as the pores of our skin

Chickweed

olive
           the emblem of peace on
           Solomon's temple; to
           eat of the olive brings
           peace to our temple

Since the ancient Doctrine of Signatures has not been widely known, it's easy to understand why many would scoff at the idea of relating plant and body parts, yet the more aware one becomes of life's garden the more relevant this doctrine appears.

The ancients—Hippocrates, Pliny, Galen, and more of course—had no laboratories. There was only that which nature and her ways provided. No synthetics, no elaborate medical institutions of massed machinery and paper, just the everyday interaction, reaction, and observation of nature that will ever keep us involved when we work with her.

The Doctrine of Signatures still awaits full discovery, as many medicines have yet to be discovered, but there is validity in the belief that nature provides at the time of need. The doctrine also holds that small increments over a long period of time are better than large doses all at once. We must condition ourselves to moderation.

In the past decade in every part of the world, especially the United States, new interest has arisen in our wayside friend, the herb, called weed by many; defined as aromatic, possibly tonic; shrouded in stories and old wives' tales; for eating, curing, or ritual, much has been said and volumes written about the humble herb. Many seeking new paths toward a more natural means of existence have learned of families of plants that have fed the peoples of the world since recorded history began. Many of these foods have become medicines, some widely used in their time and now forgotten, many remembered and used even now.

These hardy perennial plants grow better without much attention from man. With the aid of modern pathology, we have found that they consistently show the presence of natural concentrated nutrients. Old stories are being traced to their sources. We find a plant being used for this disease or that, and we discover yet a new property, a new plant having origins as old as the culture using it. This appears to be true in every area where one could possibly have a need. At a time of need what we need is at our feet. Ironic as it seems, with all our modern technology, there are still discoveries to be made about plants. Within their structure exists a property that we cannot yet duplicate; what nature does so neatly anyway—growing in balance.

A new way of cooking, or possibly an old remembered way, is arising in accord with nature's way. It is a change from the "bulk processed," "fully balanced," and "enriched" foods that bombard us daily.

To greet nature's foods, the essences and spirits, with enthusiasm and reverence will lead the seeker to higher forms of cooking appreciation. The gathering, chopping, grinding, blending, simmering, boiling, and other processes involved in the preparation ritual reaffirm the knowledge that each thing we touch when working within nature's balance has a unique action, and the final dish is a work of art, with soul, in tune with the universe.

In many countries today, the daily preparation of food is in tune with the natural cycle of things as reflected in nature. There are Chinese dishes presented at the commonest of tables that are the seeds of perfected thought; each dish is its own medicine, evolved from three centuries and more of balancing.

The people of the world who have experienced longevity know the planting of good thoughts, the proper cultivation with good air and water, the harvesting exercise and rest, the body's mind and soul. They regard themselves in the balance of nature's hand. Elsewhere highly technological societies are just becoming aware that nature exists— and our awareness moves us closer to her balance.

We who forage for our foods and prepare our daily sustenance from them have long sought foods and waters that were more concentrated forms of nutrient. Such foods as seeds, fruits, pollens (honeys) and the wayside plants contain those concentrated nutrients. The plants share their being.

There is an inner voice, an inner nature that runs within us, through the plants. Animal-Mineral-Vegetable—Air-Earth-Fire-Water. Our bodies, minds, and spirits naturally become more in balance as the plants act on us, giving us their air, their aroma, their fiber, and their life.

As in past centuries, many are beginning to "hear" and "see" relationships between the plants' anatomy and their own. This relationship begins with the gradual incorporation of plants in one's daily diet. Being with the food from seed to tabled harvest is but one complete ritual. Everyone, alone or as a whole, is connected to that same center, our source, our creation and creator, by an invisible frequency that carries what may best be called Life Force. There is an inner hearing and seeing relationship that requires the will to be in balance with nature—a commitment certainly—and a lifelong path toward harmony.

People sensitive to nature feel this Life Force. They feel in each food, no matter what form, a different frequency.

There are places on earth where people live in harmony, and in those places we see foods being prepared in harmony. But man has so abused nature that disharmony seems to be rampant. The symptoms are expressed by disease in both animal and plant life. Extinction of whole species of plants and animals continues, while countries boast of peace as they arm the world. There must be alternatives that will lead to a more harmonious place about the table. Suppression of cures that use raw plants, though there are many working validly in the field, is not fair to nature or ourselves. Finding a better way to adapt, use, and correct this imbalance is one reason for this book. Each meal of life can have a more apparent meaning if each of us will take more responsibility for ourselves and our environment.

There are many reasons why people are becoming aware of their inner hearing and sight. Pestilence often affects cultivated crops while the weeds are still standing well-rooted and strong. Drought strangles the upper growth of many of our cultivated plants, yet weeds thrive because their root structures thrust many times deeper into the earth to seek water. They become, at a time of need, a supplemental source of food once very primary to man's early existence.

One such plant is the alfalfa—the Arabs call it "the Father of all Foods." It is unique in the plant world because its root structure may reach as much as six hundred feet through the earth. What a marvelous thing to have such a structure of roots! How much greater is the absorption area for minerals and vitamins of such a plant.

In Arabic al-fal-fa was named before laboratories knew anything about its innards. Is it not ironic that these people without scientific apparatus and technology could be so aware? They watched their animals eat alfalfa and work hard, and when they ate the plant they too could work hard.

Today alfalfa and seaweed products occupy an honored place on our shelf of herbs. Ground into meal or sprouted, made into tea or tablet, eaten as seed, or as a food

supplement, alfalfa provides the organic minerals magnesium, calcium, phosphorus, and potassium, plus all the well- known vitamins and the newly discovered vitamins K, B_8, and P. They are used as an organic base for today's ubiquitous high potency vitamins. But why buy a bottle of tablets for two dollars when you can get a pound of alfalfa seeds for the same price, and sprout a *living* product?

Many are beginning the nomadic journey toward raising their consciousness. To do so with foods requires an understanding of the everyday use of our plant friends. Preparation is as important as the gathering of a food for medicine. The ground, our earth, our magnetic balance, centers us and our daily bread.

When picking from the garden tomatoes, parsley, plantain, comfrey, and radish for my dinner salad, a poetic thought:

> *Somehow I am uneased,*
> *to eat,*
> *Whatever has a soul.*

TWO

The Planting, Picking, Gathering, Drying and Storing of Roots, Barks, Berries, Flowers, Leaves and Fruit

Planning and growing a garden is best accomplished by observing nature's way and following her plan. Utilize rock for boundaries, create a forest by mounding a corner plot and planting a hardwood with some ferns beneath. Observe the many native varieties of plants, the more common of which can be gathered as you learn. Seed collected soil is most applicable for cultivated varieties of herbs. I would want a dry spot for those from which to receive the oils. For vegetables and flowers, a rich nitrahumus soil is best. There is no mystery to observing plants. Each time you walk be sure to notice the varied climes and natural habitats. Imprint this on your mind and transfer the thought to your garden.

Like the everbearing plants, the hardier are the varieties of herbals. Medicinal, culinary, psychic. Annual, biennial, perennial. Each climate is different as is each garden's walkway. Cultivate according to your own needs. Place mints in cooling corners of your home or near faucets or troughs where water is received. But with all plants give their roots some natural irrigation; to do otherwise is to drown them. Mints and pennyroyal like water areas, but sage would not. Mulching your garden with nature's materials, manure and so forth is great. Horse droppings and oat hulls—primo. If rice hulls are available, excellent. Your own excrement if properly digested. Accord the food from the land back to the land. Chemicals cause bacteria that make much waste until totally recycled. But we're getting closer. In the Orient, *Yakto* (night dirt plus seed) is a word for human waste that is digested naturally into the field, aerated, and then produces the richest foods to be seen. This is done every three years for proper soil amending, naturally, with such plants as comfrey and ginseng.

Composting directly into the ground in pits, or special bins is natural. There is much information available at many hardware stores. The old compost piles, as grandad's, were just in a heap, or over the

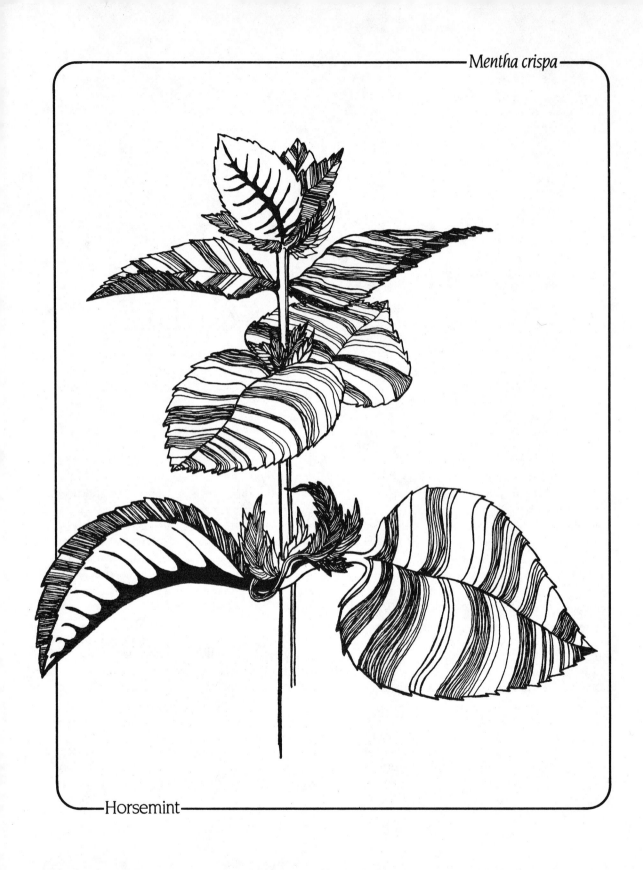

Mentha crispa

Horsemint

side of the hill. Huge vegetables, herbs and fruits have sprung from many a compost pile, unbeknown to the keeper. The bottom was rich, digested from a few years' grass clippings, field leftovers, tree leaves and an occasional bucket of kitchen waste. Racoon food. Rat food. Beware of neighbors and city ordinances.

Cultivating planter boxes in an apartment in the city can be accomplished given some light during the day, proper watering, and a breeze by the leafed friends. Spray now and again. Hardier types which will grow in cities are parsley, chives, oregano, mint, thyme and sage. Last year in a desert city I observed how a friend had placed book shelving next to a window and instead of books there were growing several terraces of potted herbs. Wonderful. I've seen lettuce done this way but for more nutritional utilization of space, sprouts (seed sprouts as alfalfa, mung, soy, red wheat, etc.) or dandelion are compact in their growth. All there for your needs.

Arrangement is totally up to the beholder of the space. Square—a circle—a triangle or rectangle. Because of drought in many parts of the country I saw where people who had lawns, but could not water because of rationing, turned their lawns into gardens, cutting a pattern, leaving grass for walkways. A beautiful symmetry was seen, utilizing space, and because a garden was permitted, hand watering was allowed.

Most herbs don't get too hassled by bugs. Many have too much resin and the aroma given off is too strong for the little buggers. The snails like comfrey, but placing fireash around will hinder them. They stay away from pennyroyal, tansy and rue. The lady bug is one of many garden friends to help with balancing diseased plants.

When collecting seeds observe the plant's habitat. Your own experience is the best possible guide. If you're hobbying about, then growing herbs is fantastic for the air you live in. There are five main families of herbs:

BORAGINACEAE

Includes borage, forget-me-not, heliotrope and alkanet.

COMPOSITAE

Includes the artemisiae as mugwort, wormwood and dusty miller, chicory, chrysanthemums, tansy, calendula, and daisy.

LABIATAE

Includes mints, spearmint, peppermint, orange-mint, pineapple-mint, basil, sage, rosemary, lavender, horehound, and thyme.

CRUCIFERAE

Includes watercress, peppergrass and mustards.

UMBELLIFERAE

Includes anise, caraway, chervil, coriander, dill, fennel, cumin, lovage, pimpernil, parsley, carrot, myrrh. Many good pamphlets and catalogues are available from the sources listed under "Procurement" at the end of this book.

The tool which is used is as important as the foraging and gathering itself. A sharp knife has always been companion to the outdoor person. The obsidian glass of mountain stone chipped till sharpened will strip off hide or bark of root, and cut the branch, yielding stick to dig for tuber and roots. Yes, you may pull the root of the plant, but as with the bark, let it yield its being to you. Don't force or yank but rather, if you need, dig with a stick. If there is a forge available (or hardware store) then a small pack shovel works well. Remember the military supply stores that sell old relic war trench shovels— good bargain and well made, small and available for our utilization. Although we cannot ascribe to war, some tools that man has developed are of use and benefit to evolution. The stone mortar and pestle, and stone milling blocks for grinding grain into flour are timely wonders.

There are really no set rules for cultivation or foraging. Best to seek out those who work with the tools in that area, seek their knowledge and as you gain experience the daily lesson will be your guide. There is a reverent agreement among those who forage of inner commitment to do so in the most harmonious way we know with nature and her products.

Stories of the ginseng being hunted at night tell of spotting the glow of a blue aura about the plant, and placing an arrow marked with a red swatch by the plant to gather on the morrow. Never touch the root with hand, it is said, for thus it may loose its power. Take a gathering stick with forked point and dig about the root so it gives of itself for your spirit. Or how the best growing garlic is planted in the full of a moon and before the frost; or the cabbage planted so the roots are on a slope to grow better.

When you cultivate your wild plants keep the area weeded of other weeds. Potentize the soil with compost, the essence of the plant. Some, such as mints, should be moved every now and again as they leach the soil. But as you work with these you will see, as in olden fields, that much nitrahumus (good natural manure) high in nitrogen or active life force bacteria—and

love—with good water and pleasant surroundings best serve your cultivated medicinal, culinary and psychic herbals. Observe every organic and inorganic situation (environment and stimuli) that is about the plant you are taking from the wild to the cultivated state and insofar as possible recreate that habitat. When you know this mundane chemical (organic or inorganic) relationship you begin to transmute your life force (psychic and parapsychic) through the alchemy of the herbal.

The different parts of the plants yield each their properties according to a divine plan of nature. A plant, such as dandelion, has its roots, stem, leaf, flower and seed, each yielding different strengths. A tree has also these parts but bark becomes a more apparent entity than it is on smaller herbs.

Throughout this book the word "herb" is used and the following definition, from Webster's Dictionary, 1930 India edition (The Merriam Company), is entered to help align our thoughts toward reverently fathering the meal:

(1) . . . herbs are annual, biennial, or perennial according to the length of life of their roots.
(2) Grass or herbage collectively.
(3) A plant of economic value; specifically one used for medicinal purposes or for its sweet scent or flavor.

Within the structure of plants we see many properties given to us for our aware use. Through the extracts from the gums and balsams of plants and trees come oils, in each of their structures are their salts, minerals, and earthy substances. If we were to extract all the properties mentioned we would be left with the gross matter. This, in turn, upon proper preparation will yield ash; then, a growth of the plant in the

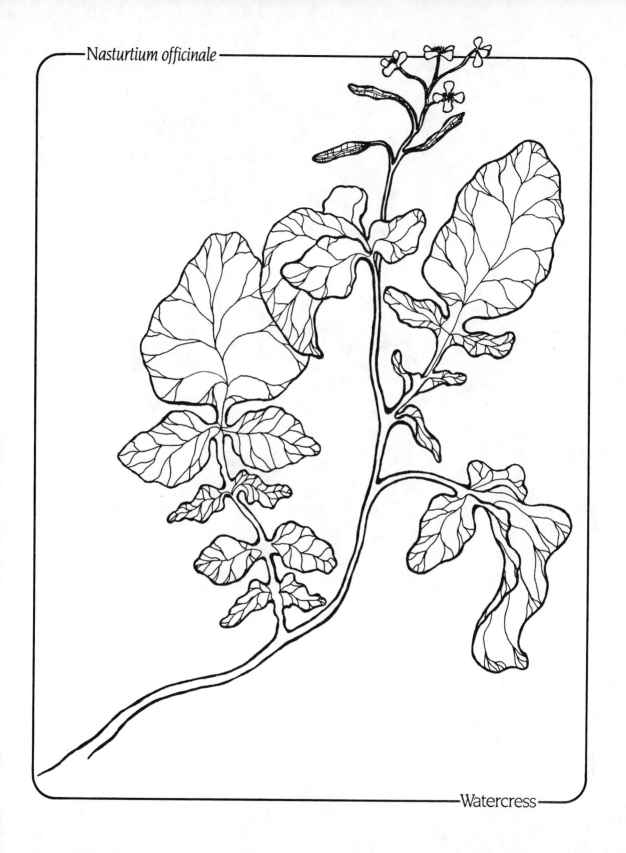

Nasturtium officinale

Watercress

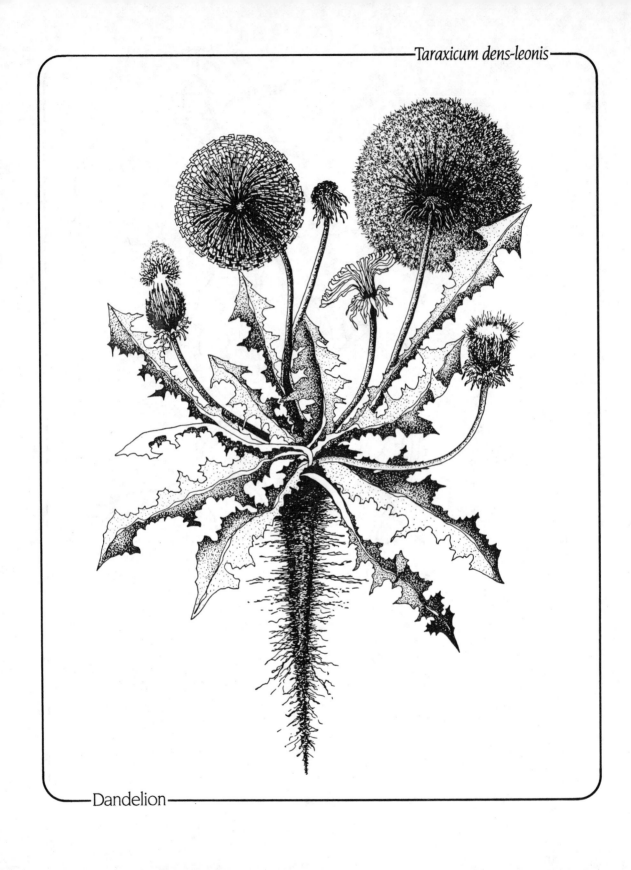

Dandelion

form of crystals or clarified salts. All may be aligned to read simply as:

The plant itself:

> *its root*
> *stalk*
> *leaf*
> *flower*
> *seed*
> *or   bark*

> *yield gum*

> *oil or balsam*
> *salt*
> *mineral*
> *earthy substance*
> *crystal*

Do not fear that which you are about to do. Interact with the thought that the exchange is as vital as is the final product for consumption. This will allow all those little, reverent thoughts to compile a fine collection of nature's products. Your interaction will stimulate the growth of the plants when properly applied. Like digging comfrey. If you want it totally out of the ground a potato digger or pig will do the trick. Machine or animal. No matter how hard your hands may work, getting the comfrey to completely yield itself seems almost as impossible a task as getting out all of a dandelion root. A weed is a weed, and a weed indeed is better than a bird in the bush. Depending, of course, on its final use, your interaction and involvement and the way the plant part feels about your using it. Why not ask the plant next time you begin to forage it or its products, "Ah, pine tree, will it be all right to have some of your pitch?" or "Hey, dandelion, may I have some of your leaves?" Sure. But asking first always seems to be such a nice thing to do. Even though those fruits on someone's ground look nice, don't you think we

ought to ask and thank? Good manners help for better spiritual intonations between plants and persons.

TO GATHER THE ROOTS:

Roots must be gathered in spring or fall while the sap is rising or as the sap is falling. As the first green leaves peek above the ground, the essence within the plant is rising. The best time to gather would be on a day in early spring when the weather has been dry so the root does not rot when drying. Many of our more oiled plants, as seal or seng (golden seal and ginseng) are best gathered in the "fall dug" (as it is called by the forager) when the ground is dry and the plant has had its full cycle for the season, making the oils therein stronger. Certainly many spring tonics, as dandelion or poke, yellow dock or plantain may be gathered during the spring. But if the plant is not as abundant and patience can be afforded, wait till the fall when the sap is falling.

TO GATHER THE BARKS:

The best time is during the fall when the bark may be stripped without hurting the skin underneath. Many trees and shrubs yield their barks at other times of the year. Thus, it is best to gather when the bark may be stripped and the sap prevents it from adhering to the wood. As with a scab formed on a cut on the body, we would not want to pull away new tissue. A tree or shrub has the same feeling when we gather its bark, though not as pronounced as our own. Be aware. Many old practices required the whole tree be lost just to get its bark or sap for production. Some trees had to be completely dug up to get their roots. Reverence in using only what one needs is certainly the rule.

To Gather the Leaves

Pick leaves just before the flower blooms when the essence is at its height. Many leaves can be smelled merely by their emitted aroma. Others need only be touched to give off an aroma so strong that you'd believe they held a message for your nose. Like flowers and seeds, gather leaves at the rising of the noonday sun, after the dew has dried but before it gets so hot the essential oil is dissipated or traveling back to join the plant to rest at night. In this way you prevent mold or rot when drying and the oils are not diluted with water. The more you are within the fields the more you will become aware of this right time. If you watch for the light this renaissance is inevitable.

To Gather the Sap of Trees

It is best to observe a native or local forager in their techniques. Maple syrup is gathered in the winter months and pine pitch during the summer months. Each tree yields according to its own design within nature. We all know of the frankincense and myrrh—saps also. The first item in trade between man may very well have been amber, also a sap. A bruise on a part of the tree yields, like a scab on our body, the sap for protection. All saps, like our blood, contain cleansing properties.

To Gather the Flowers and Seeds

One should gather flowers and seeds at the height of their ripeness, or essence. Only patient and sensitive observation will teach you this. But for the novice, understanding that there is a proper time will be sufficient. The more time you spend in the field the more significant the statement, "pick at its height," will become to you. You will see the flowers color more uniquely, some see this as an aura; the seed will darken when it is about to drop. Many plants, especially the herbs, will never bear seed all at once. Thus constantly returning seed to the earth prevents the loss of plant life which gives these herbs their everbearing quality. Some herbs, such as basil, are annual and loose their seed about the same time. But by careful observation you should have enough for the next year. Other herbs need never be reseeded. For this they are called weeds, and will always bear multiple amounts of seed.

Preparation for Building the Home Herb Picker

If you have a great deal of seeds or flowers to gather then building a homemade picker will help since hand picking is laborious. A wooden box serves the purpose well. The exact size is up to the handler but take a box approximately twelve inches wide, sixteen inches long and six inches deep. Take off one end, and attach a strong strip to act as a handle to the remaining sides. Use a strong piece of wood about one inch wide and place nails (2½" long) approximately ½ inch apart in a line to form a comb. This is swung through the flowers or seed to snap off the part to be gathered. As you fill your picker you can transfer the gathered material into another, larger container. Or simply use a beater, such as Scotch broom or chaparral tied together, and a gather bag or basket.

Some seeds, such as fennel, anise and coriander, are harvested a bit before ripe in order to retain a good appearance. This is especially important if you're marketing your seed. Dry your seed as you would roots; spread them out to dry and turn regularly. When stored dry they will not rot.

To Gather the Fruits

One almost has to be on top of the fruit as it falls. It should be firm but tender. Ripeness shows itself by color and aroma depending upon the fruit. After the dew has dried gather the fruit at the rising of the noonday sun. Many times observance of the wildlife, especially the birds, will show the picker when the time is right. Their instinct is a bit more sharply developed than that of the human species and they are aware when the fruit reaches its fullness. Your awareness will expand as your experience increases.

To Dry Roots

Roots require a thorough washing. Hang roots so the oil runs into the root and in the same direction as you pulled it from the ground. Some, as seng, are strung through the root with string and hung to dry solidly. Immerse in dry sand for long term preservation or place on a drying rack, in a moderate oven (250° F) till dry. Large roots are usually sliced or split, spread thinly on a clean surface.

It is a good practice to gently stir the roots as they dry on screens. Both roots and leaves require good ventilation while drying. To protect the color from changing don't expose them to the sun. Mold or browning will manifest if you have harvested the root wet. When dried, each will be greatly less than the original size when gathered. When you, the forager, are there for a time in the actual doing experience you will observe these truths and develop much insight.

To Dry the Leaves

Place leaves in a paper bag (upside down so oils run into leaf) and out of the sun where there is a good air flow. In about three days you may crush the bag so the leaf looses itself within.

Preparation of the Herb Drying Box

Or, you may wish to build a drying box. This is done by using a wooden crate which has a top to protect the leaves from sunlight. The bottom should be of wire mesh (preferable nonrust and not aluminum) or linen, or any material which allows good passage of air through it. Raise it off the ground at least a foot by legs or other means. Place the herb inside giving the leaf ample breathing space. The weather will determine how fast the leaves will dry.

A simple and convenient alternative is to hang them upside down in your kitchen and use when cooking as the spirit so desires.

To Dry the Flowers

The same methods employed for roots and leaves may be used for flowers or you can use drying powders. Use alumroot powder, plaster of paris, chalk, baking soda, powdered sugar, orrisroot powder, borax or there are many others. The flower should be as freshly gathered as possible. Put down a layer of powder and place the flowers on top. Then cover with another layer of powder and so forth. Some powders will change the color of the flower but repeatedly borax seems to yield consistently good results when using a drying powder. The gentleness of the flower and purpose for which it is to be used will determine the best method. I have crushed flowers by the weight of the powder at times. Tissue paper will tend to flatten also.

The method which I have found to work best, over and over, is the simplest method, hang drying. The flower should be gathered at its height, then, when dry, separated from the stem and placed in an airtight container.

Herbs should be washed to rid the leaves of pests. Some have residue from the garden washing which tends to dissipate their taste and quality. Pick off the dead or old leaves. Rinse, and drain till dry. It is always best to work with one herb or fruit at a time thus not to confuse and mix the scents.

To Store Properly

Make sure the container you use has been thoroughly cleaned and dried for if any water remains in the container, mold and rot is sure to follow. You will also want to make sure the product to be stored is also totally dry. It is said that when properly stored products of nature may be kept indefinitely. Often insect insurance demands the addition of dried bay leaves, mugwort and/or aromatic leaves as pennyroyal. Season to season use is preferable. In the case of some of the rare seeds only a small amount may be available until who knows when. Then proper storage becomes even more important. I have found the products of nature will keep longer at higher altitudes as opposed to being stored at sea level, the difference in air and moisture.

An interesting lesson was learned about altitudes of ten thousand plus feet and loving seed sprouts. I gathered many different seeds to sprout for a backpack trip into the mountains. However, I found even alfalfa would not break for at least five days. Later I learned the lack of air set back the germination time so it takes longer than at sea level. Now when I go into the high country I start seed before my departure and let it continue as I go higher.

In storing, a label will help to determine what it is you've done as the years go by. This is true of any recipe you concoct. After all, if it turns out well it's nice to know how to repeat the performance. This helps you and those to follow you.

Before one even gets to my front door the smell of herbs sends greetings. Upon entering the house hundreds of bottles may be observed in various stages of herbal development. Herbs, dried, drying, vinegars, beers, sachets, and the like are all about. I have learned to keep a running notebook, and instead of writing information on labels, ascribe a number or code and if I need, refer to the book for clarification. I've had a few years to develop this method. A simple label is all one really needs. It may seem a picky point but is essential—for memory can play tricks on even the most attuned of eyes and noses.

If none of these methods appeal you can freeze your herbs if you so desire. But when properly gathered and prepared freezing seems overly technical. A root cellar is closer to the spirit.

Drying Techniques for Vegetables, Fruit and Most Foods in General

Most foods can be dried quite successfully in the sun. Your own ovens, would be ideal. Modern ovens work well however and gas is preferred to electric. Both are incredible energy sources although gas causes smog inside the house! If you have a wood stove the flavor is never to be beaten. Include some herbs with the burning wood and notice the different aromas in the smoke as the foods are drying. But for simplicity the sun will never be replaced as a center of energy. As with the earth and its moon, there is a push and pull that seems better than all of our ovens, save maybe

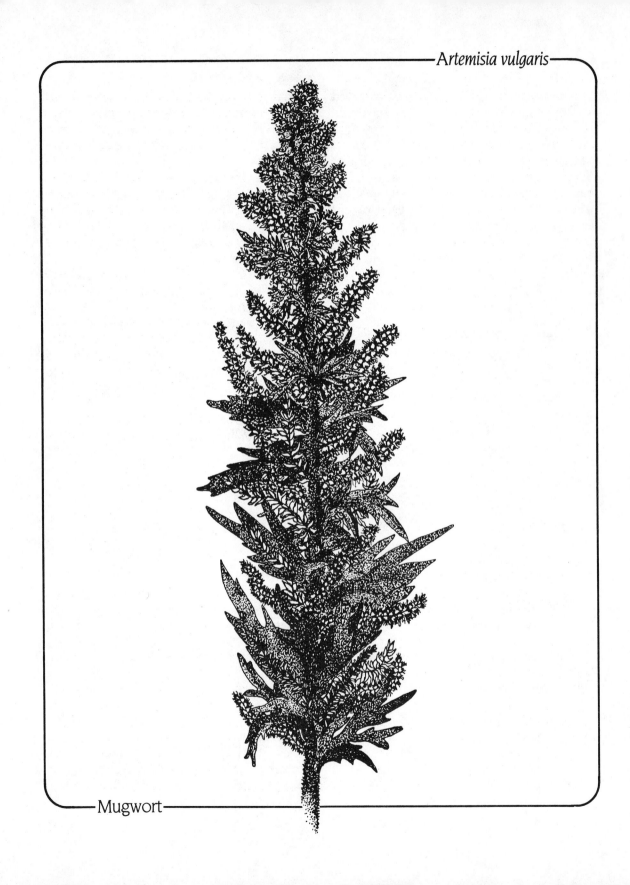

Mugwort

our woodburners — but then there is the wood to be considered.

I remember first seeing fruits of my grandparents, trays filled with figs drying and grapes (turned raisins). I recall even to this moment the taste and smells as I ate during the winter months. But we are talking of the techniques of drying. Ah—the aquarian!

Another sun drier may be built according to your own needs and space. As mentioned, cloth or quarter-inch wire mesh for the bottom of the shelf or total enclosure is best to keep out flies and bugs. The fruitfly will always be here it seems but hanging pennyroyal or tansy about the dryer will help. Do avoid touching the herb to the drying fruit or veggie as this may slightly change or taint the taste! An old refrigerator, or upright freezer that has been discarded makes a fine dehydrator. Build your shelves four to five inches apart, install a small heater-type fan in the bottom and many hours of dehydration time will be eliminated. Of course it will use more electricity unless you have solar batteries or windmill storage units. Provide some vents in the roof of the dryer for better air circulation and load the trays so there is ample space between the fruits or vegetables. The old shelf covered with cloth works well and saves loading and unloading time. When drying in electric or gas ovens 140° F is about right. Stir or turn food regularly and shift the trays every half hour or so if needed for even drying. Fruits retain from ten to twenty-five percent moisture, vegetables slightly less, when they are dried. Seeds usually don't have to be dried because they are sun ripened when harvested and ready for planting or grinding.

Store all dried foods in a cool dark storage space in airtight containers. If you have stored grains, rices, beans or seeds and they become moist, heat them in a 200° F. oven for about a half hour to dry, then repack. In Seymour, Indiana, I saw onion skin and garlic skin used as a moisture retardant instead of saltine crackers or silicon bags. When I got a cooking space of my own where I stored grains, I tried this. It works and I still use it to this day. More aesthetically pleasing than the modern techniques.

Following are a few of the fruits and vegetables that I have charted for reference when drying. This was done in a coastal area and when tried inland it took less time. The drying test works best. Touch it! Then taste it!

NATURAL PRODUCT	PREPARATION	TOUCH TEST
Apples	Peel and core. Slice ¼" rings.	Springy and pliable.
Apricots	Cut in half and remove the pit. Pit may be dried off to the side and used later.	Pliable.
Beets	Peel and slice ¼" cubes or rings.	Brittle.
Berries (gooseberry, blackberry, raspberry, strawberry)	No preparation. Strawberries should be halved.	No longer moist to the touch.
Carrots	Peel and cut ¼" slices or strips. Steaming first speeds drying.	Very brittle.

Natural Product	Preparation	Touch Test
Cherries	Pit and drain well.	Pliable but still sticky.
Grapes	Need no preparation, but steaming. to break the skin helps.	Pliable.
Wild greens	Cut off the tough parts to prevent the leaf from bunching up.	Crisp.
Mushrooms	Trim and remove tough parts. May be dried whole or sliced to ¼" pieces.	Crisp or brittle
Onions	Peel the skin and slice to ¼" pieces or rings.	Crisp.
Peaches	Peel if you desire but not necessary. Halve and remove pit. Dry with the pit side up.	Pliable.
Pears	Peel, core and discard woody material. Cut into ¼" slices.	Pliable.
Plums	Leave whole or cut. Halve and remove pit.	Pliable.
Rhubarb	Cut lengthwise into slices about 2" x ¼". Cook by placing in rapidly boiling water for a few moments. Wipe dry before placing in dryer.	Hard and brittle.

These are but a few of the fruits and vegetables we have dried both in the sun and electric dehydrator. The dehydrator is a bit quicker but the results are not as tasty. Remember they all have a lot of moisture and must be reconstituted with water at time of eating. Fifty pounds of fresh apples yield about five pounds of dried fruit. Twenty pounds of fresh carrots will yield about five pounds when dried. The dried, cubed vegetables are good mixed together for taking on backpack trips to use in soups to augment the wild greens you forage.

There are many other ways in which to gather, dry, store and use. The Indian shares his principles with us, "For every seed gathered, scatter two." "When you gather be sure to leave half as much as you take." In this way the plant is allowed to reseed and spread naturally. If not already ingrained within our reverent thoughts, "Take only what you need, and only at the time of need."

This is a good time for us to observe nature's way, for now the world's foods are still traded. Learning while there is still an abundance of food will provide us with a better understanding when a natural or man-made crisis strikes. There are very basic foods that have always had great value in crisis:

Water

Honey (In which fruits or vegetables may be immersed for use later as the conserve. Honey being antibacterial acts as a preservative. In the Orient, ginseng and honey are often found together, the honey makes a fine base for a tonic—naturally.)

BEANS   (Navy, soy, kidney, green, split, etc.)

WHEAT   (or other equivalent grain)

SALT

Having lived on only three of these items (beans, honey and water) plus greens which I foraged for many months I know they will very adequately suffice. Your knowledge of picking and foraging properly and reverently will certainly aid if a crisis occurs. For the moment, be as content as are the windy grasses, blowing their heads about freely. But be aware of where you walk—it may be your next meal. Do not fear nature.

SURVIVAL FORAGING RECIPE
*(Use during times of stress
or need to determine edibility.)*

A certain mental state and the willingness to experiment are required to survive through foraging for the uninitiated. Many have died because they could not stomach the thought of eating a wild food. Under stress this can kill a healthy and strong-minded person lost in the wilds. As you become aware of the wilds, a sixth sense of your surroundings develops. An inner seeing. By thinking simply—the simples appear.

At the time of need or stress, when you are about to eat a food with which you are unfamiliar, be aware in the first place of noticeable reaction. Oxidation takes place, due to the plant part coming into contact with the air when separated from the plant. Many plants as well as fungi rapidly change color when separated from the source of growth and exposed to the air. Experience the plant first. How does it feel? Is this abundant or scarce? How is your instinctual consciousness? If it does not feel right, leave it alone and seek another.

If it feels right, proceed with cautioned awareness. Taste and reaction in the mouth should be noticed. The air and the mouth are signposts. Place a small amount in your mouth (discretion please, a small amount is ¼ teaspoon or less). Become aware of the action in your mouth. Is it burning? Dry? Acrid? Bitter? Does a great deal of salivation occur? I would not proceed to swallow but would spit it out if these characteristics are present. Usually any toxin will cause the mouth to form a natural resistance, as heavy salivation when masticating (chewing), thus causing a washing effect to get rid of the foreign material. If the plant part does not cause this salivation, or only one or two of the characteristics appear, proceed with caution if you need a food source. Usually one try is not an efficient test so chew well and swallow the amount. Wait an hour for reaction. If this is a strong poison and you ate a small amount, vomiting is the worst that will occur. If nothing happens do not assume edibility but repeat the procedure (recipe) increasing the amount and waiting again. Then proceed according to your taste and attitude.

Be assured that the number of people who die from poisoned mushrooms and other plants is minute in comparison to the number of foragers in our culture. *Positive identification* is a good standard rule. The responsibility for many poisonings should not be blamed on the source so much as the prejudices of edibility. It usually is quite hopeless to try to tell this to people unfamiliar with plants because newspaper articles tend always to sensationalize poisonings. If the new force wants to make an effort to curb bias, a good practice would be to include the name of poisonous material, its effects, antidotes and proper treatment. This would help inform people as opposed to frightening them.

Early man did experiment. Today there

are so many sources of food about us this seldom happens. But by law of averages random experimentation does occur. By becoming aware you will learn of the potentials within plants, as well as an instinct toward survival foraging.

Many people think poisons will kill you. Yes, some will. But usually this happens because they eat too much and do not listen to the body's natural instincts. Would you believe some plants that are edible are also poisonous? Unless *properly* prepared the following are but a few:

> Tomato leaves are toxic before the fruit forms.

> Potato shoots and green parts are poisonous raw.

> Garlic, onion and leek oil are toxic in large doses, yet we eat the flesh often.

> The mature leaves of bracken fern are tough and chewy and to eat a great deal can be toxic. Yet the young, tender fiddleheads are a delicacy in many countries. They are eaten raw or with other foods.

> Elderberry berries are wonderfully delicious but the pith, leaf and stem are poisonous.

Physicians of the past, and some today, use poisons as antidotes. Several of the most common toxicals in the field are Buttercup (*Ranunculus*), Meadow-saffron (*Colchicum*), Hemlock (*Conium*) and Deadly Nightshade (*Atrope Belladonna*). The first two are good soil conditioners and within their structure exude products into the soil that aid the grasses to rise. If an individual were to get poisoned by any of these four, Angelica root tea can be given in quantity—or milk if no root is about your area. Dilution of the toxin seems to be a key to any poisoning, flush with water or

an equivalent substance. Hemlock is often mistaken for parsley or wild carrot, and mingles freely among these. One good rule with these is to smell the root. Hemlock root smells bad whereas the others smell sweet. It takes relatively smaller amounts of toxin to cause serious, if not fatal, situations with children though adults may be just as vulnerable. It seems early education here would be an essential part of any program. Some simple thoughts about poisons: until known, leave plants with milky sap or unknown white or red fruit alone. Wild seeds have the greatest concentration of substances within their structure, oftentimes potentizing their action. So eat sparingly. Be cautious about bulbs lacking the garlic/onion smell. If you must experiment with eating the unknowns and the survival foraging recipe does not appeal to you, then cook the plant material in several changes of water. Taste a small amount, observe its taste through a small ingestion. Then your sensible reaction will be a bit better. If all else fails, call a physician or if in a city, call a botanical garden, or look in the phone book under poison.

The best guide is your own awareness. Trust in listening to your inner self. If it feels right—do it—you will find that your own individual nature is not vindictive.

Written words will never teach the lesson to be learned as well as actual experience. Learn by touching. A deep rooted feeling is established by working with a life (spirit if you wish) from one season to the other. People who have accompanied me on foragings often comment that this season is different than the last—and so it is. Yet each season has its yield. "Eat according to the season." Ideal as it may seem, probably the best interaction with these wild foods is just as that statement implies. After all, we don't want to do as many have done—hear of an item that has a market value or

mythical use and just go running out to pick because it's there. This does neither you nor the plant any good and will ruin, if not destroy, the essence as well as the area and plantlife. For herein lie the secrets toward a good recipe (with medicine or spirit within) as opposed to a product that has no essence. Though we may prepare a plant's yield, the quality nutrients may still be in another part of the plant and even have retracted because of the lack of awareness on the part of the picker. I realize the debate between pathologists on this idea, yet man has still to define vitamin as well as what truly is a nutrient. Discovery indicates a more inherent knowledge contained within the plants structure each day. The soil, our water and sun, our air, our varied vibrations each play an integral part in this wondrous being, the wild edible.

When I was living in Mississippi I had the opportunity of collecting "yarbs" with a black gentleman from Hattiesburg. They were his source of food as well as income. Jim would always comment that his people before him had instilled the thought that as man has changed the world and become more insensitive, then feeling the earth was the most important thing he could do to overcome that insensitivity. To get in touch with the earth and its plant life somehow grounds us and each other.

In Mississippi, as well as throughout all the South, the Blue Ridge and Rockies, the "yarbs" are as important as coffee is to a majority of the world's population. Jim could not afford coffee, so his roots, such as dandelion and chicory were his coffee, and the white man paid a good price to have these. Other things he would gather throughout the southern states were sassafras, poke root, yellow dock, golden seal, seng (or ginseng), wild potato, onion, cress and snakeroot. He had no car but those

who knew him were always glad to travel with or take him because of the stories he could tell, the information he would share.

My friend died in 1968, having lived nearly ninety-one years. I understand he helped many whites (as well as blacks) with their gardens. We should pay attention when it comes to learning about the proper ways of gathering and foraging, drying and trading. We must learn from our elders, no matter the color, race or creed. We're all from the same source!

In Peru I met another forager, Carlos Arroyo from Huancayo. He would spend from three to six months each year gathering the herbs that were traded among the twelve thousand or so inhabitants of his town. Sarsaparilla, life-everlasting, dandelion and cress, some of the few. His philosophy was always to take a younger person with him if the weather accorded. Otherwise no, for the elements at those altitudes could be very strong, as he was. He said he had to meditate with the plants to be gathered. He remained until the plant yielded, accorded a vibration, its essence. He said he could see this as light that would appear about the part needed.

Today as I travel and walk the earth's ground, the plants each take on their own light. If one is aware of this, the light becomes like the oils of the plant, an aromatic essence. Some plants, as golden seal, the mints, thymes and sages throw off a color within the heightened (maturing) growth of the leaf; the color within the veins is the color of the flower. We each have the potential to develop this light sense as we become aware of the plant parts. Individually there is something still to discover, something still untapped. Like the vitamins the smallest unit of life-giving properties, which hold quietly their mystery.

THREE

Simples: Medicines which Consist in Their Own Nature

ALFALFA

As previously mentioned the Arabs called this the father of all foods. Because it is such a deeply rooted legume we find an untold amount of rare trace elements not found in cultivated garden foods. The protein content is exceptionally high (comparable to meats and nuts). Dr. G. Chaney, a renowned food scientist from Stanford University, discovered Vitamin U, seemingly a remarkable healing agent and preventive of peptic ulcers. There are eight essential enzymes that dissolve, oxidize and convert starches, sugars, proteins and fats. All this within one plant.

Alfalfa Tea

Infuse 1 tablespoon of leaves in a pint of water. This serves two. For variation add some mint leaves.

Alfalfa Seeds Sprouts

This takes three to five days. The nutritional value quadruples from the seed to the sprout. Keep some going by your sink. Take some

along for backpack trips into the wilderness areas or for your survival food stash.

NOTE: Alfalfa seed is not the only seed to sprout. Be *imaginative* when you are preparing sprouts. Such seeds as watercress, plantain, flax, soy, mung, lentil, radish, sunflower, buckwheat, garbanzos, dandelion, and fenugreek are delightful, each having its own unique taste. Remember though that the seed is the potential whole of the plant. Thus, since it is concentrated, it's better to use a little over a longer period of time as opposed to using a large amount at first. Watercress seed is very hot. Mint seed is cooling.

In Chile, alfalfa has become known as Chilean Clover. There, people pick the sprays of the plant and lay these about the house to drive away fleas.

DANDELION

How many of us remember the first plant we met? Most may recall the dandelion — the yellow flowered, tooth-leaved friend seemingly found everywhere. Often pulled as weeds,

29

1. Start with an amount of seeds—
or beans (unhulled).

A jar (or two or three) with open
top lid, to place nylon screening,
preferably cheese cloth + H_2O H.

2. Measure ⅔ tablespoons of
seed/bean into jar. Cover with lid
or use band to hold cheesecloth.
Rinse seeds—Then fill the jar with
water and soak overnight.

3. In the morning, rinse seeds again
(use H_2O for plants or as soup
base.)
Strain water thru lid or screening
and place jar on its side—slightly
sloped so water may drain. Place in
a cool dark spot.

4. Rinse and drain your seeds twice
a day, for two days. Some require a
longer time to sprout—in altitudes,
much longer.

5. Continue to rinse seeds till
sprouted (average two days).
Now place in sunlight so sprouts
will become green and energized.

6. When ready—enjoy in avacado
sprout sandwich, as a dressing, for
soups, a vegie on a meal plate or in
a green drink.
Sprouts are a live food. Say hello—
or use sprouted grains for an
addition to bread dough.

Sprouts on plate & in sandwich.

believed to be of no use, you may have wondered why it so abounds about our planet.

This "weed" takes no special attention by man to flourish. It sits sunbathing most of its days just absorbing the sun, water and minerals. As with many of its close "weed" friends, this attribute creates a hardier plant, thus more essential properties, which causes it to be of great nutritive benefit.

Monks spent days and years contemplating this plant's energy, oftentimes ending the season with a dandelion wine that today is still recognized as a fine spring tonic. Philosophers sought its knowledge. The Myddfai physicians prized its curative properties, recommending it for the treatment of kidney complaints, liver trouble, and circulatory disorders.

And today, we many times begin our cooking by simply picking a handful of spring dandelion leaves to eat raw or enjoy in salads or in soup.

Simple Dandelion Salad

One handful dandelion greens. Add one teaspoon lemon juice, garlic to taste, and a tablespoon of olive oil.

Dandelion Coffee
(A frontiersman's must.)

In August the root of dandelion contains much of its active principles (taraxacin and inulin). Dry the root well for about two weeks. Then chop into one-fourth to one-half inch pieces. Place in 250° F oven for ten minutes or more, turning occasionally. When roasted, powder, run water through this and you will have dandelion coffee or, if you prefer, grind and simmer in a pot until taste is full.

To many, cooking need be only the act of your hands in contact with the part of the plant to be used, yielding a meal.

Feel the leaf breathe as you pick to partake of sharing this new experience, between you and the leaf.

CHICORY

Another "weed," chicory, is closely related to the dandelion. This perennial grows in most countries as a "pot herb" (one which can always be found in the cooking pot). High in vitamin A and C, chicory is known as the companion to the forager and is used in salads and soups, on bread or eaten raw.

When I was with the Air Force and stationed in the southern part of the United States in 1967, I met an elderly lady living near New Orleans who taught me an alternative for coffee. As I was not a coffee drinker this became a favorite substitute and it is certainly an economic resource.

Chicory Root Coffee

Follow the same recipe given for dandelion coffee. For variation combine the two roots, chicory and dandelion. Although the taste is different you will have a better coffee than many present on the market today.

After traveling several days to Huancayo, Peru (altitude twelve thousand feet), Alberto Villoldo and I were tired, dirty and thirsty. Carlos Arroyo, the herbalist who met us, looked at us and realized we needed something local to pick us up. He took us to a little juice stand where we were greeted by a sparkling woman. She too looked at us and ventured to say she knew what it was we needed. She gathered:

One large handful of chicory greens, one carrot, and half a handful of watercress. She placed these in a clean cloth and crushed the vegetables together, then twisted the rag thus yielding a beautiful herb drink that did indeed sparkle our spirits.

It is delightful to watch the chicory bloom sporadically during the day; the light-blue flowers are seen from July to September. An old favorite to preserve these is:

Pickled Chicory Flowers

2 cups chicory buds or flowers
3 cups apple or white wine vinegar
½ teaspoon sea salt
¼ teaspoon ground ginger (or ¼ teaspoon clove or ¼ teaspoon cassia)
½ cup honey

Wash the flowers in icy water, then drain. Place in a clean (sterilized) jar. You could use a canning jar. In a separate pan, bring the salt, vinegar and spice to a boil. Simmer for five minutes. Remove from heat and stir in honey till dissolved. Pour this over the flowers in a jar, seal and store in cool place for at least one week before using.

Spanish folks rarely go without the leaves or root of chicory. In salads and soups the leaves offer a delightful taste. The root has always been a substitute for coffee or added to coffee as an adulterant. Many times chicory itself is adulterated with acorns, dried carrot, roasted wheat or rye. Succory, another name of chicory, likely was derived from the Latin *succurrers*, to run under, because of the depth to which the tap root penetrates the earth. Chicory attests to the almost universal influence of Arabian physicians. European writers including French, Spanish, Portuguese, Italian, German, Dutch, Swedish, Russians, and Danish wrote of chicoree, achicoria, chicoria, cicorea, chicorie, cichorei, tskikorei, and cicorie. And if you have ever wondered about those bachelor's buttons of old, then observe the blue flowers so tender that even on cloudy morns throughout midsummer their blue eyes blink at you. Emerson, too, in his "Humble Bee," sees only the beauty, writing of *"succory to match the sky."*

COMFREY

A plant definitely making a comeback is comfrey. From Russian descent, and also known as knit bone and boneset, it derives its name from its use in helping to set and knit bone or tissue that has been damaged. It contains the remarkable healing agent called allantoin, which is not produced during the flowering cycle.

Written about through time, in such notable books as Turner's *1568 Herball*, Gerard's *Herball* of 1597 and Parkinson's *Theatrum Botanicum*, 1640, this plant is spoken of as a wonderful cleanser for ulcers and wounds. The leaves, raw and beaten into pulp are applied or laid upon the troubled area. The roots taken fresh and beaten small are said to ease pain.

When I first met this remarkable plant some eight years ago only the old timers seemed to know of it. Now, throughout the world, this plant, a fine source of nitrogen for the soil, is finding its way back onto the table and into the body of earth, as well as man.

When many areas are feeling the effect of a water-short summer, this plant seems, by the appearance of its leaves, to be wilted during the day. But the minute the sun stops beating on it, the comfrey leaves spring up as though there were some magical force within their veins. Why even bother to cultivate lettuce when such a wonderful plant with such fine qualities is available, and requires little or no tending.

Comfrey Coffee

Comfrey root
Dandelion root
Chicory root

Scrub the roots, and roast slowly for four hours till brown and crisp. Grind and make as other coffee substitutes.

Comfrey

Since we are working with the dandelion, mustard and mallow in this section let us simply blend the following for a super concentrated lunch:

Wild Green Goo

Chop very fine, mash or grind:

2-4 comfrey leaves
2-4 dandelion leaves
2-4 mustard leaves
A handful of mallow
(or any other of your favorite greens)

Mix one tablespoon agar-agar (a glutinous seaweed) into boiling water until dissolved. Add the chopped leaves, one cup of lemon juice (lemonade is milder) and one cup alfalfa sprouts. This will jell at room temperature and will not melt. A fine item for your picnic or backpack.

Leaves of comfrey, large stems and veins removed, are wonderful steamed, with a bit of garlic and oil, plus a dash of powdered dulse (all sea minerals).

At a recent conference, devoted just to comfrey, Lawrence D. Hills, the British agronomist involved with research, and certainly a leader in compost gardening and comfrey, offered what he calls "delicious:"

The Vodfrey

one part vodka
four parts comfrey juice

If you would like the non-alcoholic approach, he offers pineapple juice as a substitute for the vodka as a nice healthy "nip."

Comfrey is raised successfully from root-cuttings. It offers great potential in under-developed areas and protein-short countries. Its deep taproot allows comfrey to thrive in dry areas. It's valuable in your compost heap because of its high nitrogen and potash content.

HONEY

There is evidence that bees existed as many as fifty million years ago. Hieroglyphics record honey being gathered by cavemen. Monuments of ancient Egypt describe the use of honey. In Hindu mythology, bees were considered honorable beings. Vishnu, personifying the sky giving life to the universe, is seen as a bee that rests within the lotus flower. The Ayur-Veda mentioned a diet to prolong life composed of milk and honey. The Greeks considered this a gift from the gods. There are details in *The Iliad* and *The Odyssey* of how Agameda prepared a most refreshing honey drink for the Greek warriors. Pythagoras lived to be ninety which he credited to eating honey; and Hippocrates ate of the honey daily—using this combination (honey and water) within his medical practice as a remedy against all sorts of disease. All this indicates (and there are hundreds of other references) honey was considered an important curative agent in many popular medicines.

Throughout the book I indicate the use of honey as opposed to sugar. I am in no way endorsing sugar, the overly refined, gross bastardization that is one of the major contributors of the dis-ease presently rampant in highly technological societies. When you have worked with the natural entities, as honey, then refined sugar just doesn't have the taste or the nutritive benefits. But as with the section on meats, fowl and fish . . . I recognize the transition for many and thus only for clarity and alternative do I mention it within this work. The chief element of honey is glucose (as grape sugar). This is such a widely used product in medicine that it's hard for this layperson to imagine the use of anything other than honey. If man were to cultivate bees, and all natural products, as opposed to the many chemicals, the earth might be a better place to inhabit. Unfortunately, the new age has reached only a minority. Yet in time its qualities will be recognized. Honey, like sea water, is also a prime source of mineral salts and organic acids necessary for life. Its therapeutic value should be clear. The first time I ever realized its real ability to heal was when I had been backpacking for several weeks in the Sierras. A blister had formed on the heel of my foot and was so raw I could not continue without some relief. I knew the plant yarrow (named after Achilles, and being referenced as heal-all) would help. Wanting an adhesive, I took the only pan I had at the time and mixed some honey and pine pitch. I incorporated all this into an ointment. (See extracts section.) Rural, I realize, but at the time it was what was available and that is what is best used. The blister was raw where many layers had been worn and the center looked like another blister. For the next five days I placed this ointment on the wound and the relief, as well as the appearance and the healing, was remarkable. Again, I am not saying one should do this but if it is all you have and no medical advisor is about then you must trust your own good judgment. I did have a doctor look at it when I got to a town and he said it looked fine. He said he remembered his old medical books speaking of honey but he had never really thought of using it this way.

I could ramble on about honey for some time, another book really. But to give you an idea of the pleasures of honey, let me share this—mead was considered a medicine by the ancients. Honey bread retains moisture and the ancients would make a cake that was highly nourishing and remained fresh longer than normal breads. A honey cake takes the hunger away quickly when backpacking and especially during times of prolonged exercise or walking. Honey has often been attributed with disinfectant and antibacterial properties (which helps to prevent spoilage of bread as well as self). Aside from tasting good, it is a prime replacement for sugar and contains all these qualities. The change should not be difficult.

Bee Pollen and Wheat Grass Juice

4 cups sprouts, juiced
2 tablespoons bee pollen

Mix together and enjoy or blend as juice.

Cooking with honey instead of sugar offers great joy and taste in jellies, jams and preserves. The various fruit berries such as gooseberry/cranberry/mountain ash/quince are a delight.

Try this. . .

Clean the fruit to be used by paring, coring and seeding. Place the fruit in a pan, cover with water and cook till it becomes tender. Remove fruit and strain the remaining juice. Throw nothing away please. Mix two parts of honey with one part of the cooked fruit in a preserving pan. A cup or two of the juice is added back and boiled till a syrup forms. The rest of the fruit is added back and this is simmered together till it becomes translucent. Delicious on pancakes. Try adding nut meats (to the preserves).

Other ideas include making lemonade and orangeade with honey. Milk and honey is great for children. Honey on cherries, raspberries, blackberries, and gooseberries. Once I ate a honey and milk barley soup. It was smooth and soothing and I've often tried to duplicate it—alas, to no avail. Each time I make the soup it has a familiar taste, but not quite the same—must have been a rare and exotic far away spice or honey.

A thought evolved many thousands of years ago by the Chinese in preparing their foods as medicines: each type of extract was designed to take care of those partaking of the meal. Hopefully, those partaking helped in the production of the food, thus enhancing the properties of the plant through the vibrations during the ritual of gathering and preparing.

PINE PITCH

(ABIES CANADENSIS *yields burgundy and Canada pitch*)

This sap is a source for turpentine and is used to make oil paint. The spruce *Pinus nigra (Abies nigra)* yields an *Essence of Spruce,* prepared by gathering the tender young branches, decocting, then evaporating.

This in turn may be added to beer (which is another fine summer beverage with considerable vibration). Taking this on long outings is said to be good for scurvy. The following was formulated by several men while packing on Shasta mountain. It was given to me when they saw me staring at a pine as they walked by—a common sight, me, looking at or hugging trees!

    ¼ pint essence of spruce
    2 ounces ginger
    2 ounces hops
    1½ gallons river water when available

Gently boil this together for seven minutes. Set a moment, strain. Add:

    5¼ gallons water
    ½ pint yeast
    3 pints honey

Mix and let this ferment for three days.

Spruce sap is often chewed alone or mixed with mallow as a substitute for conventional chewing gum.

MALVA (MALLOW, MARSHMALLOW, CHEESEWEED, SLIPPERY TONGUE OR FAIRCHEESES)

This plant has found its way freely into soups, salads and such. From centuries of use and practical experience, the Spanish often refer to this plant as a good food and a good medicine.

Another perennial, Malva grows from six inches to six feet in height with deep green, slightly serrated roundish leaves on long slender stems of a deeper green than most of the wayside plants. An unequaled source of natural Vitamin A, minerals and chlorophyll, this plant grows abundantly in moist fields throughout most of the world. It is also known as marshmallow, because of the soft and soothing mucilaginous quality.

In the Bible, in the book of Job, irony touches the mentioning of mallow, as some seventeen or so species of mallow grew in Palestine, concerning who was the critic of rank to name the species eaten, saying:

> *"for want and famine they were solitary, fleeing into the wilderness . . . who cut up the mallows by the bushes and juniper roots for their meat."*

A woman in one of my classes asked, "Rob, if you had a child with a sore throat, and wanted to use a local plant what might you use?" I thought, and then put the question to the group. They, in turn, brainstormed the problem then offered the following recipe, for which I want to say thank you.

Malva Mellow-jello/or Slippery Elm Food Beverage

(All measurements approximate.)

2 ounces slippery elm powder or
2 ounces crushed & powdered malva root
2 quarts boiling water (or mucilaginous liquid as agar or carrageen)

Put slippery elm in boiling water, turn off heat and allow to infuse. In fifteen minutes bring to a boil again and then let stand for a few more minutes.

Blend in a little at a time:

¼-¾ cup nuts
¼-¾ cups raisins
(NOTE: raisins should be soaked in hot mallow slippery elm while waiting to blend.)
(cashews, sunflower seeds etc.)
¼-⅓ cup honey
¼ teaspoon ground corriander
¼ teaspoon ground anise

Blend until smooth and chill. Add chopped fruit if desired.

MUSTARD

This ancient and widespread plant has a variety of uses. Most important in many cultures have been its purifying and strengthening effects on the blood. It is no wonder this yellow spring bloomer abounds for our winter blood!

Excellent as a source of Vitamins A, E and C, mustard is also high in chlorophyll. The tenderest of the green leaves make a fine salad. The buds, containing nitrogenous pollen, are an excellent source of protein.

Steam the buds three minutes only and place on top of mustard leaves (either cooked or raw.) Simple, yet rewardingly warming—Hummmmm-

Mustard Flower Salad

Gather your favorite collection of wild raw edibles. Place in a bowl and sprinkle the mustard flowers lightly on top. Add your favorite oil. Delightful subtle flavor to warm your being.

Mustard Seed Cakes

(The California Pomo Indians mixed mustard seed with cornmeal to make this.)

1 cup mustard seed
½ cup cornmeal
water enough to make a thick paste

Taking the freshly gathered seeds, parch and grind to coarse consistency. Mix cornmeal and water to make a thick paste. Place on a clean rock in the sun and cover with cloth for approximately four hours or until hard. These were carried on long migrations for their nutritive and energy producing qualities.

Unlike many of the cultivated plants, mustard and a number of other weeds have extraordinary properties that improve the soil. They are humus producers and stimulate growth of friendly bacteria. They are unique in drawing the nutrients upward through the soil. If only our cultivated plants could have but half the nutrients as many of the wild plants.

Mustard Leaf Syrup

Juice any amount of mustard leaf (depending upon how many partake). Combine with honey and lemon to thicken. Great if your voice is fading.

ROSE

The word "Rose" is a simple anagram. From the rearrangement of the letters is derived the word "Eros"—the Greek God of Love.

The rose, and its eastern equivalent, the lotus, like all beautiful flowers represent spiritual unfoldment and attainment. Thus many deities are shown sitting upon the

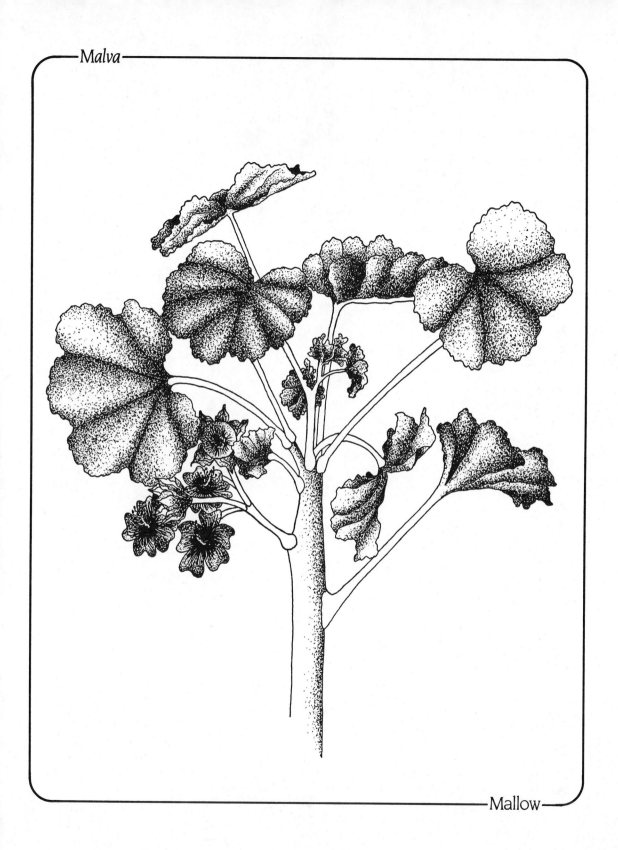

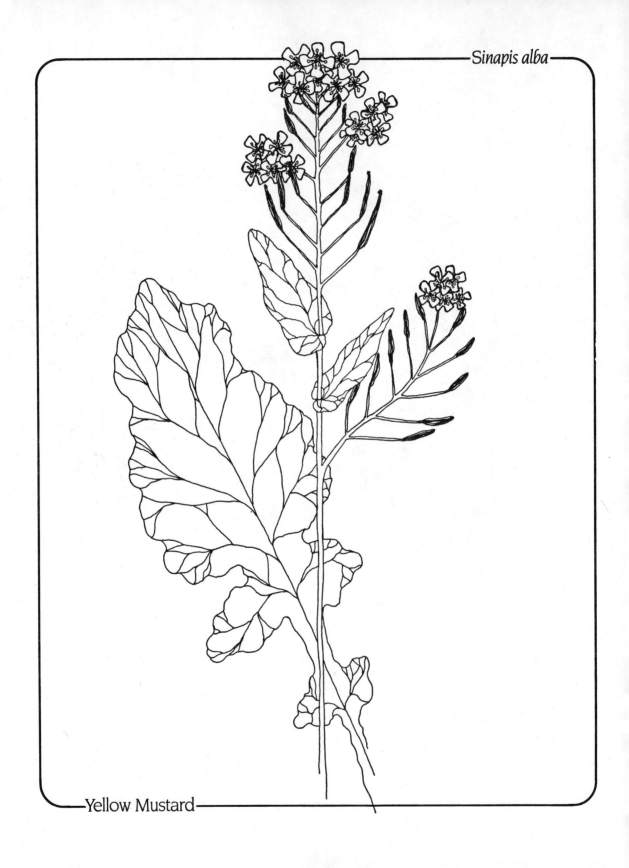

Sinapis alba

Yellow Mustard

rose or the lotus. The Rosicrucians used a garland of roses to signify the spiritual vortices (ironically) referred to in the Bible as the seven lamps and the seven churches of Asia— representative of the spinal column, (like the seven chakras).

A thorny bush, the plant embedded within the earth seems symbolic of divine nutriment. In fact, this plant's hip (the bud ripened after the flower petals have fallen off) taken raw or as a tea, is very high in Vitamin C.

All varieties are fine to use but the Japanese Rose (*Rosa rugosa*) with its deep pink or white flowers and Pasture Rose (*Rosa carolina*) with pale pink flowers are the most fragrant. The Sweetbriar Rose or Eglantine (*Rosa eglantaria*) is seemingly the most beloved of the poets; possibly because the leaves are thickly covered underneath with sticky fragrant pores which give a marvelous scent about the bush. But for all intended purposes the wild rose varieties are the preferred.

Rose Vinegar
(Yields about a quart)

2 cups fragrant rose petals
½ cup honey
4 cups apple cider vinegar or white wine
    vinegar

Wash the petals and pack into sterilized canning jars. Add the honey and then pour the vinegar over. Seal the jars. Let stand approximately two weeks. Strain out the petals. Return the vinegar to the canning jars, a vinegar cruet or bottle.

Rose Hip Conserve

The preparation of Rose Hip Conserve is renowned throughout European countries. The well-ripened wild hips should be gathered and spread out to ripen fully in a dry shady place, making sure they do not lie on top of each other since this will cause rotting. When nice and soft, pulverize with a mortar and pestle (or a mincer) to obtain a good red puree. With a wooden spoon, rub this through a sieve or cloth to remove the seeds (or pips). The result is of jelly consistency rich in Vitamin C. Mix with half as much honey. Because honey is such a fine preservative this uncooked conserve will keep well. Use as a spread. A spoonful a day is nature's answer to the chemist's Vitamin C tablets.

We have the pips, some pulp and skin left. Dry this out and have Rose Hip Tea. Ideal for the winter months. This tea has a delicate flavor that becomes subtly enhanced when you add your favorite fruit juice (try lemon) or milk.

When you believe in what you're preparing, the quality of the preparation is more fully enhanced by your belief. The Green Drink is one such example. Many have spoken of this green drink, but those who teach throughout their lives a *reverence* for the natural use of plants, teach always the use of The Green Drink. Popular plants for the green drink are mint, lamb's-quarters, alfalfa, comfrey, chard, dandelion, malva, and chickweed.

Wild Green Drink
(My own version)

Several:

    dandelion leaves
    dock leaves
    malva
    comfrey
    miner's lettuce
    parsley
    chickweed
    1 cup alfalfa sprouts
    2-4 cups lemon or orange juice
    and other veggies you would like
        cut stems into ¾-1" pieces

In a blender, (osterizer) blend for five minutes or until equal consistency. If you like, banana may be added or other greens of your choice. Great for constipation of the body's mind and spirit.

This, as a food in itself, is a blended simple and is practically free for the picking. If you have no blender, remember God gave you one when he was designing the human body, the mouth. A bit cruder perhaps than our modern technological types but certainly as efficient—with less downtime, waste and energy output. But if you don't want the fiber then our technology is fantastic.

CATTAIL

GENUS TYPHA. This narrow leafed cattail stands above our heads beaming a known frequency for our awareness. Cattails are found throughout the world. The velvety seed pods, slightly cooked and buttered have a subtle tastiness. When they have been cultivated, cattails thrive. As with many other plants, they are receiving much attention in chemical research. The rootstocks are edible and recent studies indicate the food value of this plant is equal to that of rice or corn. When dried they are ground into a flour and since there is little starch in the rootstock they make a fine substitute for cornstarch. Originally the name was derived from Russian, and was called "Russian asparagus." Cattail pollen as a protein source has often been acclaimed. In spring when the new shoots are rising, like asparagus, they will enhance a salad or make a soup dance.

The North Coast Indian tribes have many uses for the tuft from the top of the plant. They use it as a wound dressing, pillow stuffing, for diapers, cradle padding, extra insulation of the house and caulking barrels. Floor mats are woven from the leaves.

PLANTAIN

Another universal weed is plantain. The common or broad leafed varieties seem underfoot almost everywhere.

When I was very young I observed the grain blown from shaft of stalk into an old Indian mortar stone. I wondered—and thought about how perfectly these two seemed to go together—just so. Then came too many years of enriched technological white flour.

To feel again those wonderful textures and run my hands through the many grasses, learning each day. So many that whole books are devoted just to grasses. It's too bad not many people are still gathering, tribal-like, the grains we have about our country. So much to the wind then, it is nature's way!

In 1967, walking among those beautiful Shenandoahs of the South, I remember distinctly the moment I confronted an elder because the grass she was pointing to and describing she called "plantain." "Indian buckwheat," I contradicted, because grandad had always pointed to this plant and called it Indian buckwheat. "No, this is plantain," she answered, and each of us was correct. In fact it was a staple among the North Coast Pacific Indian tribespeople; the Indian buckwheat with the abundant shellfish, the seeds eaten either raw or cooked—native style.

Indian Buckwheat Bread or Plantain Seed Mush

(Two from one.)

Gather one handful of plantain seed (scattering two to the wind).

Crush (or grind) and mix with enough water to form a thick paste. We could eat just this, but better, place it on a nice, warm rock and leave it in the sun till hard. Carry in pack and eat as desired.

Typha latifolia

Cattail

Plantago lanceolata

Broad Leaf Plantain

The leaves are good in salads; the broad leaf is tastier. It is a treat in soups and makes a highly prized tea which has been popular for many centuries. Volumes have been written about just this plant alone. It is used successfully as a poultice for stings or for washing poison oak. The seeds are eaten raw or slightly browned and made into a mush. This plant has been used in combination with dandelion as a spring tonic. The roots are a good survival food. Time and space here limit a full description of plantain's uses.

NETTLE

In Scotland the tender tops of the nettle are steamed to make a warming soup. The minute the nettle is heated the formic acid dissipates and no sting will manifest. The Oriental people as well as many other cultures claim nettle to be a good plant to rid the joints of deposits. The soup is considered good for tired women. It provides an alternative source for rennet, and like most of the greens is a fine diuretic. When I got a good sized cut on my foot I personally observed the binding and cease of bleeding when this plant was crushed and applied to the wound. It even felt good. Oftentimes the most simple interaction with nature manifests when utilizing the simples.

Archibald Menzies, the able naturalist with Captain Vancouver, writes in his journal in the entry for June 11, 1772; "...(we) stood in for a large Bay where we came to an anchor... about half a mile from Shore ... (and upon landing, found) the scite of a very large Village now overgrown with a thick crop of Nettles and bushes ... along the Beach ... we found a delightful clear and level spot cropt with Grasses and wild flowers..."

MINER'S LETTUCE

Miner's lettuce is but another of those abounding weeds. Found about many a field, the leaves are used for salads and soups. Ground and made to flour the seeds are a delicious substitute for buckwheat. This plant is not utilized as much as the other plants for flours however. The dried root is a good pot herb and on the trail it makes a good munching companion you can forage or take along.

There are thousands of simples but these seem to be the least complex. A local plant person would certainly be of value to teach identification and techniques of use.

WATERS

Many of my guides in this life have spoken of the importance of water when infusing or decocting anything. Water is of extreme importance because it is the vehicle of your preparation. The following are some of the better known waters:

DEW WATER: Lick or collect from plants—a subtle, often refreshing spirited essence.

TAP WATER: Can be improved by sitting in sun for from one to three days (solar tea).

DISTILLED WATER: Useful when you want a neutral water (one without minerals) to flush mineral deposits out of the body. Continued use will flush out too much. Add herbs to obtain multiple trace elements.

SEA WATER: Proven to contain all trace elements and minerals. Highly acclaimed by healers as nature's best water. Use sparingly as too much may cause dehydration. Dilute one part sea water to seven parts distilled.

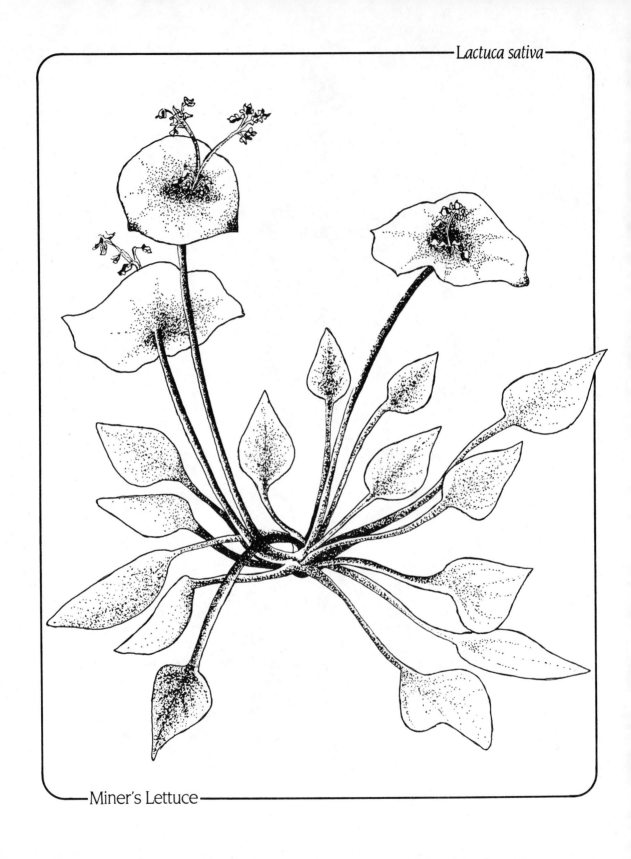

Miner's Lettuce

RAIN WATER: Don't use the *first* rain water of the season because it will be too polluted. It is very good if there are no wells or springs about. In some countries where rain occurs but once or twice a year, artificial reservoirs, called cisterns, are used as holding tanks.

SPRING WATER: How many times in our wanderings or readings do we hear or read about spring water. Pilgrims would travel for hundreds of miles for this spiritual essence. Baths, for bathing the spirit, were springs; others springs were reserved for drinking. Each spring has its own mineral type. Iron water is great to mix with lemon and honey. Sulfur is good to bathe in.

WATER OF LIFE—URINE: This, our own water can be recycled and is high in biochemic salts. A survival drink well-known in the armed services, life sustaining to motorists stranded in the desert, and people downed in the oceans. Take only your own and fresh. When exposed to the air, oxidation occurs causing bacteria to form.

Here it is appropriate to discuss the recycling of our water. Chemical soil amendments are beginning to be seen as "hindering" rather than "helping" the soil for vegetable or herbal production. An infusion of five parts water to one part urine is wonderful addition of nitrogeneous substance to organic soil. The dilution allows for very little odor and prevents burning the plants. A light or aura seems to appear about plants receiving this recipe. One may also use it to make a special herbal compost which provides a good mineral-oriented base. No matter how you recycle, you should be aware of the others that be next door and if you live in close city-type dwellings you will need to be in tune with city ordinances.

Now that we have explored a few simples, let us move to teas.

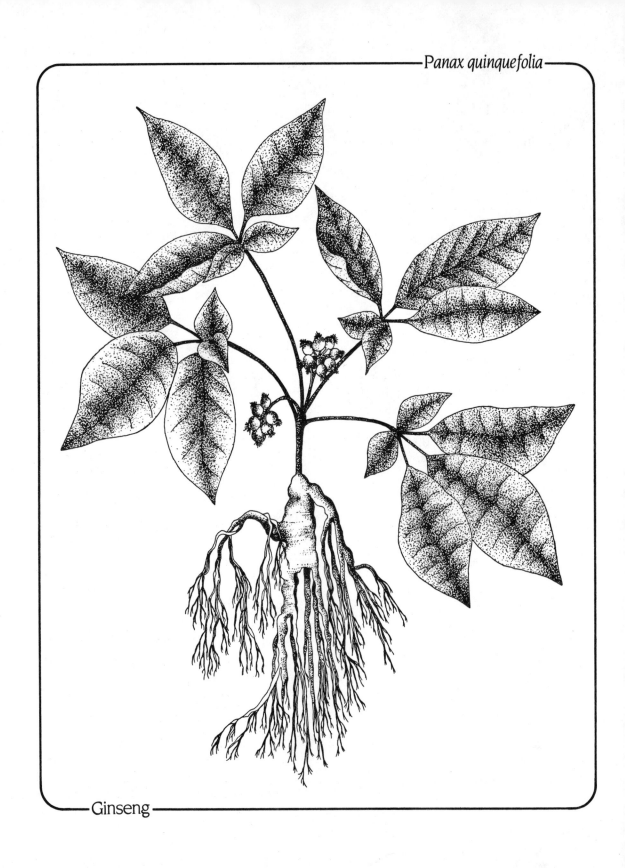

Ginseng

FOUR

Teas

Any of numerous plants more or less remotely resembling tea in appearance or properties; also an infusion prepared from their leaves and used medicinally or as a beverage; commonly with qualifying adjective or attributive, as Abyssinian tea, Laborador tea, sage tea, etc.

Webster's New International Dictionary

INFUSION

Infusion is a gentle way to blend a leaf or flower as tea. The usual formula is:

One teaspoon of herbs (leaves or flowers) to one cup. Warm the teapot. Place the herbs in the pot and pour boiling water over them. Allow three to seven minutes to infuse (some require longer—your own experience is your best guide). Strain and add sweetener if desired.

In some countries the herb is tied in a thin cloth and placed in the pot. A nice variation is to use tea in your tub.

DECOCTION

Decoction, the method of making tea from roots, barks, and seeds.

Place the whole root, bark or seeds in a mortar and with the pestle bruise until broken into fine pieces (thus allowing the essence to become ex-

pressed more readily). Bring the water to a boil and add the crushed root, bark, or seed. Boil momentarily, then simmer from ten to fifteen minutes. Strain and serve.

Herbal Tea Bath

Tie a handful of your favorite herb (lavender, mint, chamomile, etc.) in a cloth or clean sock and place it in your bath. Relax and let your skin absorb the beneficial properties.

This is not the *conventional* way to take your tea, but it is certainly a pleasant alternative.

There are virtually unlimited methods and variations of preparing tea according to your own brewing ideas. What about. . .

Sun Infused Tea or Solar Tea

Let the sun be your heating agent to vitalize the water. Take one quart of water and add half a cup of herb (e.g., mint). Let it stand in the sun one day. Cover the jar to prevent stuff from falling into the sun infusion.

This sun tea has been a favorite of mine for many years. It was inspired by a close friend, Hugh Read. Those fortunate enough to know this gentleman never forget their first visit to his kitchen. It is an array of bottles of leaves, roots, barks, berries, and flowers in what seems a hodgepodge of nature, brewing, stewing, and bubbling. In the sun on the windowsill, on the floor, in every cupboard, there are things growing, literally and in full essence.

Many who have been using the wayside weeds as herb tea for years agree that taste becomes refined as one experiences these plants. Grandma always had her rhubarbs and quince; granddad his heather, figs, and grapes. Some like comfrey, and others love orange flowers with a twist of lemon. No matter. Your taste will be your guide. Your stomach will let you know what it likes. But don't get carried away and unknowingly start pouring amounts of herbs into a pot for tea, or you *will be* conjuring the spirits. Be prepared for possible flight should you do so unwittingly. Flight refers to the light-headedness that results from blending too many spirits into one pot of tea.

The word *tisanes* originated in France and is also used by the English to refer to herb teas as opposed to ordinary teas. Some are reputed to have value for both internal and external use; some are very specific in their internal therapeutic value; some have specific cosmetic or bathing value. Whether for breakfast, nightcap, or bath, the herbal tea, or tisane you blend will enhance the spirit of your existence.

You may be just beginning to experience the many ways of cooking herbally. Don't let this be overwhelming. Your willingness to experience the world of wayside weeds comes when you first become aware of where you walk or sit and when you begin to think of the uses of plants. Herbs such as burdock, dandelion and chicory root all have been used to add to the flavor of coffee. Mint and lemon balm leaf are often used in iced tea. The flavors of herbal (leaf

and flower) teas are usually delicate. Some, such as Valerian root, smell like old socks, and wormwood leaf, for example, is as bitter as the name implies. There is an endless variety awaiting you.

For the best flavor, never, never use aluminum to brew your tea. Use only earthenware, china, or glass. Don't steep the herb too long, because this can ruin the delicate flavor.

The following teas include brews that range from the simple to the complex. Beliefs from several countries are included. Whatever feels right for your fingers to touch and infuse with water is fine for you. When I have been with companions in areas isolated from civilization we have created blends from the plants we know, then tried to establish an historical recreation of what might have been used in the past. Amazing realizations occurred when we ritually prepared tea this way. Try it the next time you go on a walk. Gather three of your favorite wayside friends and make a blend. Envision past roots from this blend. Give it a name—you may have just discovered a new "tonic." Such a "tonic" appeared when several of us had been camping for a number of days. We had seen little water, and when we did we wanted only to drink and bathe. As we were drinking we became aware of the plants about us: mugwort, life everlasting, and nettle. We decided to take a nettle bath. We would step from the cold water, brush with the nettle, and get back into the water. We repeated this several times. You might think we were crazy, but in healing rites, nettle is prescribed as a fine antidote for pains in the joints of the body. Refreshing. After our bath we gathered the fresh leaves of mugwort, life everlasting, and nettle for tea. We used about a quarter ounce of each to one quart water. This became known to us as *creak*

Monarda

Squaw Mint

Heuchera americana

Alum

tea—jokingly, the "creaker's" tea, for the creaks from hiking.

AGRIMONY. The herbs and seeds have been steeped in wine for a pleasant alternative to tea. An infusion, with the addition of honey, is a gargle as well as beverage.

ALDER. The fresh leaves have a gentle feeling when applied to the skin. Placed in shoes it will help you walking, and when you have walked too much it's a nice footbath. It also makes a great gargle, and try steeping alder nuts in brandy to "keep out the cold."

ALMOND. A protein tea used by diabetics, or one could make Almond Milk by blending together one ounce of almonds, half an ounce of honey and six ounces of warm water. A delight.

ALOE VERA. A plant that is grown in your home not so much as a tea, but as a living lotion for burns that occur about the stove. A biblical plant, aloe is mentioned as having been brought to prepare the body of Christ. A good emollient, internally and externally.

ALUM. Probably our best known astringent and mordant for fixing colors to cloth. Used as a powder and applied to shaving cuts. The root makes a good gargle. The juice mixed with vinegar and a little salt may be bound about the feet to relieve fever.

AMARANTH. Decoct the flowers as a general astringent. The leaves in salads and the seed for cakes or bread are a fine source of protein and minerals.

AMERICAN MANDRAKE. Also known as mayapple, mandrake is a slow but certain cathartic. The root is often used in healing rites for purification because it resembles a man.

AMERICAN SCULLCAP. As a tea strengthens the stomach and is also good for overexcitement and fatigue.

ANGELICA. A pleasant gargle is made from the roots. Also known as Dong Kwai in the Orient. The species has long been used by American Indians for all dread diseases. Many times this plant is called "woman's ginseng." This name is said to be derived from its asserted power to make the female "revert" to her husband or to stimulate the generative organs to increase the opportunity of bearing child. In poisoning by such toxicants as meadow saffron, buttercups, belladonna or hemlock, the angelica root tea is immediately given.

ARNICA MONTANA. Mostly used as a tincture externally. For internal use, this herb has also been boiled in beer or wine to purify the blood. The tea is used to wash sores, and the Arnica Salve (made by heating one ounce flowers in one ounce lard) has often been used as a general cream.

BARBERRY. Also known as Oregon Grape Root. The tea is employed in small doses for weak digestion and in all cases of general debility. The berries aid to check thirst and keep up energy. The tea of the root can be used as a gargle for sore mouth.

BAY LEAF. Also known as Sweet Bay. The leaves, used in cooking, aid the stomach. The fruit can be crushed and smelled if the lungs need stimulating. The oil is placed about the home if fleas are about.

BEARBERRY. Also known as Uva Ursi. The tea is a general tonic. The leaves can be smoked as a pleasant alternative to tobacco. This is also known as Kinnikinnik and is found in many smoking mixtures.

BEE BALM. Also known as Lemon Balm or Melissa. The herbalist's delight. The plant smells like lemon. The tea of leaves is most enjoyable. Add lemon juice for colds and fever. When one is running

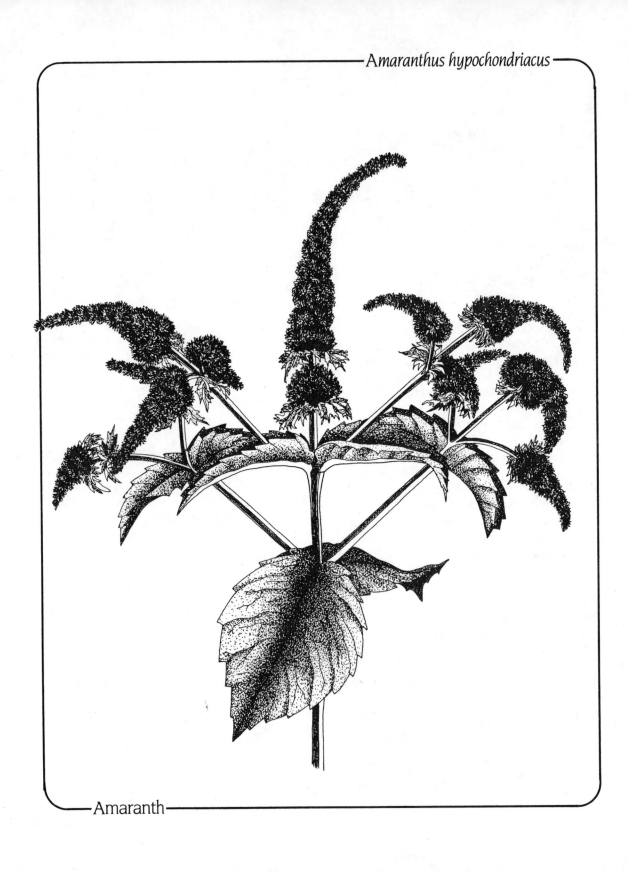

Amaranth

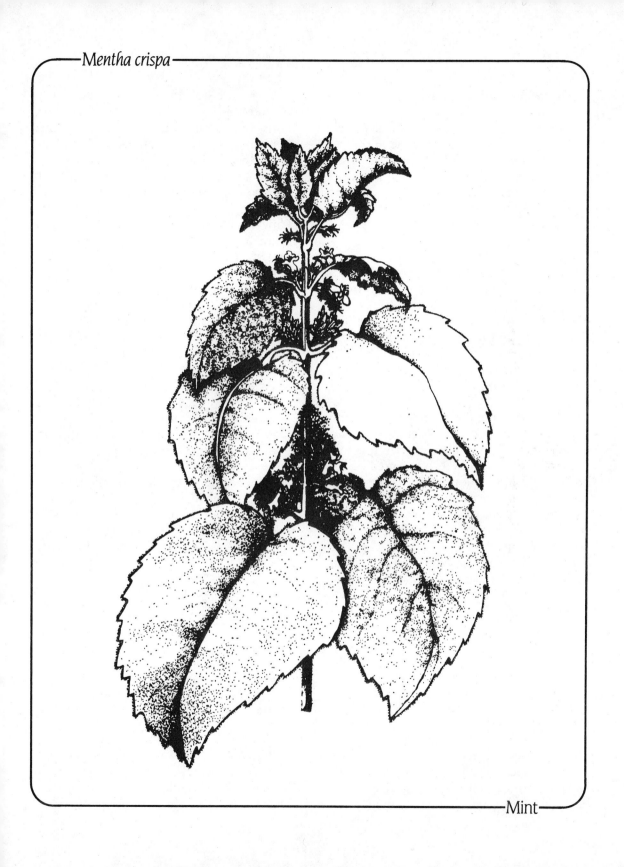

this can be inhaled to alleviate shortness of breath.

BLACKBERRY. We all know the fruit when eaten raw. Used to flavor wine and for a fine syrup. The unripe powdered fruit mixed with wine makes a great vinegar.

BLACK COHOSH. Always considered a tonic tea from the plant, the roots are more widely known as a tonic for the liver and kidneys.

BLESSED THISTLE. The fresh juice is very helpful for poisonous bites; the cold infusion for loss of appetite and sour stomach. The tea increases mothers' milk and is in great value as a general debility plant. Too much may cause vomiting but then that's true with all plants really.

BLOODROOT. The powdered root has often been a foot doctor's blood cleanser. As a powder this cleans putrified skin disorders. Once used as a snuff for relieving sores in the nose. Has been very useful for dysentery. In South America this was given for diarrhea often and worked well.

BORAGE TEA. Infuse for five minutes and strain. This, like comfrey, has been called boneset. For variation try the flowers infused three minutes and strained. Add a touch of honey.

BROOM. The flowers and seeds when steeped in water and honey act as an internal sauna, inducing perspiration. Or mold the fresh flowers for ten days, dry, and smoke for an old Indian euphoric.

BURDOCK. Another blood purifier. This is often heard of as a root decoction for arthritis. The root canned, in honey, is used for dysentery. A leaf tea is good for indigestion. The burdock leaves are good for children's nervousness. An excellent burn salve is made by gently boiling the fresh leaves and root for an hour in butter. Burdock oil rubbed in the hair, with rosemary oil, is fine for falling hair.

BURNET. Often used in salads, the fresh leaves are also applied with much reputed benefit to skin that has been hurt or wounded. Steeped in wine, burnet has a reputation for being a good blood rejuvenator.

CASCARA BARK. You can still drive through Oregon and see store windows with signs reading "We buy cascara." This bark is a fine laxative when decocted, or in tincture form.

CALENDULA OR MARIGOLD. A mild and pleasant tea, often used for the stomach. The flowers make an enjoyable hair wash. For calendula ointment (that has been used for almost everything) take six grams of the marigold juice mixed with thirty grams unsalted butter.

CHAMOMILE FLOWERS. The gypsy's delight. In Spanish *Manzanilla*. Many still find this to be the herb for rekindling the heart's light. At night a beautifully relaxing tea. Unless following specific instruction, the normal amount of tea to water is one teaspoon to one cup infused and strained. Or, why strain? It is food! Each with its own flavor. I remember a story Bob Gumpertz told:

In 1963 I was living in a small town in central Mexico. Two significant things happened that year, both related to herbs. When I came down with my first illness, the usual aches and cramps, the maid, who I inherited with the house, went to the marketplace, came back with Te de Manzanilla, Camomile, made a large pot and told me to drink several cups. The next morning I was quite well, and more than pleased that I had found something far superior to the various prescription pills that I had in my satchel, and which barely worked, if at all. The camomile was pleasant tasting, relaxed me, and took away the aches. I viewed Leovina and her herb teas with great interest that year.

CHICKWEED. Another of the common "weeds," this small tender green is a delight fresh or infused—one teaspoon to

one cup for five minutes—with a bit of honey added. The name comes from the small flower that looks like a chick-pea.

CLUB MOSS. Better known as *lycopodium* or tree beard. This, when rubbed on external cuts or bruises, aids to clean and strengthen. Steeped in wine this has been used for kidney and bladder upsets. Externally the powder is good for chafing on infants.

COLTSFOOT. The fresh leaves are wonderful for sore feet as well as general sores. For cases of giddiness, the powdered leaf is used as tea. A wash for the eyes from the flowers, well strained, or for your hair. A wonderful smoke and, in fact, a British tobacco used for lung problems is made from coltsfoot, eyebright, betony, rosemary, lavender, and chamomile.

COMMON SORREL. Also known as Oxalis weed. The tea quenches thirst and the leaf eaten raw is useful for its anti-scurvy effect. It should be noted that this plant contains a lot of oxalic acid and people with a rheumatoid condition should see a medical advisor before ingestion.

DESERT TEA. Also known as Ma Huang or Ephedra. Of the horsetail family this is high in silica as a tea. The herb is often employed by the Indian and Oriental for fever. Used as a tea with other plants this brings energy to the stagnant. The source of ephedrine.

ELDERBERRY. The flowers are made into a tea that opens the skin and produces a good sweat. The tea aids to eliminate impurities through the skin, and is used a great deal for colds and coughs. The wine is a fine liver and kidney tonic, as well as being used when a cold is coming on. The juice from the leaves, combined with cream or lard, makes an excellent salve for burns or poison oak.

ELECAMPANE. A wild sunflower; the root decocted is a good tonic. The leaves and seeds can be eaten raw in salad. The leaf applied to nettle rash is soothing.

EYEBRIGHT. Written of by Shakespeare and Milton for eyesight, this delicate flower grows abundantly in late summer and autumn. Infuse two minutes and strain. For very bad eyesight we're told to infuse longer strain thoroughly, and wash the eyes.

FENNEL. The root replaces celery for salads. The leaf is also enjoyable in salads or as a tea. The seed is used for flavoring foods and is a good chewing seed for refreshing the mouth. This plant is our substitute for licorice, which does not grow in the United States.

FENUGREEK. The seed taken internally as tea is said to be equal to quinine in preventing fever. A good gargle and an excellent poultice.

FEVERFEW. The warm infusion of the leaves is good for a cold. The tea acts like chamomile and if decocted with honey is of great use in breathing. Or bruise the herb, mix with vinegar and honey and eat with your meals.

FLAXWEED. The fresh plant makes a good poultice. The seed is used for a demulcent tea. Linseed oil is extracted from the leaf; linen is made from the leaf; and if boiled in milk the leaf also yields an excellent fly poison.

GENTIAN. The tea is excellent for a generally debilitated condition and gives force to the circulation.

GINGER ROOT. The wild varieties are best, more subtle, yet invigorating. Gather the root in early spring or late fall, bruise, decoct but a few moments, and strain. Use again till flavor departs. A Renaissance proverb tells us that if the "stomach stinketh: ginger unstinketh."

GINSENG ROOT. This root was once supposed to grow only in Korea, but it has been discovered to be also a native of

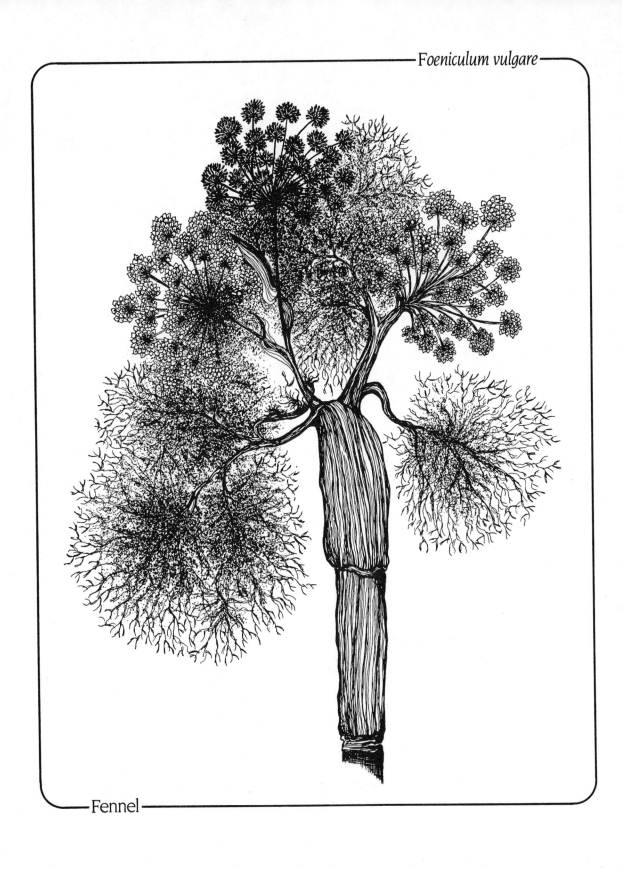

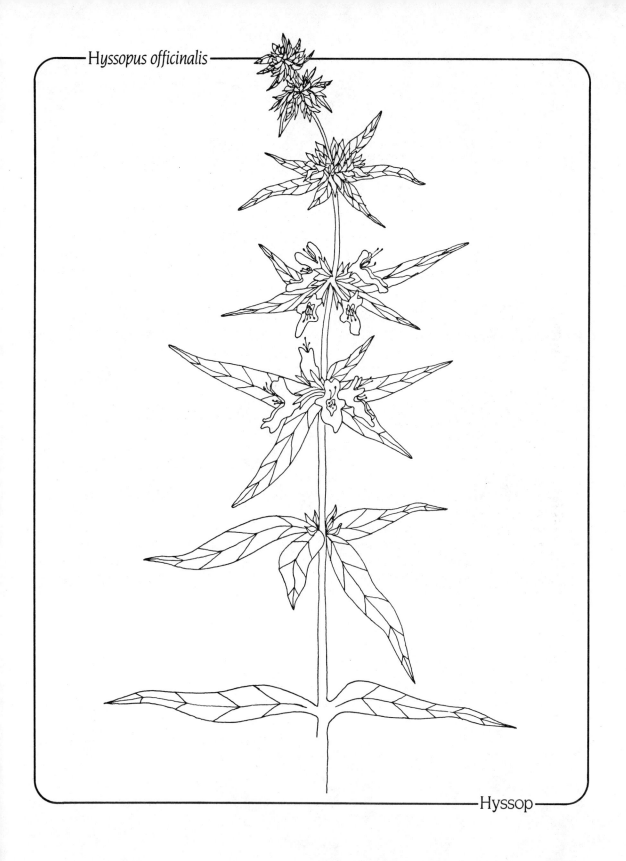

Hyssopus officinalis

Hyssop

North America, where it grows to a great perfection and is equally valuable. Its root is like a small carrot, but not so tapered at the end; it is sometimes divided into two or more branches, and in all other respects it resembles sarsparilla. The root tastes bitterish. In eastern Asia it is considered a panacea. When chewed it certainly is a great stomach strengthener.

GOLDENROD. The flower is a fine smoke for the throat and lungs. A tea of the leaves and flowers is a good tonic. Externally the tea cleans mild bruises and wounds. When goldenrod is hung about the home the air becomes clearer.

GOLDEN SEAL. Extremely popular herb whose uses are widely varied. Claimed to be one of the best blood purifiers, the root can also be decocted, strained, and used for an eye wash. Powder on wounds is great.

GRINDELIA. Resembles the sunflower, but exudes a sticky substance that gives the two varieties from California the nicknames "tar weed," "gum weed," and "rosin weed." Both varieties have the same bright green leaves and grow up to three feet tall. The *Squarrosa* has a yellow flower the *Robusta* an orange. The leaves and flowers of both varieties are made into a good tea. The leaves and sap are used externally for burns and cuts.

GROUND IVY. The tea increases the appetite and is useful for digestion. The fresh juice has been used as an ear drop.

HAWTHORN. The flowers and berries are decocted and are very good for the organic functions of the body. The Swiss make a good beer from the fruit and a tea for altitude sickness.

HORSETAIL: Also known as shave grass. Use the scouring rush for cleaning your pots. Horsetail is also a fine source of silica as a tea or soup.

HOPS. Infused in water, better than beer (for beer recipe see page 142). And for those hectic nights when your being needs quelling, one teaspoon hops flowers with two teaspoons chamomile flowers. Infuse five minutes and strain.

HOREHOUND. You recall those candy drops made of the horehound for soothing the throat. A nice infusion is one tablespoon honey to one tablespoon horehound and one cup of tea for those winter morns when one wants to awaken the throat. A pleasant weed that has a silver green aura.

HUCKLEBERRY. A tea from the leaves is excellent for a weak and sick stomach or as an eyewash. A decoction of the root bark or the dried berries can be made as well. A mixture of the leaves of huckleberry and strawberry make a nice combination tea.

HYSSOP LEAF. Provides the coloring found in many liqueurs. Infused and strained this makes a light and tasteful brew that is a joy when the winter blues beckon. Hyssop is spoken of in the Bible (Psalms 51:7) in connection with cleansing and purifying the blood.

JUNIPER BERRIES. A taste mildly pleasant to the mouth. Often referenced as being decocted for fifteen minutes, strained and taken alone, or mixed with mallow, parsley or alfalfa leaf. Good in effecting the flow of our water (urine).

KELP. Though this is never really considered a tea, a Piscean minister once recommended a sun infusion of one quart distilled water and one cup kelp for a gargle tea, as well as salt supplement, if one had done much outdoor work in the hot climes. If there was any left he advocated feeding it to the garden after diluting with five parts water.

LADIES SLIPPER. The fresh juice is great for using on poison oak. The leaves can be used as a wash for the skin, and the flowers make a tea for stress.

LAMB'S QUARTERS. Raw leaves are great for salads. The leaves can also be used as tea, and when abundant are good for the Green Drink. Bruised leaves are beneficial for the skin, and the seed is used on top of salads and breads.

LAVENDER. Laver means to wash, as washing the soul with an aromatic. The tea is great for headaches and once when I was nervous a close friend gave me some lavender and milk. Extremely calming. The oil has been used for loss of appetite. If one flies about in one's dreams too much the following pillow was recommended: Take a handful each of lavender flowers, chamomile, rosemary, rosebuds, sage and balm, mix gently together adding a bit of sassafras (or cinnamon and cloves). Place this by your head; it really helps.

LEMON BALM. See melissa.

LOBELIA. Although used more sparingly than other herbs because of its emetic effect, this plant has had a widespread usage. Can be used for itch ointments or snuff, or use the bruised leaves on the skin.

LICORICE. See fennel.

MANZANITA. Mountain folk make a good tonic by letting the berries stand in water overnight, and straining.

MARIJUANA. One plant that has definitely affected the spirit of many folks. As a tea the leaf tastes much like parsley tea—green. As a smoke the flowers are said to be "euphoric." One's ability to deal with spirit would determine the amount used as tea or smoke. (Smoking anything over a long period of time may be detrimental.)

MARJORAM. We don't think of this as a tea much, but throughout the European countries it is popular with the winter drinker. Zesty. It is found in foods throughout the world, smoked as an alternative to tobacco, and placed in dream pillows.

MINT. Common garden mint should be everywhere. If one teaspoon to one cup is infused three minutes, the aroma alone will verify the spirit. Like peppermint, a gentle pleasure after any meal. Cooling.

MUGWORT. The leaf is a good source of iron, and has often been used in soups or salads by many cultures. A tea of the leaves is used to expel any evil. One could also burn the dried leaf for its aromatic smoke.

MULLEIN. This very furry leaf is often burned in saunas or sweat lodges to relieve congestion. A tea can be made from the leaves, and salve can be made from the flowers.

NASTURTIUM FLOWERS. This peppery tasting flower is a warm delight during those months when warmth is needed. Gather the flowers when they are fully ripe, dry them, and prepare them as you would chamomile. A blend that requires only lemon verbena is:

> one half teaspoon lemon verbena leaf
> one half teaspoon nasturtium flowers
> one teapot water

Infuse three minutes and strain (or don't strain—the parts are good too).

NOBLE PINE. Also known as pipsissewa, noble pine in many ways is like uva ursi. The old timers used it for complaints anywhere in the body. Can also be used externally in the bath.

NOBLE YARROW. Like a hand in the meadow, this leaf and flower yields a bitter tonic. Or dry the stalk and cast your fate. A tea mixed in equal parts with chamomile or lemon balm is most enjoyable. Can also be used as a wash for sore heels after long walks.

Artemisia vulgaris or japonica

Mugwort

OKRA. Used many times as an emollient poultice. The seeds have a calming effect when chewed and also clean the breath. In the South okra was often given as a remedy for ulcers.

PASSION FLOWER. Just stand by this plant for a calming effect—or drink the tea. The marrow of the fruit is used for scurvy, the vine to tie bundles of gathered fire tinder.

PENNYROYAL. Also known as squaw mint. As the latter name implies, this plant was often (and still is) used by women to balance the water cycle more efficiently and ease their monthly discomfort. Use one teaspoon to one cup. It has been suggested that cramps can be eased by merely munching on the leaf.

PEPPERMINT

So much from such an abundant herb. From my childhood I remember the smell of peppermint, like when we mixed spruce gum and a leaf.

Chewing Gum

Gather spruce pitch (any amount) take a bit of the peppermint leaf and chew these together. This was always given to children for stomach ache.

Peppermint Stomach Essence

1 heaping teaspoon each:

  fennel
  wormwood
  elecampane
  blessed thistle
  peppermint

With mortar and pestle, powder all these. Let stand in one pint brandy ten days, then add:

  one half ounce orange peel
  one half ounce lemon peel
  several pinches cinnamon or clove

Allow to stand three more days. Filter. Use in morning—sixty drops to one cup of water.

PIMPERNEL. Often the root was given to chew for toothache. The leaf or flower is a good gargle, and a decoction of the leaves can be used on the skin.

POLYPODY. Also known as brake rock fern, this is an excellent tea alone or with mallow leaf. The fresh root in powder form is a good body powder, or take some powdered root and mix with honey for cuts and scratches.

PRUNELLA VULGARIS. Also called self-heal, this clover-like herb with shiny purple flowers is found growing in wild areas. For a subtle tea, infuse any amount of the herb in water. There is not an herbalist about who has not included this amongst his or her *materia medica*. Aside from the name self-heal, it is called carpenter's herb, sicklwort, hook-heal, and the older name brunella altered by Linnaeus.

QUERCUS. A plant better known as oak. Ruled by Jupiter as being the king of hardwoods. Throughout history, the leaf has always been used for tonic. It is found in the same area and is often used as the antidote to poison oak. The leaves are placed in a cloth and made into an astringent tea, which, when applied directly to the skin, helps dry the infected area.

QUAKE GRASS. Also called dog grass, this herb contains a great deal of silica. The tea is a good blood purifier and one can sprout the seed. In combination with chicory, mallow, and violet flowers the tea has been used to relieve water retention.

RASPBERRY LEAF. The Indians tell us that all fruit leaves are good for balancing women's cycles. Though there is no known medical data to support its use, many

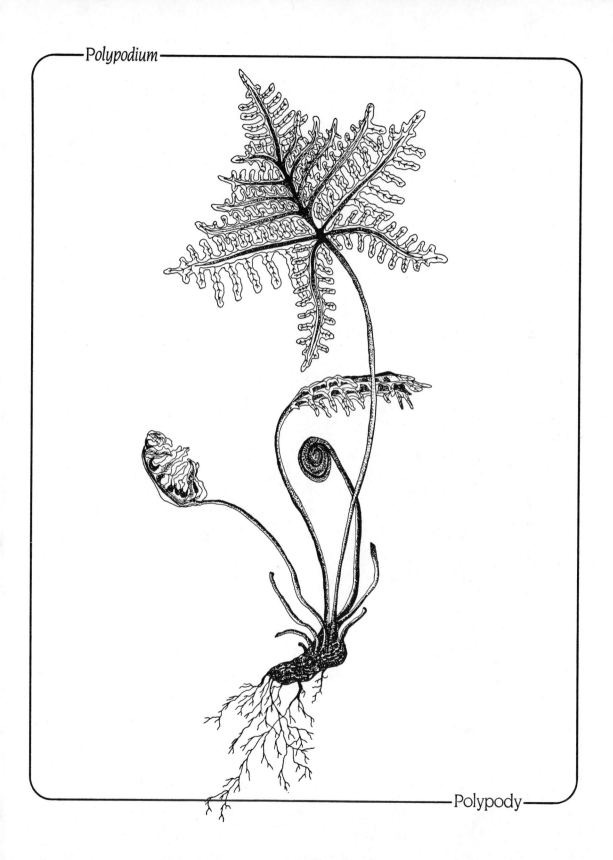

women claim morning sickness is alleviated by this tea.

To one teapot hot water
add one quarter teaspoon chamomile
  flower
one quarter teaspoon comfrey leaf
one quarter teaspoon raspberry leaf

Allow to infuse. Drink liberally.

RED CLOVER BLOSSOMS. Widely recorded as a blood cleanser. The tea used for coughs and infections of the pancreas.

REDWOOD. The Indians used the bark and sap from cones as a strong astringent. A good stain was made by infusing the gritty sap from the cones and trunk. As a furniture stain, as well as John Muir's ink, the following recipe was used: gather the pigment from about the seed and soak these in water till a rich red-brown color develops. This is mostly tannin.

RUE. The fresh bruised leaf is good if you're bothered by sciatica, a hot fomentation on the head will ease headache. Or you can take equal amounts of rue, sage, lavender, wormwood, and mint; let stand in vinegar in a sunny place for four days; filter; and use on salads.

SAGE. In the middle ages much credit was given to the power of Shalfey (sage) as both food and as medicine. When made into tea the plant has been called the asthma weed. However it is better to inhale the vapors of the tea. Sage is used more to cook with than as a tea. Sun infusion makes a good drink, or add a few leaves to soup.

SARSAPARILLA. The root of this and sassafras has often been recommended for venereal diseases, ulcers, skin disorders and in all cases of debility. The smoke of the root is used for lung congestion. A tea decocted with comfrey root and rose hips greatly aids when flu strikes.

SASSAFRAS. The first export from the United States to England, this has always been used for the blood. The root has been used as a wash for nettle rash and as a flavoring for beverages. It makes a tasty tea. Its flavor has caused it to be called our native cinnamon.

SHEPHERD'S PURSE. The leaves when crushed are good for those hard day's bruises or sore joints. Am told by all Indian medicine people that this is one of the best herbs to stop bleeding, especially internal, and all types of hemorrhages. A tea is good for congestion.

SLIPPERY ELM. One of nature's best remedies for stomach and bowel disorders. The bark as a decocted tea is a mild and harmless laxative for kids. The bark powdered is a fine emollient and poultice, for boils, fresh wounds and burns.

SOAP ROOT. This bulb was often used to clean wounds and relieve itching when applied topically. As a decocted tea with watercress this was employed as a fine digestive tonic. Use only for survival because all bulbs are becoming endangered.

SPIKENARD. Spikenard is a great blood purifier. The Cree Indians used this for syphilis. For wounds, a powder of the leaf or root is still used by locals of the South.

ST. JOHN'S WORT. The tea made from the flower or leaf has always been regarded as beneficial for the blood. It also makes a good hair rinse and is good if one is chilled. For cramps in the stomach, macerate four ounces of the tops in one pint of olive oil, and rub on the stomach.

STRAWBERRY LEAF. The strong infusion of the leaf has always been considered a potent tonic and has also been used as a beneficial gargle for the gums. To regulate those sluggish days a tea can be made from equal parts of dandelion, burdock, rhubarb, and strawberry leaf. We do not often hear of the tea simply as a refreshment.

SYCAMORE. The tea is used for the skin. A mixture of horehound and sycamore makes a fine tea for coughs. You can get sycamore sugar by tapping the tree and boiling the juice.

TANSY. The tea has been used for all stomach complaints, especially those of the female. The oil is used for sore muscles. When placed or grown about the home, tansy acts as a bug repellant, especially against ants.

VALERIAN. Ah, the smelly old socks herb, but it is also known as nerve root and as a tea the root is beneficial for nervousness or insomnia. Boiling the root with licorice (fennel), raisins, and anise makes a good cough formula. The tincture is still available from many druggists.

VIRGINIA DOGWOOD. The flowers are used during fever, and a tincture of the berries restores tone to the stomach in alcoholism. The legend of the dogwood flower tells how the tree was straight, but after Jesus was crucified on a cross made of dogwood, it became so twisted as to be of no use, and the flower grows in the form of a cross.

WINTERGREEN. A tea of the leaves every once in awhile has always been recommended by those in the Shenandoah Valley as a "strong cleanser." In small amounts it stimulates the heart.

WITCH HAZEL. The leaves are a good skin cleaner, fresh or dried. The bark should only be used when dried. When decocted it acts as a good enema, as a gargle, and for bites.

WOODRUFF. Used often as a flavoring for other teas, it is also a good blood purifier. The fresh leaves on your forehead will help headaches or can be used as a poultice for the skin. The drink often associated with woodruff is May Wine, which is made by placing woodruff leaves and strawberries in white wine for two days. Tasty. Woodruff, thyme, strawberry, and blackberry leaf tea is divine.

WORMWOOD. A bitter tonic or a tea for feebleness in the body, this should be used like lobelia: "little bits over a long period of time." Boiled in vinegar or oil, wormwood is excellent for all sprains and swellings. As the name indicates, the tea has been used to expel stomach and bowel worms.

YARROW. See Noble Yarrow.

YEW. A syrup is made from the fruit for respiratory troubles. A tea made from the green twigs is good for the stomach.

YERBA BUENA. "The good herb," is native to the San Francisco region and once was the namesake of the area. The tea has a delightful arom and a delicate mintlike flavor.

YERBA SANTA. Chew the leaves for thirst. A tea is good for congestion. The smoke of the leaves is often used in ceremonial rites and as a lung purifier.

YUCCA. The roots have been used as a source of soap by chopping and soaking in water, after which they are dried and cooked. It is a rather lightly astringent, starchy food source. The core or pith of the center stalk is a survivalist's tinder.

Blessed is the man that trusteth in God, and whose hope God is. For he shall be as a tree planted by the waters, that spreadeth out his roots by the river, and shall not fear when heat cometh, but its leaf shall be green, and shall not be careful in the year of the drought, neither shall cease from yielding fruit.

Jeremiah 17:7-8

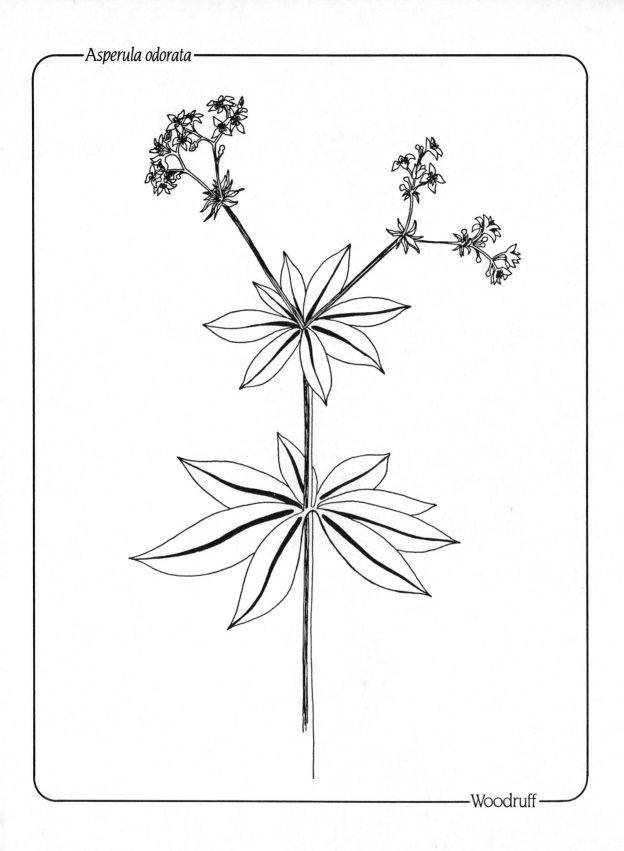

Garlic

FIVE

Soups

A Good Physician Should be a Good Cook:
His Soups the Seasonal Inspiration
Toward Healing

A Good Physician should be a Good Cook;
His Soups the Seasonal Inspiration Toward Healing

Perhaps in our minds there are thousands of uncharted recipes for soups. When we are cold, a soup is warm inspiration. When discouraged, a soup is a glorified herb tea, refreshing yet simple. Each country has "its own" soup. Each person, his own centering creation. I can pass on to you only a glimpse, a few guides as you experiment in developing, tuning, preparing a creation (possibly tradition) of your own. Be imaginative with what you prepare in accordance with the balance of nature.

When water was never to be trusted, or when the intent was to purify, the addition of onion and garlic was almost as essential as the water for brewing. Throughout my travels one soup keeps reappearing, almost as a "sign," the garlic soup. Many variations, yet one familiar taste.

In Peru, in a market place in Cusco, the Inca Capital, I observed a simple, yet upon tasting, complex soup. The woman cooking said it had been passed down to her people from the Inca rulers.

Garlic Soup

3 bulbs garlic
one pot of water

Boil garlic one minute, then simmer ten to twenty minutes. Add potato chopped into squares and torn mustard greens as desired.

NOTE: When ritually preparing food, tearing is preferred as opposed to cutting, although some argue that a clean cut is quicker, others contend that tearing allows the herbs to yield according to their own fiber contour and cellular structure, thus passing on more of their own essence which is lost when we eat of bulk processed or enriched packaged foods.

Garlic/Watercress Soup

1 cup watercress
4 cloves garlic
1 tablespoon parsley, freshly chopped
1 teaspoon sea salt

Bring water to boil. Place garlic in pot and boil for ten minutes. Slowly add the salt and the parsley. Reduce heat to very low. Add the watercress and cook together five minutes. For variation add some warmed raw mild, miso, or cream.

Miso

An Oriental staple. A thick paste of fermented soybean barley, sea salt and water. Be sure to obtain pure, as some new processes use artificial starters. So much has been said of this food by the Oriental people, that one wonders why in such a food-conscious state, many are just discovering this protein, enzyme rich food.

Garlic Miso Soup

a couple of onions, minced
five cloves garlic, chopped
4 cups water
1 tablespoon oil
5 tablespoons miso
¼ cup favorite vegetable herb, such as comfrey,
spinach, chard or cabbage

Saute vegetables in oil about ten minutes. Bring water to a boil and pour over vegetables. Cover and simmer thirty minutes. Just before finished, dilute miso in a cup of warm water and add to pot. Do not boil, as much of the delicate essence will be lost. Top with parsley or chives.

Over the last five years, while teaching historical herbal classes, I looked forward to a class where the students could conjure up experiments making use of what he or she had learned. A few of the varied soups that appeared are included here. Where I could give credit, I have done so. Never have we lost anyone from wild soup as yet, but as always, let a prudent amount of caution be the guide.

One such dinner reunion included sixty herbal folks and one soup capable of serving almost that many. You may add or subtract according to your specific serving needs.

Herby Lentil Herb Soup
(Ginger)

10 quarts water
2 pounds lentils
2 large onions
4 cloves garlic (more garlic!)
¼ teaspoon dill
¼ teaspoon sage
¼ teaspoon basil
¼ teaspoon celery seed
¼ teaspoon caraway seed
¼ teaspoon bay leaves
¼ teaspoon rosemary
¼ teaspoon turmeric
¼ teaspoon Hungarian paprika
¼ teaspoon oregano
¼ teaspoon curry powder
woodruff leaf
coriander seed
juniper berries
ground cumin
allspice or mace
ginger, pinch
salt and pepper to taste

Tie woodruff, coriander, juniper and cumin in cheesecloth. In a large (two or three gallon) covered pot, boil all the above ingredients gently for about two hours or until soup reaches the desired consistency. Then add vegetables such as carrots, celery, cabbage, comfrey, cauliflower, and potatoes.

With vegetables added cook another five minutes. Let stand to infuse the aromatic essence *por el momento* (Spanish—for the moment), then remove cheesecloth. Vegetables will be *al dente* (Italian—a little bit crisp) a nice reference to the way vegetables should always be served—a little bit crisp.

Scotch barley always comes to mind when I think of a grain that often found its way into my bowl when I was a youngster. There are many types of soups and stews. Many types and many combinations—nice really when you realize that even though there are an infinite number of possibilities, there are no secrets, really. This makes cooking something for everyone—though not everyone is reliant upon his or herself yet. Hopefully, the educational systems will start to require food survival skills that are combined (like a good meal) with the sciences, recreation and philosophy.

Scotch Barley Soup
(A grain soup)

2 quarts water
3 grated carrots
3 chopped onions
1 potato, boiled, cooled and chopped
2 stalks fennel (about ½ cup)
1 cup pearl barley
2 tablespoons chopped parsley or chives
1 teaspoon kelp flakes
½ teaspoon sea salt
2 tablespoons oil

Place the carrots, onions, potato and fennel in deep pot with oil and saute. Add the water and bring to boil, stirring in the barley, kelp and salt. Simmer one hour. Serve with the parsley sprinkled on top.

FERMENTED MILK

You may wonder why we turn now to fermented milk. Aren't we discussing the making of soups? Simply, fermented milk is yogurt. Throughout the Levant (Mediterranean) people have, since time recorded, used this semisolid, cheeselike milk—called yogurt. Research shows that fermented milk products can enhance the usefulness of some minerals, and conversions of sugar, when taken in foods, have a tonic quality beneficial to our digestive systems. Kefir, another of the fermented milk products, was called "the drink of the prophets." There are many books about these fermented foods; the Bibliography lists several. There are many ways in which to serve these products but two soups appear which seem universal in their table presentation:

Cold Yogurt and Cucumber Soup
(Cary Knozler)

1 cucumber
2 cups yogurt
2 teaspoons apple cider vinegar
2 teaspoons virgin olive oil
¾ teaspooon sea salt
2 teaspoons fresh mint, minced or dried
½ teaspoon minced, fresh dill weed or ¼ teaspoon dried

Peel the cucumber and grate it coarsely. Stir the yogurt in bowl until completely smooth. Gently but thoroughly beat in other ingredients. Chill (the longer the better). Serve plain, or over bed of your favorite vegetable.

Yogurt Beet Soup/Borsch
(There are as many versions of this as there are Russians in the East.)

2 cups beets
1 cup onion
½ cup carrots
1 tablespoon butter
2 cups favorite broth
1 cup finely cut cabbage
1 tablespoon vinegar

Cover, barely, the carrots, beets, and onion with boiling water. Simmer gently, covered, for about twenty minutes. Add to this all other ingredients and simmer another fifteen minutes. Place in bowls and add yogurt (about one tablespoon for each bowl, according to your taste for yogurt). If you like, top with cucumber and add your choice of seasoning. If it's cold, cayenne pepper is nice; if warm, dill and parsley are delightful. Once we served this soup over comfrey leaves with fresh brown bread.

In the preparation of soups, I often feel as though each ingredient that goes within the soup imparts a flavor, an essence, and some spirit. Thus when I eat, or drink a soup, a spiritual brew is infusing within my body.

When I am traveling in the Orient, seaweeds are always presented before me, including nori, dulse, kelp, kombu, wakami and hundreds more. As yet, there are no known poisonous seaweeds or sea-vegetables. But if you are going to gather these yourself, here are a few rules before cooking:

Thorough washing is important because of the tiny sea snails and their eggs which could be poisonous.

Some seaweeds are too tough to eat but can be added to soups—just more chewing meditation.

To retain their flavors, wash in the ocean water.

Summer is the best time to collect these vegetables.

Gather and wash in unpolluted water.

Soak the seaweeds five to fifteen minutes before cooking—thus softening. Then cut into strips.

 While sharing views of the seaweeds, I like to reference the alfalfa with the kelps. Both are unique in nature because of their large and ever-spreading root structures. The universal circle illustrates. Place A (alfalfa) on one side, K (kelp) on the other. One has the most unique root structure of the solid earth and other the most unique root structure of the liquid earth. Both have such absorption factors that they are fantastic-

ally full of the elements and minerals that make up this earth.

Though the kelp leaf stretches sometimes hundreds of feet through the liquid earth to the light, you may have seen from the long kelps on the beach, an "onion" or bulb does exist at the base, holding the whole into the sand at the bottom of the ocean floor. This bulb or onion is very edible, slightly salty and served as other vegetables. Hopefully we will soon have as much food from the ocean as from the land. Sea peoples in the East have always included these different types of seaweed in their food. Once we, as Westerners, start to use these, the less synthesized (processed) salts we will have to use for flavor. Natural flavors are enhanced by nature's biochemic salts. Many soups of the ocean exist. My favorite survival soup, (were I to be stranded near the ocean for any length of time) is:

Earthy Sea Soup

Gathering and preparing accorded to the simple "rules" I take:

    1 handful gathered seaweed
    1 cup sea water

Allow to infuse in the sun for approximately three to five hours. Drink slowly. Its taste is of the ocean. Salty at first, but as your body begins to utilize these waters, the more benefit you will derive from it.

Another is more complicated:

Seaweed Soupreme

    1 quart water
    1 cup seaweed
    slice of ginger
    parsley to taste
    chopped green pepper to taste

green onion to taste
water chestnuts about 4, sliced into
    fourths
mushrooms to taste
a pinch each of basil, cayenne, celery
    seed, and sage

Simmer the seaweed in water about fifteen minutes. Add the vegetables and spices, as the soup simmers (usually in last five minutes of cooking) remove from heat, dash with parsley, and enjoy.

Seaweed-Burdock-Onion
(For combating radioactivity)
(Richard Katz)

3 ounces seaweed of your choice
2 sliced burdock roots (gobo in the
    Orient)
2 diced onions
1 tablespoon oil
4 tablespoons soy sauce

Soak the seaweed and slice or cut into small pieces. Saute onions in oil. Add burdock root, then seaweed. Cover this and bring to a boil. Simmer fifteen minutes. Add about a cup of the soaking water and soy sauce and simmer this ten minutes more. Make substitutions as desired.

I remember a swim in Wiamea Bay one Easter. My companions wondered why I was lounging about the rocks in the bay—and found me eating seaweeds. What a sight—about ten people joined the sea-lunch—each offering their ideas of this old, yet new, way. We talked of man's evolution from the ocean to the land and what many are missing today, within nature's natural "soup," the sea.

The following four soups have no specific amount of ingredients. Many people have enjoyed preparing their own versions and I have included them here so you can see what others might add to their soup, herb-ally. You have received enough perception in the previous pages to properly blend these. Again be imaginative.

George Jones' Sensuous Soup

damiana	celery
garlic	green pepper
onion	salt and pepper
carrots	

Jenny Nelson's
Barley Root Soup

barley	alfalfa
celery root	comfrey
carrots	dandelion
squash	watercress
tomatoes	plantain
sunflower	

Helen Smith's Seed Soup

soy milk with pumpkin seeds
blended in
sesame seeds
dock seeds
plantain seeds
poppy seeds
alfalfa seeds (for protein)
lamb's-quarters leaves
one dandelion leaf (for fun)
kelp
Irish moss
parsley
miso

Simmer together gently.

Thrower's Jerusalem
Artichoke Soup

3 pounds Jerusalem artichokes
4 onions
    (sauted in 3 tablespoons oil)
4 stalks celery
1 pound mushrooms
4 tomatoes

dandelion greens
fresh coriander
 (also known as cilantro)
fresh watercress
wild dill
4 tablespoons soy sauce
parsley
sea salt
½ ounce marijuana herb

Green Soup
(for a large group)

As with the Green Drink in the Simples section, so likewise the Green Soup in this section. These last two recipes are as complex teas, but with a bit more flavor.

Fill a large pot half full of:

 chickweed
 wild onion
 sorrel
 plantain
 5-6 sprigs fennel
 6 cloves garlic (large)

Add a few inches water. Cook until just tender. Then blend and strain. Add some of the fiber to this stock.
 Season with:

 3 tablespoons cold pressed oil
 2 tablespoons ground cardamon
 1 tablespoon paprika
 1 tablespoon cayenne pepper
 1 tablespoon sea salt
 a bit of basil and thyme
 1 tablespoon soy sauce

Cook four handfuls of rolled oats in 2 cups water. Cook then blend and strain. Add to soup to thicken, being careful not to make too bland.
 Saute and steam vegetables. I used 1½ tablespoons chopped ginger with cauliflower, broccoli, carrot, celery and six more cloves of garlic, then more wild onion, more basil and sage. When done add to soup.

NOTE: The point here is to not cook the vegetables any longer than necessary so as to retain the vital elements. Keep covered whenever possible.

Weedy Wild Soup
(Ron and Seejoy)

Gather approximately two quarts of tender, young greens. Wash, drain, and save the water for your plants. Stir the weeds into a large pot containing about five quarts of boiling water. Cook the weeds for two to three minutes. Drain the weeds (again, this material left is great for your house plants). Chop to desired size. In soup kettle cook four to five tablespoons minced onion or garlic in four tablespoons oil until the onion or garlic are translucent. Add five cups water and bring to boil.

Add goodly share of diced potatoes and 1½ cups of tender greens, cooking the mixture to a rapid boil, gradually stirring in three-fourths cup quick cooking oatmeal (or oatmeal of choosing). Reduce the heat. Simmer for three to five minutes, adding salt and pepper to taste. This yields slightly less than two quarts.

The soup you may have left over can be frozen and saved for another time. Fresh is always the rule when possible. There are so many nourishing soups that volumes have been devoted just to them.

Perhaps it is futile to ask you to write down your discovery of a new recipe. After all, what really is a recipe? A formula—a set of instructions—a symbol of nourishment? Possibly a souvenir of the time, no more. Perhaps it's vain to set down in amounts an evocation of good times—perhaps it's not the soup or the recipe that counts. But rather the gathering, the working with your hands and the many varied flavors that go into the soup that make it all worthwhile.

The rest is up to you. Happy souping.

Sorrel

Soup Suggestions
For Your Own Invention
(titles only)

nut meat and onion
garlic and onion
apple
apple cider with cabbage
artichoke and yogurt
cold fruit with herbs
leek
lentil and herbs
mushroom and herbs
green split pea and herbs
potato salad
lettuce and sorrel
spring greens
corn and parsley
egg drop
leek and potato
minestrone
pepper
cream of sorrel
watercress
cucumber with chives

potato onion
rice and vegetable (herb)
celery
carrot and thyme
garden pea and pepper gazpacho
seaweed broth
soy sauce broth
cream of spring vegetable
avocado dandelion
cream of parsley
spiced herb
spinach supreme
saffron rice soup
coriander and dock
mushroom curry
cheese noodle with herbs
ginger mint soup
garlic anything
herb anything
anything
anything

SIX

Salads and Their Dressings

The most significant of my teachers, Nathan Podhurst, & Emma of Nature's Herb Co. in San Francisco always say to me, "Rob, when you finish your salad (or meal) make sure that you are still hungry and leave a bit upon your plate as an offering. In this way you will never eat too much, you'll never gain much weight, and you'll always be well."

"Salade," according to Organic John is: "Nature's menu in universal form—recipes for the Family of Man."

SALAD

If we take away the water from the teas and soups, what we have left are the basic ingredients for salads.

It is now recognized that our daily requirement for salad is at least 50 percent of the day's intake. These are the fiber foods essential to the metabolic function and the cleansing and toning of our system. When we ingest the wild greens, essential minerals and vitamins are absorbed. Figure-watchers especially should have as much salad as possible.

There are many ways to present the salad, but the most aesthetic way is to lay out each vegetable separately displaying the many textures and colors and allowing people their choice. This is especially attractive to those who are just being converted to the vegetable (herbal) way of preparing foods.

The salad bowl is as important as the salad. Though we cannot eat it (unless made of a large leaf), it does impart subtle vibrations that are transferred into the salad. After each use one need only rinse or wipe dry, and with time the flavors season the wood and the salads. If one feels the need to wash the bowl, do so in cool water and add some oil to the wood afterward. This also applies to utensils. Many friends enjoy eating with wooden utensils rather than metal ones, because of the vibration factor (teeth to metal feels awful). Some prefer their fingers! (Too bad this is socially unacceptable.) The undeviated experience seems to increase the level of understanding transferred from herb (or vegetable) to person. I am convinced that we absorb some of the nutrient through touch, as well as lotioning our hands: a delight for the body, mind and soul.

It is a pleasure to experience the many different salads in this life. Many are just becoming aware that they are free for the picking, though don't be too free and unaware of where you pick or how much you take. An Indian said before I went picking, "For every leaf you pick, leave two unless the root is strong. For each seed you take scatter two, so the earth and bird may feed and reseed." A quieting thought from one who spent much of her time just "feeding on the greens, like the deer."

DEER DEW MEADOW SALAD
(inspired by children playing and animals eating)

This is another of those unconventional ways in which to sup. If you are an evolutionary thinker, take yourself or others into a dewy meadow in the morning. Knowing the basic herb weeds, such as dandelion and plantain, notice if any of the tops of the plants have been eaten off by the deer. If there are no deer, look for other signs. Getting down on all fours, become like a deer for awhile; stick your nose to the dewy grass; don't mind the dewy knees or hands (they'll dry—good form of dew hydrotherapy). Smell the dew, inhale slowly, slowly, slowly—the everlasting breath of life's watery morn. When you feel fulfilled this way, with your fingers, face, and tongue lick the dew water. Then prepare to eat what you have identified. To start the day with this meadow salad is a unique pleasure. Something the whole herd would love to do. A dewy morning picnic maybe?

At times we may feel there is only lettuce with which to make salad. Some may know no other way. Practice with the greens. There are more besides lettuce. Dandelion salad anyone? In a marinade?

Marinated Dandelion Salad for Four
(a meal in itself)

four cups freshly picked dandelion greens (washed and dried so no water remains to dilute the taste)

In bowl, mix thoroughly

½ cup lemon juice
1 teaspoon salad herbs
(equal amounts of rosemary, sage, thyme, oregano, marjoram)
1½ teaspoons herb salt*
½ cup olive oil

Let marinate 15 minutes, then place on a bed of crisp lettuce. Dash the top with cayenne or paprika.

*HERB SALT (one half cup sea salt, any combination of favorite herbs, powdered & added)

Miner's Lettuce Luncheon Salad

A plant that received much acclaim during the gold rush and was called the scurvy weed. It was given to the miners in the spring by the Indians as a source of vitamin C (found lacking during those potato and onion winters).

Any amount miner's lettuce leaves.
Season with
olive oil
pepper*
vinegar
lemon
spices to taste.

*The pepper we usually use is cayenne, as the black pepper has not had the acclaim of the red. Dr. Jeff Anderson, of Mill Valley, California, writes of this plant—testimony of the use of red to black.

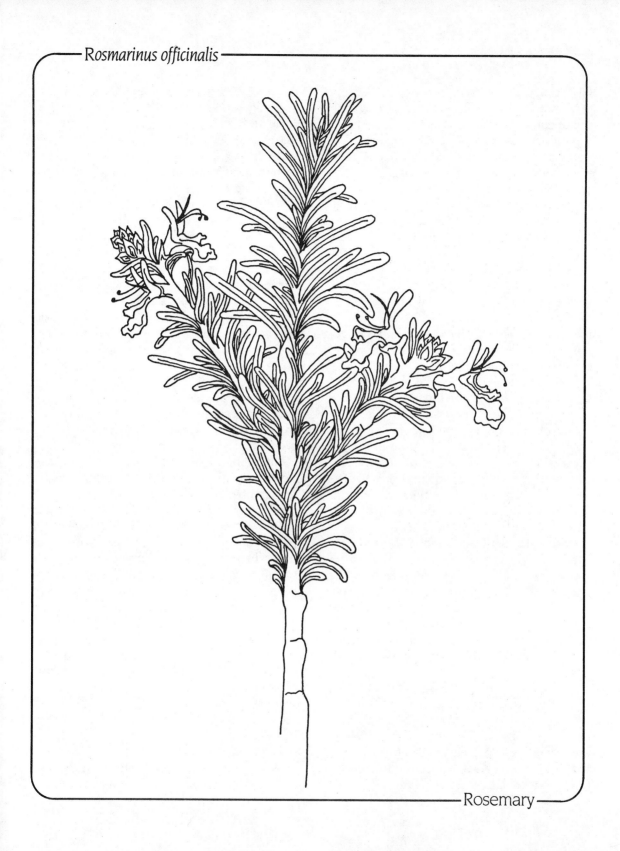

I have in the past five years employed approximately fifty different herbs for both therapeutic and preventative effects. From this variety of herbs one has proven itself the most outstanding and efficacious with the widest scope of uses: capsicum or cayenne pepper. This extraordinary plant is, I believe, the classic "prototype" to which all others may be compared. It manifests the *sine qua non* characteristics that every therapist seeks but seldom finds in choosing his or her natural medicines: a high degree of efficacy in a wide variety of diseases; very low degree of toxicity or adverse reactions; reasonable availability; equal effectiveness used internally or externally, very rapid onset of action; and highest degree of effectiveness in *raw* form.

Capsicum is the highest known source of vitamin A in the plant kingdom. It is also one of the richest in vitamin C. Although much of this plant's medicinal action derives from its content of these vitamins (especially its antiviral and antiinfectious, as well as its preventative, qualities), I believe that there is at least one other active principal as yet undiscovered. For example, capsicum's unique action in alleviating acute internal hemorrhage cannot be entirely based on its vitamin content. This other active principal (or principals) may be the pungent fraction known as *capsic capsicum*. In any case, more basic laboratory investigation would be of benefit in further elucidating the plant's active principals, intrinsic catalysts, preservatives, and modes of action.

Capsicum is a potent antiviral agent of the first order. As stated above, its high content of vitamins A and C are at least partly responsible for this action. When used daily as a preventive tonic (¼-½ teaspoon of powdered dried fruit sprinkled on food or mixed in juice or water) the inci-

dence of viral illnesses is markedly reduced. This phenomenon could be due to direct repression of intracellular virus replication or to enhanced host resistance through release of endogenous interferon, stimulation of nonspecific antiviral antibodies, or possibly both mechanisms.

Undoubtedly because of these same factors, capsicum is also heralded as a treatment for active viral infections of all types. I suggest capsicum for such diverse viral illnesses as herpes simplex types 1 and 2, herpes zoster, colds, flu, bronchitis, etc. Because of its potent decongestant qualities (once again related to its vitamin A and C content), as well as its vasoconstrictive action on mucous membranes, it is also very valuable in any condition resulting in inflammation and congestion of the upper respiratory passages, such as in allergic disorders, ear and sinus infections, and sore throats due to bacterial rather than viral origin, e.g., strep throat.

For adults ¼ teaspoon of powdered capsicum mixed in juice (fresh carrot, tomato, or lemon with honey) should be *sipped slowly* four to five times a day. Most people soon become acclimated to the pungency. (Capsicum appears to be much more effective through contact with the mucous membranes of the mouth and throat as opposed to absorption through the mucosa of the stomach and small bowel. This may be due to partial inactivation or alteration of active ingredients by stomach acid or digestive enzymes. Therefore I recommend that capsicum *not* be taken in capsules when treating viral illnesses.) Because of its marked pungency, it is difficult for small children to take it internally. Fortunately, however, it is readily absorbed through the skin of infants and children. For viral illnesses (and other indications discussed above) foot baths in warm water to which capsicum has been added (about ½ teaspoon in a small pan of water) for 15 minutes two to three times a day may be helpful. As an alternative the herb may be mixed in a light vegetable oil and massaged into the child's feet. After each treatment any excess oil should be washed off so that the child does not spread the mixture into his or her eyes.

Capsicum appears to be one of the most effective agents in treating skin diseases, especially those of viral etiology, such as warts, herpes lesions, and molluscum contagiosum. I prescribe as follows:

To ¼ cup fresh or bottled aloe vera gel, add ½ teaspoon powdered dried capsicum. Mix well to form a paste. Apply to lesions every six hours, washing off previous application first.

Variations on this recipe are many and varied; all are effective. Some of my own are: add ¼ teaspoon of powdered sarsaparilla root and/or the juice of fresh comfrey leaves for skin lesions with a severe itch associated. If aloe gel is difficult to obtain, coconut oil may be used as a vehicle by heating ¼ cup in a pan to about 150-175 degrees (use candy thermometer). Add ½ teaspoon powdered capsicum, mix well, and remove from heat. Cool to solidify and apply to lesions as an ointment.

Another marination, one often enjoyed while in Korea, is offered by Hui Dok Chun of the Korean Roof, in San Francisco.

Kim Chi

2 medium-sized Chinese cabbage
⅔ cup of hot pepper
¾ cup and 1 tablespoon of salt
1 tablespoon of honey*
1 clove garlic squeezed
3 stalks green onion (sliced)

Her recipe calls for 2 tablespoons sugar.

Add ¾ cup of salt to 3 cups of water and mix until salt dissolves. Cut cabbages in half and submerge in salt water. Let stand 3 hours and then wash in fresh water and drain. Mix well the hot pepper, the remaining tablespoon of salt, and the honey, garlic, and green onion. Cut cabbages into 1½ inch. Put the cabbage into a large container and mix well with the other ingredients. Let Kim Chi stand 2 days at room temperature before serving. For a better taste leave in the refrigerator 2 days and then serve.

A Greek salad called Tabuli (or Taboolie), which originated in the Mediterranean, mixes grain with vegetables and herbs. It is not cooked, which makes for a cooling salad. When preparing, you will experience an aroma that almost takes you back in thyme. (A staple in the Middle East.)

Tabuli (Greek Pilaf Salad)
(serves six)

2 cups raw cracked wheat, bulgur, or pilaf
1 cup warmed water
1 cup lemon juice (may use less if you
    desire less acid)
½ cup chopped onion
1 cup chopped parsley
2 tomatoes, diced
some fresh mint to taste
salt and pepper and spices
    (such as thyme or oregano) to taste

Soak the wheat in warm water till water is completely absorbed and cracked wheat (bulgur or pilaf) is soft. Add other ingredients and store in cold place till time to serve.

There are many variations:

Leave out the tomatoes, and substitute carrot, cabbage, or comfrey.

Leave out the parsley, and substitute dandelion greens (or any other foraged green).

This recipe goes very well with the Tabuli and provides the receiver with a "complete"

Thyme

protein, almost all vitamins and minerals, roughage, and laxative qualities, plus all the benefits of garlic, onion, and cayenne.

Chommos

(Approximate recipe, prepare
to your taste)

6 cloves garlic
1 teaspoon sea salt or kelp powder
⅓-½ cup lemon juice and rind
4-5 tablespoons sesame tahini
1½ cups garbanzo beans that have been
   soaked or steamed *al dente*

Place all the above in a blender in the order presented and blend. Refrigerate for several (at least two) hours. Bring this to room temperature.

Garnish with cayenne and cumin or pickled vegetables; or serve with raw vegetables and bread (preferably the Middle Eastern Pita bread p. 122.)

Since we are exploring the Middle Eastern influence in our salads, here is another that is great alone or with either Tabuli, Chommos or Sesame Tahini.

Hummos

2½ cups chick peas
5 cloves garlic
olive oil
½ cup Sesame Tahini
2 tablespoons tamari (soy sauce)
1 lemon

Boil chick peas with garlic until tender. Blend in tahini, tamari, lemon, and oil.

Pickled Vegetables

(a salad variation by Michael Farrell)

16 cups gathered wild greens or vegetables
   of your choice
10 small onions
¼ of a red pepper chopped fine (the
   hotter the better)

½ cup sea salt (or kelp as an alternative)
2 quarts water
3 cloves garlic
a couple of bay leaves
4 sprigs dill or fennel

Wash the veggies. Dry and place in a big jar with onions. Bring water to boil in a pan; add salt, let cool, then add pepper, garlic, and bay and pour over veggies and greens. The liquid should completely cover them. If not, bring more water to a boil adding a bit more salt. Cover the jar with a cloth or cheesecloth and keep cool for one week (preferably in a dark place). After five days you can serve, but you'll find the taste will improve if it marinates longer.

Sesame Tahini

Sesame tahini is made essentially from the hulled seed of sesame. Because of this it is not as high in minerals and vitamins as sesame butter. You make both tahini and butter by grinding the toasted seed into a paste. The butter is stronger because the outer hull is present. The tahini is milder, and if by chance it gets runny, *adding* water will make it get thicker. A reverse to what you would imagine. Try it. It's fun and tasty.

Tomato Jam

(Felicity Kirsch)

½ cup honey
1 pound tomatoes
¼ teaspoon ground cloves
1 teaspoon basil
salt or kelp to taste

In a ¾ quart pot, simmer the honey over a very low flame for 5 minutes. Wash and trim tomatoes, but don't peel.

Cut an opening in each and squeeze over a bowl to remove much of the seeds and juice. (Set juice aside for something else, or drink it.)

Cut the tomatoes into small pieces and add them, along with the cloves and basil, to the honey.

Cook uncovered for 40 minutes, or until thick. At end of cooking taste to see if kelp or salt are needed.

This salad has a cooling effect during those hotter days of May through August, which will make the preparation enjoyable. If you make your own yogurt (see p. 77), gather your own greens, and prepare with friends—fantastic!!

Yogurt Potato Salad

⅔ pound potatoes
½ cucumber
a pinch of garlic (preferably fresh)
2 tablespoons chives
½ cup onion stalks
touch of salt, add to your liking while cooking potatoes in veggie broth (which one should always keep about frozen)
spices
olive oil
apple cider vinegar
yogurt—diluted with the veggie broth that the potatoes were cooked in

Cook the diced potatoes in vegetable broth until tender. Drain off and save the broth to be mixed with yogurt. While the potatoes are hot, pour on the vinegar and spices to your liking. Let the potatoes stand twenty minutes or so. Then add olive oil. Mix this and add the yogurt, diluted by the veggie broth. Add just enough yogurt to make a dressing of pleasant consistency.

Sandy's Salad

(serves two)

1½ cups mung sprouts
1 carrot, grated
as many dandelion leaves as you want
salt and cayenne to taste
miner's lettuce
green onions

Mix everything but the dandelion flowers together in bowl. Place the flowers on top of the salad, and serve with your favorite dressing. Or try ours:

1 tablespoon olive oil
juice of one lemon

A simple salad, yet our first using the flowers.

Kathy's Herb Salad with Green Dressing

1 cup miner's lettuce
½ cup dandelions
½ cup plantain
1 cup Romaine lettuce
handful of wheat sprouts and alfalfa sprouts
½ cup parsley

Dressing:

½ cup safflower oil
¾ cup watercress
4 tablespoons cider vinegar
½ tablespoon thyme
1 clove garlic
1 sprig fennel
½ teaspoon date sugar

Mixed Herb Greens

Crisp lettuce, sliced almonds, alfalfa sprouts, chopped spring onions, mushrooms, cucumber, fennel, miner's lettuce, dandelion, chicory, borage, and celery. Any amount depending on foraging time and the number of mouths to feed.

Dressing:

⅔ cup safflower oil
½ lemon
pinch of sage
pinch of oregano
¼ teaspoon honey
1 clove garlic
dash of Worcestershire

FRUIT SALAD

When making a fruit salad, it is best to eat in accordance with the season (as with anything, really). This recipe appeared at a class with no known contributor but certainly boosted the spirit of the class.

1 apple sliced
1 pear sliced
4 oranges sliced
2 bananas sliced
1 cup of strawberries
1 cup freshly grated coconut
1 cup freshly picked marijuana leaves shredded
⅛ cup mint leaves
½ cup brandy

This mixture was labeled, *"Tranquility Fruit Salad."* Since we were discussing the historical applications of "spirits" or "spiritus" (solutions of gaseous or volatile substances) that night, it seemed appropriate. One student suggested making a "Punch Bowl" by increasing the spirits and lessening the fruit. Smoking Indian hemp was also mentioned, but because of present laws this could only be discussed theoretically.

Mother-in-law Salad

I never really knew where this originated, but it was named at an herbal reunion dinner where parents, friends, and relatives joined in the festivities.

1 large head red leaf lettuce
equal amounts of plantain greens, dandelion greens, and alfalfa sprouts
2 medium-sized onions

All greens are torn into bitesize pieces and tossed with chopped onions and alfalfa sprouts.

Dressing

Blend thoroughly:

1 part apple cider vinegar
1 part spring water
2 parts lemon juice
2 parts safflower oil
cayenne pepper and garlic to taste

This is the first recipe to use "parts" as opposed to the conventional measurements. Many of our recipes from past generations did not give specific amounts, because it was too limiting. "Parts" depend on the size of the group for whom you are preparing, or if preparing dressing to be stored and used over a period of time, how long you want to store it and how much you generally use.

Ironically, during one twelve-week series of classes this past winter, I was stricken for the first time in many years with the flu. Marty Benedict, a healer here in northern California made a salad that was especially prepared with the sick in mind. I had not eaten by nature for six days and I ate of this salad very sparingly. The effect was quite relaxing.

Marty's Salad

From the garden, gather: malva, green onion, nasturtiums, radish, fennel, chickweed, wheat grass.

Mix all the above, then toss cut greens with olive oil, and add mushrooms and parsley.

Add:

minced peppermint
garlic
coriander
½ tablespoon honey
½ tablespoon cider vinegar

Eat, knowing you are getting better.

About a week later, I found myself craving these foods again, so I made Marty's salad and tried my hand at making a guacamole for the dressing. Since I am from California and have always had avocados, this has long been a favorite.

Guacamole
(fairly large)

1 onion (including the green onion tops, if desired)
2 ripe avocados
1 tomato
1 teaspoon herb salt (p. 84)
½ teaspoon minced garlic
½ to 1 teaspoon lemon juice

Cut the onion and tomato into small pieces. Add the salt, garlic, and lemon juice. When blended, add the avocado, making it into an even paste. Serve on lettuce, on Marty's salad, or with crackers. Greatly gooey!

Cathy Panke has given me an elegant recipe for using guacamole.

Guacamole Nasturtiums

2 ripe avocados, mashed and seasoned with
2 minced cloves of garlic
2 tablespoons of lemon juice
pinch of cayenne
1 tablespoon fresh oregano
6 cherry tomatoes
2 tablespoons chopped onions

Blend to make guacamole and stuff the centers of nasturtium flowers. Garnish with borage flowers or ripe olive. Place each blossom on a slice of cucumber.

LEMON GARLIC THOUGHT

Often while traveling, I have found the following almost as important as washing my hands. In fact, many times when the water was infested with parasites and amoebae, or we were unsure of the water, washing hands and utensils with garlic and lemon juice was just as essential as eating. Garlic contains disinfectant, and lemon contains citric acid. Washing with lemon (though possibly not in favor with sterile therapeuticians) is captured (albeit diluted) with a slice of lemon floating in a finger bowl. Less sophisticated perhaps is taking a lemon that's been cut in half or sections and squeezing until about ½ tablespoon of juice freely disperses about the hand. Gently rub this into the hands, continuing until all the juice dries. The first time I did this I thought the lemon juice would never dry, or that if it did it would be sticky. But it does dry, and it is a marvelous new use for the familiar fruit. If you have been out pickin' berries through the day, those small cuts will feel sparked, then soothed. The citric acid "cleans" the area, then a softness appears, and a pungent smell begins to waft past your nose stimulating the appetite even more by this ritual.

It's a simple ceremony before a salad, or any part of the meal. Even ending the meal with this cleansing process is a wonderful, feeling experience, even better when you and your friends share by rubbing each others hands with the lemon juice.

In this age of space travel we should take note from our ancestors' ocean voyages. Ships destined for distant ports were supplied with concentrated juice, or crystallized citric acid with the oil of lemon. Prevention of scurvy was the reason. Much different from those advertised "instants" presently accompanying the astronauts into space.

Concentrated foods, such as oils and powders, will be shared later. We start with the simple things in life, nature-oriented.

Long forgotten-remembered? Possible, because the "time of need" was never more crucial than it is now. We must begin to harvest our roots, our essences, before more of the real things are lost to technology. Man's sciences have yet to duplicate the process by which a blade of grass grows to give us nourishment. When he does, he might accomplish what the physician cooks (alchemists) try to do—blend an art of elements with science to yield a medicine with spirit.

DRESSING

Mayonnaise

A recipe using lemon juice keeps appearing as a dressing, in multiple variations, called mayonnaise. It is familiar to us all as a dressing on our salads, sandwiches, and fruit salads and is generally found hanging out in the refrigerator, waiting to dress again. I have several hundred ways to make this recipe. Some simple rules seem to endure. You need a cool area in which to fold the ingredients together and lots of patience for the slow and careful blending. This recipe yields about 1½ cups mayonnaise when done with hand rotary beater or circle stirring (a family or friendly group in which the bowl and spoon passes from one to the next, each contributing to the hand action, until it's light and fluffy).

> 2 egg yolks
> 1 tablespoon cider vinegar
> ¼-½ teaspoons dry mustard
> ½-¾ teaspoons sea salt
> ⅛ teaspoon honey (¼ teaspoon if using sugar)
> dash of white pepper
> dash of cayenne pepper

Place all the ingredients in a bowl that is not too large. Beat till well blended and of an even consistency.

Take 1 cup unrefined salad oil (remember each oil has its own taste that can alter the taste of this dressing).

Add the oil, a teaspoon at a time at first, beating well after each teaspoon addition. Increase the amount added until half the salad oil has been used. Then take 1 tablespoon lemon juice and alternate the remaining oil with lemon juice until thoroughly blended.

If all has gone well, and the stars have been in a favorable position, this will be buoyant, fluffy, and even in consistency. If the mayonnaise separates, due possibly to temperature, temperament, or adding the oil too quickly, you can correct in a couple of ways:

Slowly beat in another egg yolk, 1 tablespoon cold water, and a small bit of vinegar.
Beat in some of last week's mayonnaise.

This should do it. Store covered in the refrigerator and use within seven days. For better flavor, add the leftover to the next batch. Serve it *fresh* whenever possible.

A bit simpler and more modern perhaps is the blender method of preparing this dressing.

While I was growing up my mother went from hand blending to the electric blender. It was always a treat to hear the motor move and watch the mass of ingredients go around and around until a smooth mixture emerged. Many times the mixture changed color according to what was blended: red from beet, orange from carrot, green from olive oil or parsley. Once I stuck in some raisins just because they were there. They did not taste so good alone but over carrots I became hooked.

Fantasy Mayonnaise

> ¼ cup unrefined oil
> 1 egg (locally produced—we have "Petaluma white or brown")

2 tablespoons lemon juice, or orange
(which sweetens the mayonnaise),
or lime
½ teaspoon dry mustard
(gather mustard seed from your local area)
½ teaspoon sea salt (could substitute
seaweed powder [kelp])
¼ teaspoon cayenne pepper or
⅛ teaspoon fresh red pepper ground
with mortar and pestle

Place all the above ingredients in your blender, seal, and mix at moderate speed until thoroughly blended. Your mayonnaise should appear creamy and smooth as the flowing roll of the sea—cloudlike, possibly—for this fantasy mayonnaise.

NOTE PLEASE: When working with a blender, be sure to have the lid on properly. Some blends require the machine to be off before you stir, then on again. If by chance you forget (forgot again, eh?) then the ceiling gets dressed not to mention everything and everybody. Oh well, it's a great facial pack!

As with the previous mayonnaise recipe, use fresh if possible, keep it refrigerated, and store for no more than seven days. Again, use to enhance the next batch if you like.

Thousand Island

There are numerous ways to make thousand island. Whether you make your own pickling or add a commercial product, changes this dressing like the weather.

½ cup mayonnaise
1 to 3 hard boiled eggs, chopped
2 tablespoons chili sauce
2 tablespoons finely chopped wild onions
and tops
2 tablespoons chopped sweet pickle
½ teaspoon fresh lemon peel grated
½ teaspoon paprika

Mix well and serve over salads or whatever the palate fancies.

A simple way, more homey, was shown to me one evening several years ago by my friend, Budge. I was going to use some fancy spices such as curry powder and Angostura Bitters. Have you ever read the label on a bottle of this old tonic? (Incredible what appears before us each day in small print.) Budge took ½ cup mayonnaise, a drying tomato (about 4 tablespoons worth) and a pickle chopped with a bit of lemon juice, and mixed it vigorously, which yielded a runny but homey mayonnaise. "It's all music" often comes from Budge's kitchen when he prepares blends. A good blender's philosophy—everything fits.

Another mayonnaise variation is to mix about ½ teaspoon of horseradish root that has been dried and ground, a tablespoon of chopped onion, 3 tablespoons chili sauce, and ½ cup mayonnaise.

Roquefort Mayonnaise

This is another of my favorites. Mix ¼-½ cup crumbled Roquefort cheese with 1 cup mayonnaise. For those "blue mold" freaks, use 1 cup moldy blue cheese and a dash of cayenne. Mix and delight to the blue mold light.

The nice thought about cheeses is the bacteria they breathe that we in turn eat. Roquefort is an original growth and in order to be so called must come from Roquefort, France and be made only of ewes milk. The mold is penicillin.

To sweeten your mayonnaise fold in ¼ cup heavy sweet cream for each cup mayonnaise and a couple of freshly chopped parsley tops.

The salad that most often comes to mind at our house is a simple garden green salad for four. Gather a medium bowl full of lettuce, carrots, turnips, and beets. Tear, slice, and grate respectively and add thinly sliced cucumbers, zucchini, celery, and tomatoes. Sometimes we have peas, other times cauliflower. Over this goes Roquefort, Thousand Island, or oil and vinegar.

Oil and Vinegar

Combine in a jar with a tight lid:

> ¾ cup salad or olive oil
> ¼ cup lemon juice or ¼ cup vinegar
>   (cider or wine)

Cover jar tightly and shake with vigor. Serve.
For variation add 1 clove garlic cut in half, to above mixture. Chill overnight, remove the garlic, mince and return.
Or make the above mixture and add ¾ teaspoon sea salt, ¼ teaspoon paprika, ¼ teaspoon cayenne pepper.
Or make the above mixture and add ¼ teaspoon grated lemon peel, ½ cup honey, and ½ teaspoon fennel or celery.

As the cooks of the world take great pleasure in their bowls and blades, they dream, as conscientious cooks do, of entertaining the most memorable compliments when the salad and its dressing become one. In nature one herb or spice will complement the other if one does not try to overpower the other. Thus cayenne, chili powder, curry powder, fresh ground mustard, or pepper are suggested in making salad dressings, but they can overpower the essences of the milder herbs. So, instead of cayenne use nasturtium flower power. Lemon is preferable to vinegar and also enhances the flavor of herbs. The most healthful oils are cold pressed, such as corn or sunflower oils. Olive oil is strong but it is probably one of the older oils still being manufactured by cold press through the centuries.

SAUCES

There seem always to be the hardy tomatoes about the end of summer. This is Leslie Pfardresher's version of a golden oldie. Goes well with the Herbal Barley Burger.

Tomato Sauce

> 4 pounds tomatoes (cut up and
>   blended to liquid)
> 1 red onion sliced
> 2 tablespoons honey
> 2 tablespoons oil
> 1 tablespoon sea salt (or 1 tablespoon
>   powdered seaweed)
> 4 tablespoons basil
> a pinch of oregano
> 2 large cloves garlic (more, depending on
>   your taste)
> 1 beet including greens

Place this altogether in a pot with water and simmer 20 to 35 minutes.
After this is cooked, blend, adding about ¼-½ cup chopped bell pepper and plantain.

If you'd like a change and have a bit of goldenrod about, then this sauce is one to entice the blender's taste buds. Use it on potatoes and fish.

Goldy's Goldenrod Sauce

> 5 tablespoons freshly gathered and
>   chopped goldenrod flowers
> goldenrod flowers
> 5 tablespoons butter or ghee
> 1½ teaspoons lemon juice
> sea salt, cayenne pepper and spices to
>   taste.

Melt the butter (or warm ghee) in a pan over a low flame. Add the goldenrod flowers and simmer 7 minutes. Remove from heat and add lemon juice and salt, cayenne, and spices to taste. Enjoy.

GHEE

In many countries without refrigeration, ghee, clear buttter or clarified butter is

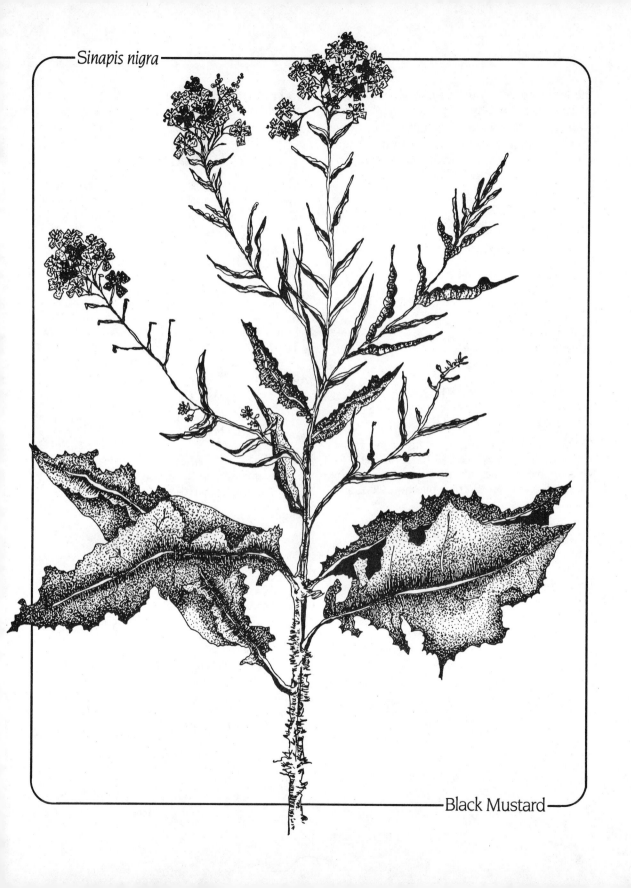

Sinapis nigra

Black Mustard

made to prevent rancidity. Fresh butter is placed in a container in a warm place, or over a low flame till the milk solids have precipitated. Pour off the clear butter that has separated from the milk solids. This clear oil is less susceptible to spoilage. Chopped onions and garlic in ghee, with your favorite combination of herbs, provide the beginning of many Eastern recipes.

Gooseberry Chutney

4 pints gooseberries
¼ pound dates
¼ pound raisins
1 pound onions
3/8 pound honey
2 pints cider vinegar
½ teaspoon cayenne pepper
½ teaspoon turmeric
2 cloves garlic crushed
1 tablespoon ginger
1 tablespoon prepared mustard

Chop fruits and onions to a fine consistency, mix with honey and spices in kettle. Cover with vinegar and simmer for 2 hours or until the mixture is very soft. Bottle while hot, serve over rice and veggies. . . Thanks, Mom.

HERB VINEGARS

Always nice to use your fresh herbs from the garden or window sill. Clean the leaves from stems and pack the jars about ¾ full. Heat cider vinegar or wine vinegar to just before boiling, fill the jars, and let stand steeping for several weeks. Strain or leave herbs within, corking tightly for storing.

Combinations of Herb Vinegars

Rosemary leaves, basil, and thyme
Mint and basil leaves
Tarragon on stem with chamomile and
   rosemary flowers
Borage, rosemary, and marigold flowers
Woodruff leaves and chamomile flowers
Woodruff, comfrey, borage, and burdock
   leaves

The combinations are endless.

Garlic has appeared and reappeared throughout this work, so why not:

Garlic Vinegar

Crush 7-10 cloves garlic into a quart jar. Add a dash of lemon and cover with a pint of cider vinegar. Pour into jars and let stand two weeks. Strain, bottle, and cork.

Stuffed Squash Blossoms
(From Bonnie Coleman, Sacramento's herb expert)

Soak wheat berries 20 hours or more. Then heat slowly in top of double boiler until soft. To these, add: ½ cup of sliced mushrooms, 1 medium onion, and 2 cloves of garlic sauteed in oil or butter. Then add:

½ cup fresh cherry tomatoes, chopped
¼ cup chopped watercress
¼ cup chopped parsley
½ cup sunflower seeds
¼ cup minced chives
2 tablespoons fresh oregano
tamari if desired

Stuff mixture into squash blossoms.

Rose Petal Salad
(A small feast for four)

2 cups rose petals, wild preferred
2 cups mixed dandelion and plantain
   leaves (very young, with tender souls)
2 cups potatoes, cooked and cooled and
   diced
¼ cup lemon juice or rose petal vinegar
½ cup salad oil (fresh-pressed olive is nice)
1 teaspoon fresh tarragon
½ teaspoon sea salt or kelp powder
¼ teaspoon cayenne pepper
1 clove garlic, crushed
Optional: 2-3 hard-boiled eggs

With wooden salad bowl in hand, rub gently with crushed garlic, saving a bit to dash on top later.

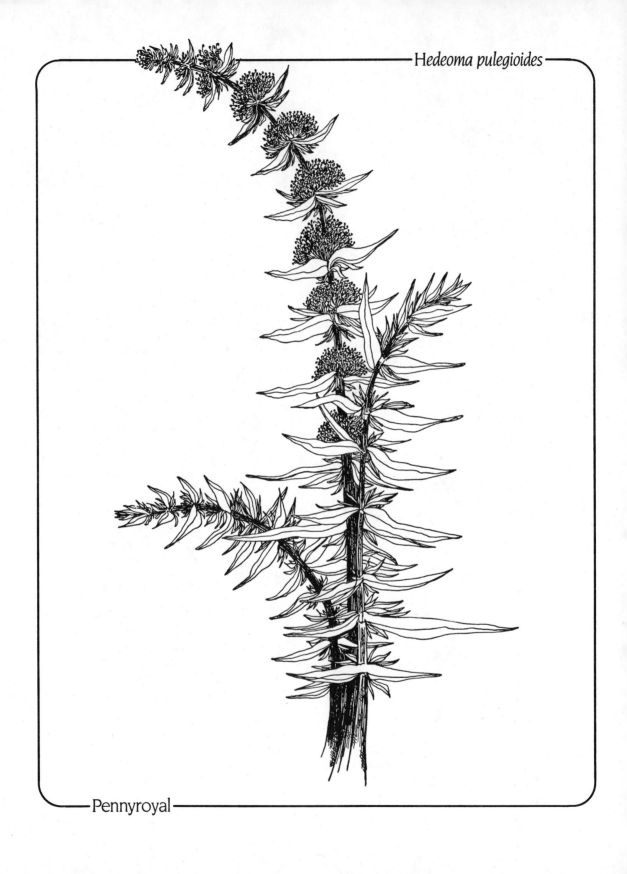

Hedeoma pulegioides

Pennyroyal

Arrange a circle of rose petals, saving some to sprinkle on top. Shred the dandelion and plantain greens on top and add potatoes and eggs.

Stand aside from bowl and inhale the essence.

In another bowl mix together the salad oil, tarragon, sea salt or kelp, cayenne, and the rest of the garlic. Pour this over the salad, mixing with thy heart.

Place the remaining rose petals on top and have served by six court bearers.

Flower Power Flower Salad
(Inspired by Denni McCarthy)

Gather in August and September the flowers for this salad.

> 2 cups, and that is an amount of flowers!
> tarragon, pennyroyal, oregano, marjoram, lemon balm, yarrow (pink flower), mint, spikenard, tansy, borage, comfrey, collinsonia, a pinch of flax, bergamot, rosemary, rue, wintergreen, sage, and nasturtium

This recipe is for quite a group, we've served seven or thirty or seventy (always using two cups flowers). One must simply adjust the major portions accordingly.

For four:

> 1 cup picked greens, such as dandelion, chicory, or fennel (or just alfalfa sprouts)
> 1 cup watercress (if not available use parsley or chard)
> 1 green onion chopped fine
> ¼ teaspoon sea salt
> ¼ teaspoon cayenne pepper
> 4 tablespoons oil
> 4 tablespoons lemon juice
> 1 tablespoon lemon peel, grated
> 2 cloves garlic, crushed

Place all the above in a garlic-rubbed wooden bowl. Rub hands through this and the flowers till finely mixed. For more power, eat with fingers in the meadow or garden near the place where the flowers were picked. This recipe has always been expanded or contracted according to the preparer. Essentially one may enjoy flowers whenever. Just be aware that some do contain strong essences. The following is a list of some of the many flowers that have been enjoyed through the years in salads.

apple blossoms	dandelion	grape hyacinth	mustard
agrimony	daisy	hawthorn	nasturtium
amoranthus	day lilies	heather	orange blossoms
bay	caraway	hibiscus	passionflower
bee-balm	celery	hops	pansy
betony	chia	honeysuckle	peony
borage	columbine	hollyhock	plum blossom
burdock	comfrey	hyssop	primrose
burnet	cranesbill	horehound	rosemary
carnation	damiana	hemp	rose
catnip	date	huckleberry	poppies
cattail	dill	lavender	squash blossom
chicory	dittany	lemon blossom	sunflower
chamomile	dusty miller	linden	thyme
chrysanthemum	elder	marigold	sage
clover,	echinacea	melilot	savory
red & white	fennel	melissa	violets
coltsfoot	figwort	meadowsweet	verbena
costmary	goats beard	motherwort	woodruff
cowslip	goldenrod	mugwort	wormwood
coriander	groundsel	mullein	yarrow
celery			

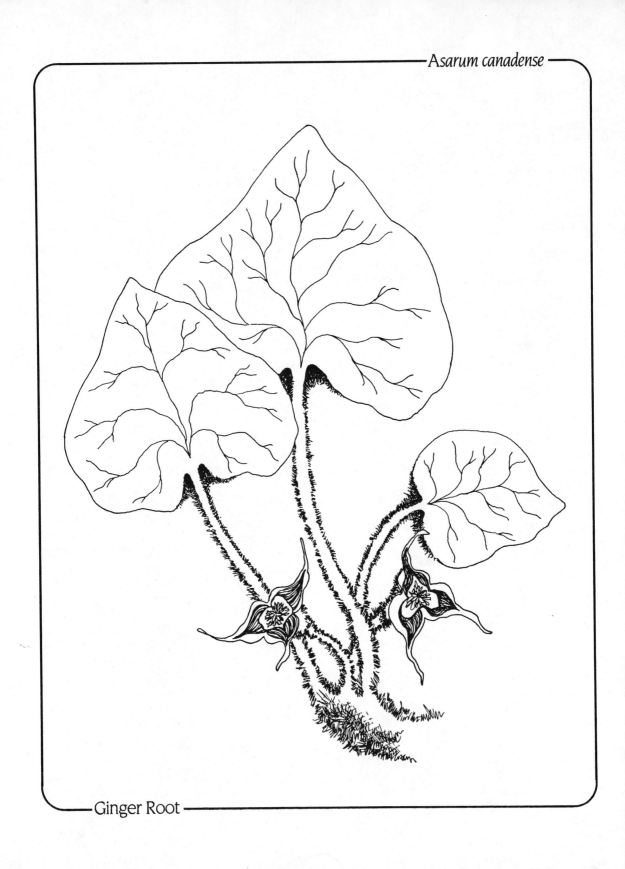

Ginger Root

SEVEN

Grains, Rices, Cereals, Beans, and Nuts

They're all seeds to me
—old Phoenician saying

Staple items, that is, grains, nuts, and beans, feed two-thirds of the world's population. They are better used whole than refined as in our milling and enriching processes. In their natural states, they contain more nutrients than their commercially refined by-products.

Cooking these products of nature requires the user to be aware of what he is procuring. If gathered from nature directly, then the freshness is certainly known. If not from nature, then where from? A package? Season to season is the rule for storage and use unless a survival situation requires longer storage. We usually have an abundance of these products in our local groceries or for gathering, according to our locale.

There are many methods of preparation. As we move along the list of grains, beans, and nuts, I'll try to share the most popular or easiest method of preparation. For example, what might once have been prepared in a heavy-lidded steamer, might now lend itself nicely to a pressure cooker.

GRAINS

Grains found in tombs have shown modern man their ability to germinate after centuries. With proper handling, these seeds, centuries old, still produce true to type.

When the germ is cracked or ground grain should be used immediately, because oxidation rapidly changes the nutrients and oils present in the prepared grain. Several means have been developed for cooking whole grains: soaking; cooking until tender; and, more recently, sprouting. The grains are then ready to eat in salads, soups, breads, or however you desire. Whole grains are a valuable source of vitamin B as well as protein. Some of the more common grains used in cooking are hulled barley (unhulled is very difficult, if not impossible, to cook), yellow and white corn (maize), millet, oats, buckwheat, rye, and wheat. Then we have common white rice (really brown rice with the outside coat removed by polishing) and wild rice. When cooking these grains, the yield is four to six cooked servings from each cup of raw grain.

Barley

1 cup barley
3 cups water
¼ teaspoon sea salt

In a pot, bring water to boil. Add barley and cover. Bring to boil again, adding the salt, and reduce the heat. Simmer approximately 25 minutes.

Yellow or White Corn

Remove corn from cob, place in water just to cover. After it boils, lower the flame and simmer 15 to 20 minutes. Serve hot.

Polenta
(Cornmeal)

Often associated with the southern United States, yet the Italians do more with this than any Southerner I've met. It is often fried or sauteed and served with fruits or nuts.

1 cup polenta
3 cups water
¼ teaspoon sea salt

Bring water to a boil. Gradually pour polenta in while stirring. When water boils, add salt, cover, and simmer for 30 minutes or more, stirring occasionally.

Millet

Whether dry or moist is up to the taste of the soul eating. The drier type goes well with salads; soft, moist millet is good for cooking. There is a slight bitterness that is soon forgotten as you learn to use this grain.

1 cup millet
3 cups water
1 teaspoon oil
¼ teaspoon sea salt

Place millet and oil in a cast iron skillet and roast till golden in color, approximately 15 minutes. Stir constantly to prevent burning and to achieve an even consistency. Place water, millet, and salt in a pot; cover; and cook over high flame. When this boils, lower the flame and simmer, covered, for approximately 30 minutes.

For softer millet add one more cup of water. Toast millet as above and put in pot. Bring to a boil then simmer from 35 to 45 minutes.

Oats

I like oats firm or solid, others like it creamy. Being of Scottish ancestry, I always use porridge as a hearty solid rather than just a winter warmer.

1 cup oats (rolled or steel cut)
4 cups water
¼ teaspoon salt

Bring water to a boil in a pot and add oats. When water boils again lower the flame, add salt, and cover for approximately 30 minutes.

If you are not using a double boiler; stir every now and again to prevent sticking and burning. Once I burned it and was going to throw out the crust on the bottom of the pan but found it was golden brown and cookielike. I saved it and found that just munching it was enjoyable. Later I saw folks add it to cookies to firm them up and make them crunchy. Just shows that all products—even ones we've "ruined"—have a use.

Buckwheat Groats

A cold weather grain also known as "kasha," and seldom eaten in warm weather. You can buy these raw, toast them yourself, and prepare this fluffy recipe.

1 cup buckwheat groats
2 cups water
¼ teaspoon sea salt

Boil the water and add the groats. When water boils again, lower the flame, add the salt, cover, and simmer 20 minutes.

To toast raw groats, put them in a cast iron skillet over medium flame and toast until

brown, about 10 minutes. Stir with a wooden spoon to prevent burning.

RYE

If you gather your own rye, watch out for a black or dark mold on the head of the grain. Do not eat this. It is the deadly poison known as ergot. The blight, a purplish dark mold, was feared by the ancients (with good reason), although early Assyrian midwives prepared a crude concoction from the fungus to check bleeding after childbirth. When properly extracted, ergot yields medicinally active and very useful alkaloids, one of which is LSD. This lends credence to early accounts of ingestion resulting in such adverse effects as vomiting, spasm, massive hallucinations, and death. So go carefully in gathering your grains. Most of the grains people purchase today have already been inspected for this mold, so there's less need for care with store-bought rye.

No matter where, Morocco or the United States, a good bowl of rye draws the family to the table.

1 cup rye
3 cups water
1 tablespoon oil
¼ teaspoon sea salt

Bring the water to a boil, add rye, oil, and salt. Cover this and bring to boil again, lower the flame, and simmer covered for 30 to 40 minutes.

WHOLE WHEAT,
WHOLE WHEAT BERRIES,
OR WHOLE WHEAT GRAINS

The red winter wheat grows where the soil is rich in minerals, thus yielding a protein-rich grain that has thrived on the land since the first grasses blew. Here we will

prepare it in a pressure cooker rather than soaking and then cooking it.

1 cup wheat berries
3½ cups water
¼ teaspoon sea salt

Soak the berries overnight, then place in pressure cooker. Add the water and salt. Place over heat till pressure cooker top hisses. Turn the flame down and simmer for two hours.

A nice variation in cooking the above grains is to substitute a vegetable stock (such as onion, garlic, purslane, or plantain) for the water, which enhances the flavor of the grains. With seed such as plantain, yucca, acorn, or chestnut, the addition of a stock really brings the earth element to the taste. A bit of oil and water or oil and butter will make the stock fuller and more flavorful.

Whenever we eat rice we think of that "white stuff" (unless in knowledge of browns) that "sticks to your ribs." But I got a recipe to "keep them ribs free" one evening when my friend Carter wanted to share a new-found dish: a favorite pastime when those beans and grains start pilin' up in the fridge.

Leftover Rice Over Beans Over

1 cup precooked rice
1 cup precooked pinto beans, black beans, and oats, mixed
1 cup of yesterday's lunch of wild onion, mint, fennel, miner's lettuce, and wild nasturtium
½ cup leftover carrot and raisin salad
¼ cup almond and walnut meats, chopped

Take all of these overs and place one over the other. Toss over a few times, then tote over to the table for serving. A variation is to add ½ cup water, toss over all into pot and bring to boil. Turn heat off and let stand ten minutes. Put over on table and enjoy.

Herbal Barley Burger

Frying is not one of my specialties, mainly because the fats used alter in chemical construction and personally I like the rawness of uncooked foods. But for those of us who hate to give up the hamburger, here is a variation using barley. Try repeating the name several times. Funny how the spirit keeps running tunes through my head as I make Ellie and Sparky's Herbal Barley Burgers.

> 2 cups whole barley (steamed, or sprouted and steamed)
> 1 cup walnuts, pumpkin seed, or
> plantain seed, finely ground
> (how about chia seed, prunella seed, or chestnuts?)
> ¼ cup grated raw potato
> ¼ cup minced green pepper with plantain leaves
> 2 tablespoons oil
> 2 tablespoons onion powder
> ¼ teaspoon thyme
> salt to taste
> seasoned bread crumbs to make a stiff dough

Blend the barley and ground nuts or seeds for a few seconds. Add the rest of the ingredients and mix well. Shape into flat burgers and broil on both sides till browned. Serve between buns or smothered with tomato sauce.

RICE

White rice is really brown rice, except that, again, man's polishing and enriching gets in the way. It has been said over and over by fresh food advocates, as well as nutritionists, that when the outer shell of the rice is removed, a great amount of vitamin B is discarded in the process. Granted, we have vitamin supplements today, but what of yesterday, before man's food technology? What did people do without all their fancy vitamins? Is it possible to maintain your needed allowance of vitamins eating only, heaven forbid, enriched white rice? I don't believe so. In fact, once people have tried "real" foods, most never want to go back to the "enriched" variety.

Then there is wild rice, botanically a cereal. The following account is from that old traveler, Jonathan Carver, in his 1766 work, *Three Years Travels Throughout The Interior Parts of North America.*

WILD RICE—This grain, which grows in the greatest plenty throughout the interior parts of North America, is the most valuable of all the spontaneous productions of that country. Exclusive of its utility as a supply of food for those of the human species, who inhabit this part of the continent, and obtained without any other trouble than that of gathering it in, the sweetness and nutritious quality of it attracts an infinite number of wild fowl of every kind, which flock from distant climes, to enjoy this rare repast; and by it become inexpressibly fat and delicious. In future periods it will be of great service to the infant colonies, as it will afford them a present support, until, in the course of cultivation, other supplies may be produced; whereas in those realms which are not furnished with this bounteous gift of nature, even if the climate is temperate and the soil good, the first settlers are often exposed to great hardships from the want of an immediate resource for necessary food. This useful grain grows in the water where it is about two feet deep, and where it finds a rich, muddy soil. The stalks of it, and the branches or ears that bear the feed, resemble oats both in their appearance and manner of growing. The stalks are full of joints, and rise more than

Secale cereale

Wild Rye

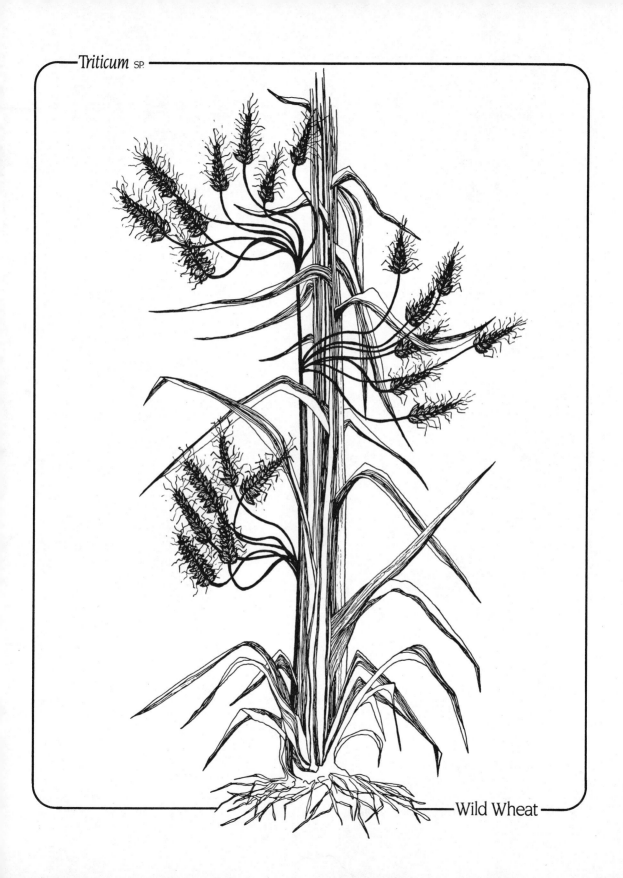

Triticum sp.

Wild Wheat

eight feet above the water. The natives gather the grain in the following manner: Nearly about the time that it begins to turn from its milky state and to ripen, they run their canoes into the midst of it, and tying bunches of it together, just below the ears, with bark, leave it in this situation three or four weeks longer, till it is perfectly ripe. About the latter end of September they return to the river, when each family having its separate allotment, and being able to distinguish their own property by the manner of fastening the sheaves, gather in the portion that belongs to them. This they do by placing their canoes close to the bunches of rice, in such position as to receive the grain when it falls, and then beat it out, with pieces of wood formed for that purpose. Having done this, they dry it with smoke, and afterwards tread or rub off the outside hull; when it is fit for use they put it into the skins of fawns, or young buffalos, taken off nearly whole for this purpose, and sewed into a sort of sack, wherein they preserve it till the return of their harvest. It has been the subject of much speculation, why this spontaneous grain is not found in any other regions of America, or in those countries situated in the same parallels of latitude, where the waters are as apparently adapted for its growth as in the climate I treat of. As for instance, none of the countries that lie to the south and east of the great lakes, even from the provinces north of the Carolina, to the extremities of Labradore, produce any of this grain. It is true I found great quantities of it in the watered lands near Detroit, between Lake Huron and Lake Erie, but on inquiry I learned that it never arrived nearer to maturity than just to blossom; after which it appeared blighted, and died away. This convinces me that the north-west wind, as I have before hinted, is much more powerful in these than in the interior parts; and that it is more inimical to the fruits of the earth, after it has passed over the lakes,

and become united with the wind which joins it from the frozen regions of the north, than it is further to the westward.

In observing food being prepared, I have learned several methods of cooking rice.

Once in Korea I was introduced to an almost meditative method of adding the rice to salted, boiling water. This is done so slowly that the water never stops boiling. The rice is then cooked till very tender, about 20 minutes. It is then poured into a wicker (bamboo) strainer and warm or hot water is run over it to wash the starch from the rice. This makes it clean, fluffy, and beautiful. (Save the water and make into bread).

You can use the synthetic forms of quicky rices but the total lack of communication between you and this impersonal type of rice destroys much of the union of cooking with spirit.

I prefer a short grain rice that grows well in the Sacramento River delta areas. As a matter of fact, short grain rice is preferred in many countries over the long grain. If you are from the northern climes, this is the best of the indigenous grains to use, unless you are fortunate enough to have wild rice. (Experts claim there are over fifty different types of rice in the world.)

A second way to cook rice is:

3 cups of water
1 cup of rice
¼ teaspoon salt

In a heavy lidded pan bring the water to a boil. Add the rice and salt and lower the flame. Let it simmer for about 40 minutes to an hour. Depending on the pot and its lid, it might take even longer. A lighter lid allows more evaporation.

A third method employs a skillet:

Warm the skillet and melt a tablespoon each of butter and oil. Add the unwashed rice and place the pan over a hot flame until the rice grains start to look white. At this point pour boiling water over the grains, totally immersing the rice. The object is to get the rice as hot as possible without burning or discoloring. When you add the water, it will continue to boil, thus yielding a totally absorbed rice that will be as porous as pieces of pumice, but more delicate for our earthly tastes.

Then there's the old standby, when no fires, ovens, or other everyday conveniences happen to be about:

    1 flat rock languishing in the sun most of
        the day
    1 handful grain, rice, or seed
    3 cups water
    salt to taste

Place grain, water, and salt in a pot with a heavy lid. Set it on the rock and let it be. It might take a few days to absorb the water totally, but the end result cannot be described. Taste it yourself. I've seen the same procedure where the grain was buried in a pot in the ground. The temperature of the soil got so hot it all burned!

Wild rice may be cooked like our domestic rice recipes. It requires a little longer to cook and more water. If one were so lucky as to have a pound of wild rice, Grandma Mazie's recipe below is a wonderful main dish for six to eight people. Serve your wild green salad with flowers on top if it's the right time of year.

Wild Rice with Fresh Mushrooms

    6 cups water
    2 teaspoons sea salt
    1 cup wild rice
    ¼-½ pound mushrooms
    ¼ cup butter or ghee
    2 tablespoons chopped onions
    1 teaspoon chopped garlic
    some dandelion greens
    (maybe two or three of your favorite
        leaves)

In a deep saucepan bring the water to a boil. Having thoroughly washed the wild rice (to remove rock or debris—this is wild you know) add it gradually to water so that the boiling continues. Cook 25 to 30 minutes uncovered (longer if the lid is on) or until the rice is tender when pressed between the fingers.

While the rice is cooking, clean and slice the mushrooms. Heat the butter in a skillet. Add mushrooms, onion, and garlic, cooking slowly and turning occasionally until the mushrooms are light brown. Remove from heat and combine with the rice. When done, garnish with your favorite herb such as parsley, thyme or dandelion greens.

When one speaks of brown rice they may recall stories of long life and well-being. I remember the many days when white rice was all I ate. Then herbs and variations of brown rice began to have new meaning as I observed the Eastern peoples and Westerners experiencing eating of both white and many brown rices. Each has a different way of preparation. Often it is the simplicity of a recipe that makes it an intriguing entity. One such is:

Brown Rice and Herbal Greens

Brown 2 cups of brown rice in 2 tablespoons of olive or peanut oil.

Add 2 cups water and place in steamer. (In an automatic steamer this cooking process takes about 20 to 25 minutes.)

When half-cooked add 2 tablespoons of sesame seeds and a handful of pine nuts (if you can afford or gather them). Just before serving add 1 pound of dandelion leaves or other greens, freshly picked and washed carefully. These should be crisp. Cook only 2 to 3 minutes. Bok Choy (chinese cabbage) or spinach may be substituted for the greens.

Curry

It is impossible to talk about rice without discussing curry. Many think of this highly spicy seasoning as the powder on the shelf that often lifts the life of foods. Curry spices are best when fresh and incorporated into a paste, ground with onion, garlic, fruits, or vegetables. In Madras, curries are incredibly hot, and yet, with only slight variation, the curries of Indonesia are mild and delicate. Every market contains the spices needed to make this dish. The curry, whether found as a powder or paste, has its best flavor when developed in oil, preferably olive, or ghee, the clarified butter used throughout India. Curry is cooked at a low temperature for several hours before adding to the dish being prepared. Your taste and tolerance will tell you how much to use.

> ⅓ cup butter or ghee
> 4 tablespoons chopped onion
> 3 tablespoons chopped celery (or fennel)
> 3 tablespoons chopped apple
> 10 peppercorns
> a bay leaf
> flour enough to thicken (about ⅓-½ cup)
> 2½ teaspoons curry powder (see below)
> ⅛ teaspoon nutmeg
> 2½ cups milk (coconut milk is preferred if available as it is on most Islands and throughout the Orient)
> 2 teaspoons lemon juice
> ½ teaspoon soy sauce or Worcestershire sauce

Heat the butter or ghee in a heavy saucepan. Add the next five ingredients at medium heat. Blend in flour, curry powder, and nutmeg, heating until the mixture starts to bubble.

Remove from heat, add milk slowly, stirring constantly. Place back over the heat and bring to a rapid boil, continuing to stir till the mixture thickens. Cook 2 minutes more.

Remove and stir in lemon and soy or Worcestershire sauce. Strain to extract all the sauce.

Curry Powder Mixtures

> A. 1 ounce coriander, cardamom, and ginger
> 3 ounces turmeric
> ¼ ounce cayenne

> B. 2 ounces each of seeds of black pepper, coriander, fenugreek, and turmeric
> 1 ounce cinnamon
> 2 ounces dry chilis
> 2½ ounces cumin seed
> 1½ ounces poppy and cardamom seed
> ¼ ounce mustard seed
> ½ ounce dry ginger

> C. 1 ounce each of coriander, cumin, and turmeric
> ½ ounce dry ginger and peppercorns
> ¼ ounce dried very hot pepper
> ¼ ounce fennel seeds
> ⅛ ounce each of mustard, fenugreek, cloves, poppy seed, and mace

Using a mortar and pestle grind together each of these combinations of seeds and spices.

A nice evening recipe would be:

Curried Rice

Saute ½ pound mushrooms with 1 cup chopped scallions and 1 pear. Add to this as it is cooking, 4 cups precooked brown rice, 2 cups yogurt and 1 teaspoon curry powder.

The following comes from Neil Hebron at Davood's, a local restaurant of international fame. Gourmet magazine says, "sensational." It took some magic to get the recipe, but it was worth the trouble.

Davood's Curry

> ¼ pound butter
> ¼ teaspoon black mustard seed
> ¼ teaspoon yellow mustard seed
> ½ teaspoon cumin seed
> ½ teaspoon fenugreek seed
> 3-4 cloves whole
> 1 teaspoon salt
> 1 teaspoon tumeric
> 1 teaspoon ground coriander
> 2 tablespoons sugar (1 tablespoon honey) or apple sauce
> 1 teaspoon cayenne pepper (according to taste)
> 1 cup yogurt

3 cups water or apple juice
3 tablespoons chick pea flour or rice flour

Melt butter in a heavy pan. Add whole spices, and saute till they pop. Add the ground spices and turn down heat. Make a mixture of the yogurt and the water or apple juice and add the flour while beating the mixture gently. Add the yogurt mixture to the spices and simmer on low heat, mixing regularly, until it thickens.

Fermented cabbage has always been a favorite around my winter table, and it's easy to make.

Sauerkraut

You'll need a stoneware crock, a round disk that will fit inside the crock (a plate, for example), and a weight (a rock will do).

For each head of cabbage use approximately 2 quarts of water or cider vinegar. Shred the cabbage and for each head add ½ teaspoon fennel, celery, and caraway seed (a variation would be plantain, dandelion, and fennel seed).

Place all the cabbage and seeds on the bottom of crock and pour the water over the cabbage till covered, but leave it at least 4-5 inches below the top. Place the plate over this, and add the rock to press the mixture. Every several days, skim the scum. In seven days, depending on the temperature of the ferment, strain and bottle. Use as garnish, a side dish, or dressing.

Apricot Banana Curry

This is a sweet curry that's best served as a side dish, along with your main portion of the meal.

4 large bananas
10 large whole apricots
2 cups chopped carrots
2 tablespoons ghee
¼ teaspoon sea salt or kelp powder
1 tablespoon ground cardamom
½ teaspoon each of powdered coriander, cinnamon, cumin, and ginger
¼ teaspoon cayenne pepper

Chop the carrots, bananas, and apricots into about 1-inch pieces. Boil the carrots gently about 20 minutes. Drain and save the water.

Saute all spices in ghee for 3 to 5 minutes. Add the cooked carrots, half the bananas, and all the apricots and saute for 5 minutes.

Add the saved water till the bananas seem mushy, which may require a bit more water. Add the remaining bananas and cook several more minutes.

BEANS

Sprouting always comes to mind when I think of beans. Then those meatless meat patties from soybean. When I was a boy Dad always made salad from precooked garbanzos (also known as chick or cici), kidney and green beans, oil, spices, and onion.

In addition to sprouting, there are many ways to prepare beans. A handy modern method is to use a pressure cooker, which saves time and water (no small consideration if there's a drought or you have to carry your water from a well a half-mile away).

One can cook beans in a pot. This requires many hours of slow cooking with very little stirring (preferably none). Add the salt *after* they have been cooked. If you add it during cooking, the beans will not soften as fast.

Most soak the beans overnight. Some beans, such as the pinto, black-eyed peas, and lentils, require no soaking. Soy beans should be soaked in a cool place so they do not ferment. We always prepare more than needed at any one meal and have some ready to use later.

You don't have to soak beans to pressure cook them, but it doesn't hurt to soak them a few hours. Make sure the skin of the bean is totally off. NEVER cook black beans in a pressure cooker. They are liable to clog the pressure cooker valve, and when that happens either the top flies off or the pressure safety valve goes, sounding

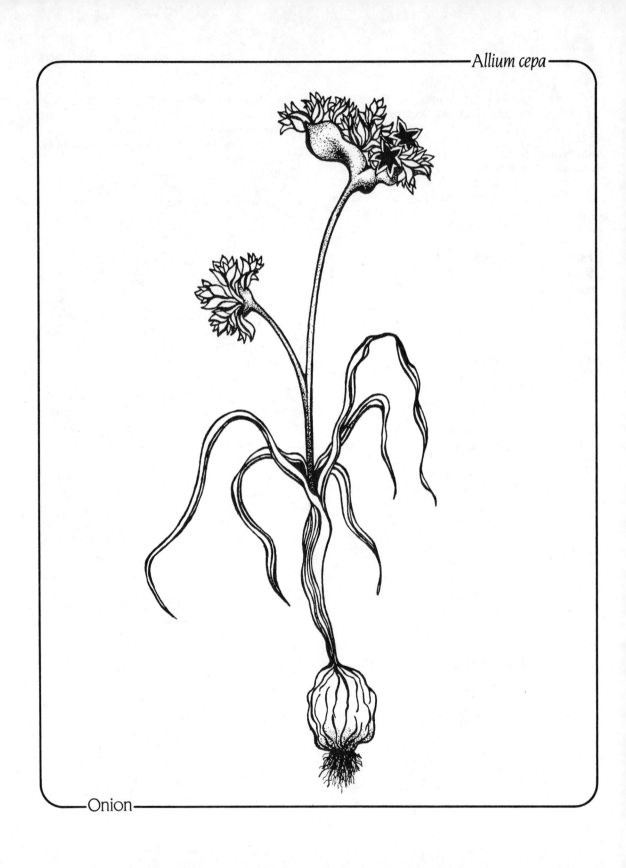

like the shot heard round the world. Both alternatives are *very* dangerous. So please be observant and careful. A pressure cooker is a good tool, but look before cooking to see that the opening is clear.

Now that we have established a few ground rules in using the pressure cooker, take:

1 cup beans
2½ cups water
¼ teaspoon salt

Place these in your pressure cooker and with the lid on, bring to a boil. Reduce the heat and allow to simmer for 1 hour. Place under water to reduce the pressure quickly. Open, add salt, cover beans with water and cook uncovered until the water is gone, about 20 minutes.

Such beans as chickpeas take about ½ hour more. Lentils take only fifteen minutes. This yields about 5 to 8 servings.

To cook beans without a pressure cooker, for every cup of soaked beans use 4 cups of water. Place these together in a pot, bring to a boil. Lower the heat, leaving a small gap for the lid to breathe, and cook for two hours over a low flame. Toward the end of cooking add ¼ teaspoon salt. If no liquid remains, add a bit more water and salt. Lentils only need 30 minutes cooking time this way. This yields 4 to 6 servings.

Save the water in which you have soaked the beans. It can be made into soup or used in a bread that calls for water. It will change the taste a bit but experiment with different tastes. If neither of these feel right, feed the bean water to your outdoor plants. They love it.

Herbs and plants that you are growing, or wild varieties, are best placed back into the soil, in whatever form, to increase the vibratory factor. That factor of light mineral element many times washed away down the drain, cannot be revitalized from whence it came — unless back to the soil given.

There are varied ways in which to prepare the beans. The soybean has become more popular recently. Those countries that center their attention on meat diets should consider the use of soybean for protein. Moving away from a diet that is high in grain-fed meats at least aids nature toward correcting the present and rising food crisis. The soybean is a most popular bean in this and other countries, especially in the Orient. When we consider that about 10% or less of the protein fed to animals is returned to us when we consume meats, and 90% is wasted, we should think how best to utilize the grain as opposed to continuing the present practice. Even though some profit is lost, a food source is gained. Especially with the soybean. To get the full benefit of all the amino acids that are contained in the soya, a necessary step is to boil its by-products, except for the bean sprouts which are eaten raw or slightly cooked. Soy bean protein is readily digestable and many nutritionists agree that a weak digestive tract or allergies can be greatly aided by this bean. When I get tired of making cooked dishes I make soya milk. After a few tries at milking your bean you may increase or decrease the amount of beans for your needs.

Richard Katz, a close botanical companion, was inspired by Bill Shurtleff, author of *The Book of Tofu,* for the following:

Cheesy Tofu Dressing
(Richard Katz)

12 ounces tofu
4 tablespoons lemon juice
6 tablespoons miso paste
2 tablespoons dill weed
1 clove garlic, minced or pressed
  (more if you are a garlic lover)
water, soy milk or soy whey (as needed)

Blend all ingredients well, adding enough liquid to achieve desired consistency. Refrigerate until used. Dressing will thicken and flavors blend while it sits.

Soya Milk

Start with a pound of soy beans, and soak them overnight. In the morning measure 1 cup of soaked beans and 3 cups of water into a blender and blend till creamy smooth. Place this in a cheesecloth or cotton bag and hang over a pot to catch the run off. Let it drip until it feels dry, and give it a couple of twists to extract all the milk. The "milked" beans can be made into tofu. The extracted juice, or soy drippings, should be boiled slowly and watched constantly as it will scorch very easily. When done you may add for every 32 ounces of soya milk 1 teaspoon of honey and ¼ teaspoon of salt to alter the bland taste. Try other variations according to your taste. Molasses is nice—or malt syrup. Store in a cold place as you would milk.

Indian Garbanzos
(Eastern style)

This tasty dish was shared with me one evening by the folks (Marcos, Morgan, Carol, and all) from Bubba Free John's Community.

> 2 cups garbanzos
> ½ teaspoon sea salt
> 4 tablespoons oil
> 4 cloves garlic
> ¼ teaspoon ground cumin
> ⅛ teaspoon ground cinnamon
> 1 medium tomato
> a few leaves of coriander
> 6 cups water
> ¼ teaspoon ground cloves
> 1 medium onion
> ¼ teaspoon ground coriander
> ½ teaspoon ground turmeric
> ¼ teaspoon cayenne pepper
> 1 small green chili
> a few leaves of parsley or dandelion

> a piece of fresh ginger about ½ finger long (optional)

Soak the garbanzos in water for a night. Next morning add the salt and cloves and bring to a boil. Reduce heat and cook for 1½ hours.

Place the oil, chopped onions, and garlic (and ginger if the option sounds good) in a pan, and saute until light golden in color. Chop the green chili and tomato and add to the onions along with all the remaining ingredients, keeping the parsley and coriander for garnish. Cook all this for 5 to 7 minutes. Combine the beans and the vegetables and simmer for another 5 to 7 minutes. Place garnish on top and serve. Spicy and enjoyable.

NUTS

The best method of keeping nuts is to store them in their shells. This protects them from exposure to air (causing oxidation), light, heat, and moisture. Nuts can be stored about the house for several months. Watching the animals' storage habits will teach you the best way. If squirrels pack them in dry earth in a cool log, you can certainly place them in jars in a cool place in your home or root cellar.

The pinon, pine nut, Indian nut, or, in Italy, pignolia is one of most delicate fortune, being right on top of the pine cones as they fall (lest you lose them to the squirrel). They must be gathered during the late summer months and early fall at the altitudes where they grow. "Good air, good nuts, good gathering, good breath upon eating," is a saying passed on by an old "feller" who instructs and oversees the cutting of trees. (Though a loss, our heritage, the tree, is being used by some at least in its entirety.)

Like beans and seeds, nuts have innumerable uses in our kitchens, but we usually think of them as snacking food. They are better, certainly, than processed snacks.

Chestnuts roasted over the fire (or right in it, but be careful of them popping) are a delight. We also have almonds, grown mostly in California, pecans and peanuts from our southern dry states; walnuts from California, macadamias, Brazils, and cashews from the tropical zones, and hickories from the East Coast. Wherever they're from they're a good addition to our diets. (As with any food, the ideal is *one at a time, or monotropic eating.*)

There are several ways to prepare nuts. Fresh and raw is, of course, simplest. Chew thoroughly and eat sparingly as nuts are very concentrated foods. Yet roasting or blanching nuts, many times enhances the subtle flavors. In addition, blanching helps eliminate the inner skin of the nut.

To BLANCH, pour boiling water over the shelled nuts. If you have a lot, cover with boiling water for a moment. Either way, be as brief as possible. Drain. Then rub or pinch the skin to separate it from the nut. The "white" meat will be exposed, thus making it easier to roast. There is some mineral loss when this method is used.

To ROAST or toast your nuts to make them crisp and enhance the flavor, place the blanched nuts on or in a 250° to 300° oven and turn often to avoid scorching as nuts lose flavor and become tough if scorched or overtoasted. Roasted nuts lose some enzyme content.

To SALT your nuts, use 2 tablespoons oil and ½ teaspoon salt for each cup of nuts. Spread and mix these on a flat pan in a 250° oven. Toast (or roast) approximately ten minutes, turning and stirring regularly so an even browning occurs.

NUT BUTTERS are good in spreads, dips, sauces, and such (optionally replacing shortenings and thickeners). *Seed butters,* such as sesame, pumpkin, sunflower, and chia make rich spread snacks. The same methods of preparation and use apply. Simply run roasted nuts and seeds through a grinder. A hand grinder works well, but if one has an electric one, it is certainly easier. Before all these fancy machines were available, the mortar and pestle, or a good grinding wheel accomplished the same result.

The other night while playing with nut butters I stumbled on a friendly recipe quite by mistake. As I was putting the almonds (1 pound) into the grinder, I accidentally knocked over some garlic powder and chia seed on the shelf above. About a tablespoon of garlic powder and ⅛ cup of chia seed got dumped into the almonds. It all got ground together, and the result was a very tasteful addition to the original snack. Prior planning could not have yielded a tastier combination. Planning anything should be done with the understanding that in the universe, all things are subject to change.

Laminariales

Sea Rocket

EIGHT

Breads, Their Heads, and the Pleasures of Kneading

Oropasa is the mother of Peru, the first place of pan, or bread, the Incas' descendants claim. The streets have no cement. Waste passes in gutters, yet the city is clean. The buildings are of the same soil as the streets, held together with wood and straw, and painted white. We arrived at Mariano's home, a simple, one-room hut with a dirt floor and a single cot spot for healing, and then moved to the home of one of the doctors I was visiting. A nun on leave from her monastery, having been within for some eighty years, never speaking but with a faint smile, served fresh-picked, dried, and ground coffee and pan. As we talked, I peered around a partition to note the corn mortar and pestle that had been handed down for some ten generations. The mortar was about a foot high at its highest, two feet long, and tapered to within nine inches of the floor. There were several earthenware pots of various sizes, all filled with different grains, seeds, and nuts. The pan we were eating came to our table from the earth via hand crushing on the rock. The candles were beeswax with wicks of hemp. The table was hand-carved wood. As the breads and rolls were brought out over the hours, an ancient craving stirred within me: "Go back to the roots, let's learn our seeds."

To gather the seed for our daily bread is a chore, yet so rewarding to feel and experience what our ancestors had to do. A picture comes to mind of the ancients as they flogged their grains (if the elements allowed good harvest), then cast their yield to the wind to separate the chaff from the seed itself. If for bread, it was put to stone to yield flour. Later, across the table, they told the story of a good harvest and partook of fine bread, maybe muffins, and possibly pastry or cookies. A pleasurable reward from nature.

There are many joys in kneading and baking. There is the contact in kneading and shaping the dough. There is an interaction like the stroking of the earth with our palms. A deeper contact and interaction imparts your own essence, sweat if you will, into what is being prepared. A meditation is felt by those wishing to experience

119

the blending of alchemy (via alchemist, or cook-physician) with the products of nature, the seeds turned flour.

A gentleman who prefers his silence is a wise man who has found contentment in his own expression. Roy Titus is a close neighbor of many years, a disciple of Meher Baha, who practices his philosophy in his weaving and kneading. His neighbors seldom see him, but when he appears it's with a fresh bread, a new philosophy about life, or a finished weaving. To know one who finds the parts and materials for his loom in nature is indeed a pleasure.

There are many such people who are my neighbors in both city and mountains. For those who have tasted of my kneading and spicing over the past years, I concede a higher source. Ignorance is truly bliss. I have reflected on my recipes and noticed a space in this four-year effort that was difficult to fill. So I asked for help with the kneading process from Roy, and Kevin McCall, a fine teacher of foods who has worked in many Co-ops (now Consumer's Co-op Basic Foods of Northern California). Kevin has appeared as a student in my courses and yet at each herbal dinner or reunion shares some of his own baking that teaches us. We are all learning—all sharing.

The following is but one example of how bread can be made. The instructions should not be followed strictly but varied according to the taste and imagination of the baker.

Wheat will always be the best product for flour, but bread can and has been made of just about every edible grain, root, seed, and nut known to man; even dried berries and some flowers can be used. A good rule is to use at least half wheat flour to assure a smooth texture and consistency that would otherwise be difficult to achieve.

This recipe will make four loaves.

Start with 6 cups of water or strong herb tea, leftover soup or the soup water, rice or grain water, or such at 105°-115° F in a very large bowl. This will feel neither warm nor cold to your wrist. Sprinkle 1 tablespoon (1 package) dry yeast into the liquid and stir in ¾ cup honey. In a separate bowl mix 8 cups whole wheat flour and 1⅓ cups nonfat milk or 2 cups of instant nonfat dry milk (this increases the protein and gives a smoother texture to the bread). Stir this into the liquid 1 cup at a time, then stir the mixture gradually and gently for 1 to 2 minutes. You may wish to add some yarrow, pipsissewa, wild sage, mint, or perhaps some yerba santa or life everlasting. For a stronger flavor, finely crush the herbs and add them to the dough. Cover the bowl with a towel and set it in a warm place, such as an oven with a pilot light, for 50 to 70 minutes until the dough has approximately doubled in size.

Have ready ½ cup vegetable oil, or whichever oil you prefer, and 2½ teaspoons sea salt. Stir these into the dough after the first rising. This should be done by pulling the spoon along the edge of the bowl for about one-fourth of a turn, then pushing the spoon toward the center of the bowl and then pulling the spoon straight up and out of the dough. Your free hand should be turning the bowl a quarter of a turn in the opposite direction of the spoon. With a little practice this will evolve into a natural rhythmical motion that will keep the dough in one piece. This and proper kneading are the secret of making a good bread. Continuing the method explained above, stir in 2 cups barley flour (or the same proportion of other flour or gathered grains), 2 cups whole wheat flour and 1 cup millet flour, one cup at a time. The amount will depend on the type of flours you use and how fresh they are. As much as a cup more or less flour may be needed to achieve the right consistency.

If the right amount of flour has been used only a few scraps will remain stuck to the bowl when the dough is dumped onto a well-floured kneading board. Scrape the mixing bowl adding the scrapes to the dough. Oil the bowl and set aside. Kneading will require two to three more

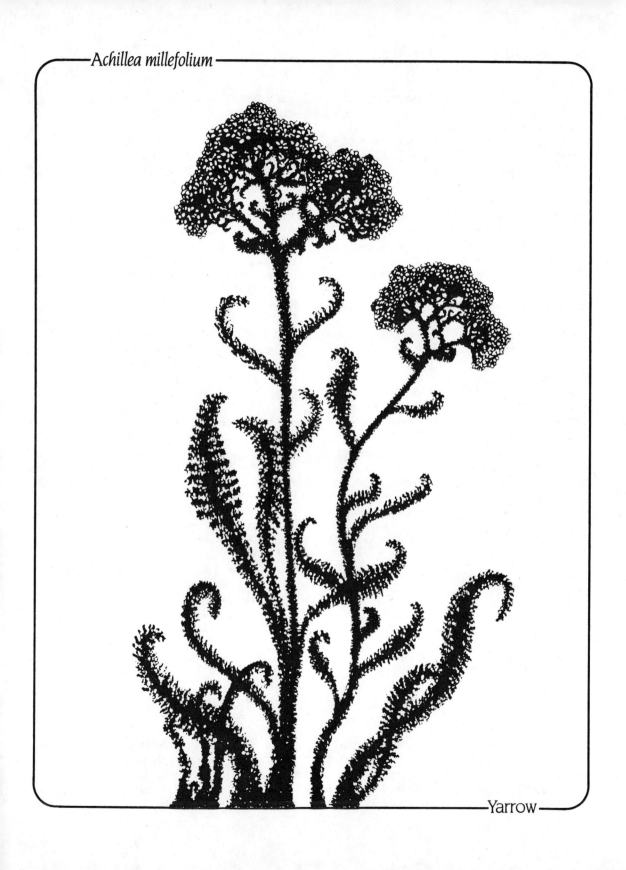

cups flour of any kind you desire. Kneading takes 10 minutes if you keep at it, or 15 minutes allowing for a short break.

Kneading is a process of repeatedly folding the dough in half and stuffing it inside itself. Fold the dough in half with one hand, then push it down with both. Turn the dough a quarter turn clockwise and repeat and repeat and repeat adding flour as necessary. Return the dough to the oiled bowl and then turn it over in the bowl to coat top with oil and prevent drying.

Let rise in a warm place for an hour until the volume has about doubled, then with your fist punch down with fifteen to twenty punches. Allow to rise for another hour.

Dump dough out on a dry kneading board and form it into a ball. Don't flour unless it sticks, which is unlikely. Cut the dough into four equal parts and shape them into balls. Allow to stand for 5 minutes. Knead each ball of dough about six times and shape into loaves as desired. Cover loaves and let rise for ½ hour while oven is heating to 350°.

If desired brush on a coating of beaten raw egg or honey diluted in milk for a shiny crust. Sprinkle with caraway, sesame, poppy, or your favorite seeds. At least one cut ½ inch deep should be made along the length of the loaf to allow for expansion and to let steam escape. Several shorter cuts may be used to create a pattern.

Bake for one hour at 350°. Enjoy—either hot and fresh with your favorite herbal jam or jelly, or if you prefer, cooled.

Pita

(by Roy Titus)

This is the Middle Eastern bread with a pocket. Great for between meal snacks or for sandwiches with a style all their own.

In 2¼ cups of water at 105°F. dissolve 2 packages of dry yeast and 1 tablespoon honey. Set aside for 5 minutes.

In a large bowl mix 8 cups whole wheat flour (pastry flour if available; it's certainly better)

and 2 teaspoons of sea salt. Next mix in ¼ cup olive oil, and add the yeast water about a ½ cup at a time mixing in each addition gently and thoroughly. An additional ¼-½ cup of water will probably be needed to gather all the flour into a compact ball. Add this a little at a time and use no more than necessary.

A lot of fine-textured flour, yeast, a little love and a lot of kneading make this amazing bread possible, so turn the dough ball onto a lightly floured board and knead for 20 minutes or until the dough is smooth and elastic. Don't give up too soon! Place the dough in the lightly oiled mixing bowl, cover, and let rise in a warm place for 45 to 55 minutes or until double in size. Punch down the dough with your fist, divide it into 10 equal parts and roll these into balls 2 inches in diameter. Cover with a towel and let sit for 30 minutes. Scrounge as many cookie sheets as you can while the dough is resting. A large sheet will accommodate two loaves. On a lightly floured board roll out as many loaves as you have sheets for until the loaves are 8 inches in diameter and about 1/8 inch thick. Sprinkle each cookie sheet with about ¼ cup cornmeal, flour, or other seed meal. Lay the loaves on the sheets, cover, and let rise for 30 minutes. Preheat oven to 500°F. If you have a gas oven, place the cookie sheet on the floor of the oven; if the oven is electric use the bottom rack. After 5 minutes move the loaves to the middle rack and bake for 5 minutes more. Wrap them in towels. Now roll out any remaining balls of dough, let raise for 30 minutes and bake. Be sure to put more cornmeal on the sheets. When finished you will have a unique bread with a pocket in the middle.

Vegetable Pie

(Kevin McCall)

This delicious pie is almost a meal by itself.

Scrub 3 medium-sized potatoes, cut into small chunks, and boil in lightly salted water 15 to 20 minutes. In the meantime saute half a chopped medium onion and 2 cloves of chopped garlic. Double the recipe for the crust from the carrot pie (see page 125), omitting the nutmeg. Press bottom layer of crust into pan. When potatoes are done, drain off the water and save. Blend several chunks of potatoes with some of the water.

Add: ½ teaspoon basil
    ¼ teaspoon ground cumin
    ¼ teaspoon dill weed
    2 tablespoons dried parsley or several pinches of fresh
    a pinch of cayenne pepper
    2 dashes of black pepper
    ¼ teaspoon salt

Blend all together well and set aside.

Fill pie crust with:
    1 stalk celery, chopped
    the sauteed onion and garlic
    1 cup broccoli tops
    1 cup carrots, sliced thin
    ½ cup peas
    4 ounces cheese cubes
    the rest of the potatoes

Add your choice of any other vegetables: Pour spice sauce over vegetables and cover with top crust. Cut four small slits in top of crust and bake at 400° for 40 minutes or until brown.

San Francisco, in addition to being a place of energy and creativity, gave us the foggy climate and air, steam beer, and sourdough bread. All go together naturally. The following recipes were presented to me by my godfather's daughter, Lilia Johnson. These, she said, had been passed to her by her elders.

Grandmother's Sourdough Starter

4 potatoes
2 cups water
3 cups rye flour
½ cup honey
1 teaspoon salt

Boil the potatoes in their jackets in clear water. When cooked, take two of the potatoes, peel, and mash them in the cooking water. Mix with flour, honey, and salt. Put in a crock, cover and let stand in a warm spot for about four days (until bubbly and odoriferous). Refrigerate.

Sourdough Bread

1 cup sourdough starter
2 quarts lukewarm potato water (or other liquid, whey is very good; could include 1 cup of sauerkraut juice)
1 heaping tablespoon of malt powder
1 tablespoon salt more or less to taste (omit if you use sauerkraut juice)
6½ cups of rye flour
5 cups of whole wheat flour
1 tablespoon whole ground caraway seeds (optional)

Mix sourdough starter with the liquids, malt powder, salt, and rye flour. Cover and let stand in a warm spot for at least 7 hours or overnight. Stir. Preserve and refrigerate 1 cup of this as starter for your next baking. Combine rest of ingredients with mixture to make a stiff dough. Turn out on a lightly floured board and knead until no longer sticky, adding more flour if necessary. Divide and shape into loaves, put in pans or on a greased baking sheet. Cover and let rise for about 8 hours. Heat oven to 350° and place a small pan of water in oven to create steam. Bake bread for 60 minutes. (If pyrex pans are used, reduce heat to 325°.)
Cool on racks.

While thinking about making bread our imaginations may wander and concoct new and exciting preparations. Once I observed an elderly lady make her bread according to simple practices previously mentioned. She lived in Sacramento, which gets quite hot during the summer. Instead of using the oven, she placed her bread in a large deep iron pan with a heavy lid. Then she dug a hole in the yard about a foot deep and large enough for the pan. Burying the pan so its top just barely protruded on the surface, she left it for the day. When we dug up the pan, the bread was completely baked and had the familiar light of sun-infused tea. She said she also made soup this way and if it were hot all the time, this would be her only way.

The following collection of recipes are from several herbal gatherings. Some are incomplete in instruction but I have included the ingredients to share several alternatives and thoughts expressed about the breads and their "heads" (those sweets of kneaded thoughts). Thanks to the cooks and their kitchens. A cooking philosopher once reminded me, "There are no secrets in the universe."

Dog Bread

(Soy-cornmeal as shown to Jenny Groat by M. Connley)

Into a quart jar put a little less than ½ cup soybeans and fill with water (about 4 cups); refrigerate overnight. Next day, strain, reserving liquid; into blender put 2 cups beans, 2 cups cold water from soaking, 1 tablespoon honey. Blend 10-15 minutes, until it has the consistency of whipping cream.

Meanwhile, into a mixing bowl put 2 cups cornmeal (masa) and a pinch of salt (rock salt grain). Mix with hands, then gently fold in other mix. Put into even-oiled and floured pan; (you can make it thin in a large pan or thick in a smaller pan, adjusting baking time). Bake at 350° till golden brown.

A *variation:* When you have a cantaloupe, save the seeds and moisture from the center. Refrigerate till ready for use. Then blend, strain, and mix with the batter, diminishing the water in the original recipe a bit.

Earth Bread

Use any amount of bread dough. You will also need a good supply of green oak, hickory,

aspen, bay or madrone leaves and a hot coal pit.

Let the dough rise at least once, preferably twice. Pat dough into desired sizes and wrap each in several layers of leaves. Make a place in the coals and place on hot fire base. Cover this with ash and hot coals. Leave for 10 to 20 minutes depending on the strength of the fire base. Test every so often with a thin twig by punching the bread. When the stick comes out clean it is ready to eat.

Munchin' Luncheon

Sitting in a close friend's kitchen not long ago, we were thinking of lunch. Wayne Kingston mentioned a simple recipe he always liked, and this is the way he did it. Truly a munchin' luncheon. We talked possibilities of substitutions, and they were endless.

Start with some finely ground cornmeal. For two we used a cup of corn flour, adding enough water to make into a dough. Add comfrey or tomatoes, and mix in a bit of cayenne and salad oil. Mix into a ball and place in a moderate oven for 10 to 20 minutes.

Serve with your favorite dressing..

Asparagus Pie

Another old friend, Felicity Kirsch, offered this delightful asparagus pie. Use young, fresh asparagus from your garden.

    2 cups whole wheat pastry flour
    ½ teaspoon sea salt
    1 teaspoon baking powder (no aluminium)
    ½ teaspoon baking soda
    ½ cup unsaturated vegetable oil
    ¾ cup honey
    ½ cup yogurt
    2 large fertile eggs
    ¼ cup nut meats, chopped
    1½ cups raw asparagus, cut into ¼ inch
        chunks

Measure flour, salt, baking powder, and soda into a large bowl and mix together well. Add the oil, honey, and yogurt and mix again. Break in an egg and beat and stir thoroughly. Add the nuts and asparagus.

Divide into two greased 7-inch loaf pans and place in cold oven. Turn oven to 350° and bake for 40 to 45 minutes.

Baking observations to share:

If you put the oil in the measuring cup first and then add the honey, it will pour out easily.

When turning a cake out of a pan, put a plate over the cake pan and turn over. The cake will come out easily.

Instead of using oil, margarine, or butter to grease a pan, use liquid lecithin (a derivative of soybean oil).

INDIAN CATTAIL CAKES—BRYSIS

As the plant easily sheds its pollen, it is best to use a gathering bag to collect the pollen. Cover the stalk and tap gently with a stick so pollen falls into the bag. Store as you would other seeds or pollen, in a cool, dry area. Pollen is said to contain *protenti* (protein), a fine addition to soups, salads, or augmented with flour, in cakes.

¾ cup cattail pollen
1½ cups fine ground flour (choice be yours)
1 egg (optional depending on diet)
1 cup milk (water if desired)
1 tablespoon honey

Mix items together in order of recipe. If too thick add more water or milk; if too runny make it into a pancake or thicken by adding more pollen or flour. Bake in 350°F. oven for ½ hour.

This same recipe has been made with plantain or mustard seeds, the latter being very warming and quite pleasant if you are used to hotter foods. I observed cattails and bamboo shoots being used throughout different parts of the Orient in various recipes, such as Kim Chi.

Carrot Pie
(Kevin McCall)

This remarkable pie tastes very much like pumpkin and it has puzzled many, since there is no hint of its main ingredient. Carrots have the advantage of being available fresh from the garden most of the year.

Take 2 cups of cooked carrots and blend with 1¼ cups of half-and-half or evaporated milk. (Put only ½ cup of carrots into blender at a time.) Pour this mixture into a bowl and add ½ cup honey, ½ cup arrowroot flour, ½ teaspoon sea salt, 1 teaspoon cinnamon, ½ teaspoon ginger, ¼ teaspoon cloves. Mix well until smooth. Pour into a 9-inch pie shell.

For a light and flaky pie crust, mix together 1½ cups sifted whole wheat pastry flour, ¼ teaspoon sea salt, and ½ teaspoon ground nutmeg. Add 3/8 cup vegetable oil and 3 tablespoons cold water. Mix together and roll out between two sheets of waxed paper. Peel off the top sheet and flip the pie crust into the pan. Press the crust into the pan and peel off the other sheet.

Bake in preheated 425° oven for 15 minutes. Reduce temperature to 350° and bake for 45 minutes more. Best served chilled.

Italian Sesame Cookies
(Rudy Paglioccio)

¼ cup soft butter
½ cup raw sugar
1 teaspoon vanilla
3 eggs
1¾ cups whole wheat flour
3 teaspoons baking powder
¼ teaspoon sea salt
2 tablespoons wheat germ
2 tablespoons stone ground yellow cornmeal
½ cup sesame seeds

Preheat oven to 425°. Cream butter, sugar, and vanilla together until light and fluffy.

Beat in 2 eggs very well.

Mix together flour, baking powder, salt, wheat germ, and cornmeal and stir into creamed mixture gradually.

Shape mixture into rolls about 2 inches long and ¾ inch in diameter. Beat remaining egg, dip cookies in eggs, and roll in sesame seeds. Place on ungreased baking sheet and bake 12 minutes or until golden brown. Cool on rack.

YIELD: 3½ dozen, more or less—less if you eat the batter.

Cosmic Honey Bars
(Susie and Theron Tuttle)

Have all the ingredients ready to mix quickly!

    1½ cups honey, or molasses, or both
    3 tablespoons butter
    2 cups whole wheat flour
    1 tablespoon baking powder
    2 tablespoons chopped orange peel
    ½ teaspoon cinnamon (or substitute
        sassafras)
    ¼ teaspoon each allspice, coriander, mace,
        cardamom, and cloves
    a handful of sliced almonds
    ½ cup more whole wheat flour

Heat honey or molasses in saucepan slowly until liquid. Melt and add butter. Mix whole wheat flour and baking powder by stirring vigorously; add to mixture to make a thick batter. Add chopped orange peel (if you have any lemon peel, add that too!) cinnamon and other spices. Add additional flour until dough is "sticky." Pat into greased pans about ⅜ inch thick. Bake 20 to 25 minutes at 350°. Don't overbake or they'll get hard! Remove from pan and slice while warm.

Apple Mint Pie
(O.J.'s favorite)

Melt 3 bars of agar agar (a gelatinous sea vegetable used to set foods or for jelling) in 1 cup fresh apple juice.

Add ⅛ cup lemon juice.

Boil gently for 20 minutes. Cool slightly and add 4 beaten egg yolks and 1 cup fresh chopped apple.

Bring to a boil again.

Remove from heat and add ¼ teaspoon lemon peel, ¼ cup honey, 1 tablespoon chopped fresh mint.

Cool and add 1 cup of yogurt.

Chill until set and fold in 4 beaten egg whites with ⅛ teaspoon sea salt added.

Pour into pie shell and chill.

Pie shell:

    Whole wheat bread crumbs
    Wheat germ
    Rolled oats
    Ground sunflower seed
    Honey
    Sea salt
    Mixed ground chia, pumpkin, and poppy
        seeds
    Safflower oil
    Cinnamon

Press into pie pan and bake for 10 minutes at 400°.

Teleport Fudge

Richard's favorites were carob n' cream, vanilla n' honey, butter n' nuts.

More specifically:

    ¼ cup butter
    ½ cup heavy cream
    1 teaspoon vanilla
    1 tablespoon honey
    ¾ cups chopped nut meats
    ¾ cup carob* powder

Combine butter, cream, vanilla, honey, nuts, and carob. Press to about ¼ inch in a flat pan. Allow to stand. Store in refrigerator ½ hour. Cut to your desired size.

*Carob, also known as St. John's Bread, is a fine substitute for chocolate, being a fine source of minerals.

Salvia SP.

Peanut Butter Cookies
(Penny Gilmore)

Cream together:

    ½ cup nutty peanut butter
    ½ cup honey
    ¼ cup date sugar
    ¼ cup oil
    ¼ teaspoon salt
    ½ teaspoon vanilla

Add and mix in:

    1 cup whole wheat pastry flour
    4 tablespoons wheat germ flour

Form into flat cookies by using a wooden spoon. Bake at 350° for 10 minutes.

Carob Nut Brownies
(Chadwick Rogers)

Cream together:

    1 cup raw honey
    4 tablespoons soy oil
    1 teaspoon lecithin or 1 egg
    2 teaspoons vanilla
    2 teaspoons lemon juice
    2 tablespoons nut butter
    1 teaspoon grated orange or lemon rind
    ¼ teaspoon salt

Add and mix in:

    ⅔ cup carob powder
    1-⅛ cups sifted whole wheat pastry flour
    1 cup chopped walnut

Bake in oblong pan at 350° for approximately 30 minutes.

Majoon

Sweets have always been the delight of the household. There are the usual fruits and dried goodies, but every once in a while one wants that extra rich goodness of honey and dried fruits, spices, and different seeds, flowers, and pollens to blend an unbeatable richness. At one such time Elabeth and Stephan blended a merry-making experience for about thirty of us. They called it Moroccan Majoon, or, this being California, simply majoon. It took years to get the recipe and after hearing it, I see why we all felt so blissful, ate as never before, and laughed. . . .

    2 cups ground marijuana seed flour
    1 cup chopped dried papaya
    ½ cup chopped raisins
    ½ cup ground sunflower seeds
    ½ cup coarse almond flour
    1 teaspoon ginger powder
    1 teaspoon cinnamon powder
    1 tablespoon anise powder
    ½ cup honey
    2 tablespoons butter
    ½ cup warm water

In a skillet, over low heat, gently toast the seed flour* till toasty golden. Add everything else except the butter and simmer till a fine puree forms. Melt the butter over low flame as the puree is finishing, then add to the puree, stirring until the mixture has an even consistency. If the mixture is not sweet enough add a bit more honey. Place in a bowl and serve with fruit, cream, or honey on top.

*The Majoon of Morocco uses Kif (the word kif in Arabic translates to quietude or rest), the powder of marijuana. Because each state has different laws concerning this plant when you find it wild, do heed your conscience and your needs. It's hard to stop the growth of weeds.

NINE

Mushrooms and Soma

When hunting this wild delicacy, be sure to keep one important thought, "identify positively." In the bibliography I have included several very good identifiers. The best, however, is the absolute knowledge of gathering passed from one generation to another or from one forager to another. There is no one rule for identification of mushrooms except to be absolutely positive. For many thousands of years the mushroom has been surrounded by myth and superstition. The early civilizations, such as those of the Romans and Greeks, used special utensils to eat their prepared mushrooms. Priests of the Americas, as well as Oriental people, used the fungi for religious purposes. In many European countries, the elders taught the children to recognize the edible mushrooms. After repeated gathering, an ingrained awareness and absolute knowledge became fixed in their minds.

To this day I hear the stories of tragedy and loss of life even of some who were experienced in gathering. But I have learned a few varieties that I can positively identify. This leads from one to another, as from one simple herb to another.

Despite misunderstandings and prejudices that lead to tragic accidents, many still persist in gathering and preparing what is often referred to as "plant meat." While many mushrooms contain protein within their fungal structure, they have a large proportion of water to solid matter. Tests have shown they are not meat, yet if you have foraged for this delicacy you will often be reminded of meat. The Oriental people have long valued mushrooms and gathered and prepared them for longevity.

There are many mycological and native plant societies in the United States and they include experts and novices. All have one common purpose, sharing knowledge and, as positively as possible, identifying native plants and mushrooms. Aside from the knowledge gained through experience, these societies from time to time find a new plant or mushroom of edible splendor, an exciting and rewarding experience. I have included this small section on mushrooms because no matter where you forage through the years you will undoubtedly find yourself running into them.

Each genus of fungi has its own preparational method. Many cookbooks describe varied and modified cooking techniques. Since the *Agaricus campestris* is probably the most common of fungi (*Agaricus bisporus* is

what we buy commercially), the following directions for preparation are given for this genus, but may apply also to other species.

To Keep Temporarily:

Clean the plant and remove the parts to be discarded. Rinse the parts to be used in cold water and dry with a cloth. Place in boiling water for 5 to 10 minutes. Drain and wipe dry.

To Prepare the Agaricus:

Clean. Cut off and recycle stems. Rinse the caps in cold water and drain. Keep in cold water with lemon or vinegar until just before using (the lemon or vinegar acidulates or makes them somewhat sour).

To Toast the Agaricus:

Dry with a cloth and dust with flour. Place a bit of butter, salt, and pepper on the gills. Lay the caps with the gills upward. Cook over moderate heat on a wire toaster for 5 to 10 minutes.

To Bake the Agaricus:

Dry with a cloth. Line a pie pan with toast, spread the peeled caps on the toast, sprinkle with salt and pepper. (Optional— place a few tablespoonsful of thick cream on top.) Cover with a plate and place in a medium oven for 15 minutes.

For variation line the dish with toast that has been dipped in hot water and buttered. Spread the caps on the toast and dot each with ½ teaspoon of butter. Cover and cook in a warm oven for 10 minutes.

To Broil:

Broil lightly on both sides under a strong flame. Arrange on buttered toast and sprinkle with salt and pepper. Set in the oven a minute. Serve hot.

To Stew:

Peel a quart of caps. Add 2 tablespoons butter, 1 teaspoon salt, ¼ teaspoon pepper, and ½ cup water or veggie stock. Boil gently in a covered saucepan for 5 to 7 minutes. Or if you like, peel a pint of cut caps and add a tablespoon butter, ¼ teaspoon salt, and a pinch of pepper. Simmer for 10 minutes in a stewing pot.

The previous methods may be applied to the other edible fungi. Experience and awareness of these edibles will be your best guide to which method is best.

I have had several experiences with these beautiful and wondrous plants that will cause any forager's expertise to grow as mysteriously as do the fungi. My grand-parents would take me, even before I could really make sense of what we were doing, out to their favorite patch: the Bear Valley Trail toward the coast of Point Reyes, California. The field was so vast and I was so small that it seemed all day was spent gathering baskets full of their favorite mushrooms. (Later I found they were the *Agaricus*.) Coming back to the cottage they would talk of such good "flushes"—such good eating. Mums would prepare them simply by cleaning, rinsing, and then cooking lightly in butter with garlic.

Last year while visiting the wine country around Lodi, California, I met with the wine master of Guild Wineries, Lawrence Quaccia, a splendid winemaker and very personable gentleman. I spent the day observing him at his trade, making wines, for research I was doing on the medicinal properties of wine. The conversation turned to *champignons* (mushrooms). We both enjoyed the picking of mushrooms, and we each had our recipes. He offered to take me to his favorite field where that year so many *Agaricus* appeared. He said he and his daughter had gathered bags full only the week before, and in fact when we went out we did indeed gather several bags full. What an experience! To hear of the years when there were very few—how this year there were many. How the best fields to gather were untouched by the till, heavily thickened by horse dung, and free-growing grasses. A joy certainly. His favorite way to prepare them was similar to my grandmother's. They never knew each other, but they knew the tastes passed from one family to another.

When you gather fresh young specimens, make sure they are free of insect infestation. Remove the base stalk and clean the caps with water, keeping the flow of water away from the gills to avoid drenching them. If a bit of time will elapse before eating, rub the gills with a bit of lemon to prevent discoloration. The following recipes have been given to me by my father.

Champignons à la Mingus
(Scottish for Menzies as offered by Dad)

Saute one minced onion in a couple of tablespoons of butter in a large skillet till golden brown. Add a pound of fresh *Agaricus*.

Add one cupful white fruit wine or champagne. (If there are several people and you want this as a sauce, you may wish to add more.

Cook over medium heat for 10 minutes. Serve over rice or with your main dish. Great for winter dinners.

Morning Mush with Mushrooms

Any amount of prepared oatmeal. Any amount of fresh sauteed mushrooms. Mix together, place a bit of butter on top and serve.

For a quicky soup after you have spent the day gathering, this recipe will warm your stomach:

½ pound *Agaricus* or other identified field
    fungi (washed and cleaned)
⅔ cup fresh milk, cream, or water
1 teaspoon sea salt

2 tablespoons butter
a dash each of cayenne and parsley

Saute the mushrooms in a deep pan with butter for a few moments before adding the liquid and the salt. Slowly bring to within moments of boiling. Garnish with pepper and parsley and serve immediately.

We have talked about the most common variety of mushroom. Others that I know and can positively identify are the genus *Boletus*. There are many *Boleti*. The *Boletus edulis* undoubtedly is best known by Europeans, and deep in our pine forests we find the *Boletus granulatus*. The ways of cooking *Agaricus* are also good for the *Boleti*.

Though fried foods seemingly are altered in nutritional value, a simple way of cooking *Boleti* is:

2 parts butter
1 part oil, olive preferred
any amount shallots (onions and garlic if
    desired)
any amount of *Boletus*
any amount of parsley

Chop the stems of cleaned *Boletus* together with the shallots (or garlic and onion). Fry these in butter and oil.

Insert pieces of garlic or shallot into the caps. Coat with a bit of olive oil. Place the fried mixture over the caps, grill at low temperature from 3 to 5 minutes, and serve.

One summer while walking in the Sierras I chanced on what *looked like* an oyster mushroom that I had often gathered. This is also called *Pleurotes* (in Greek "side"), which refers to the position of the stem on dead trees or on the dead part of living trees. This one, however, was a foot in diameter, stood about eight inches off the ground, and grew directly up from the ground. So although I felt it was an oyster mushroom and therefore edible, I consulted several volumes and several close friends to identify it. We found it belonged to the

genus *Lentinus*—edible, yet totally different from what I had previously experienced. There was so much (about three pounds!) I could not eat it all. It dries very well, to be revived by moistening.

Dried Scaly Lentinus

Clean and rub dry. Cut into strips about 1/8 to ¼ inch thick. Place on wire rack in the oven at lowest setting, turning now and again. Watch until dry.

Be sure there is no moisture in your storage jar, because it will cause mold. These mushrooms are a delight eaten dry like dried fruit out of season, and they're great for backpack trips. Powdered they are an excellent mixture with spices for the tops of salads.

Other mushrooms I can identify are:

PUFFBALLS (genus *Calvatia*): These are especially attractive when fresh, but watch for insects. They ripen quickly after picking so use them right away or store in the refrigerator for a day at most. Cook like other mushrooms or fry—they'll taste like French fried potatoes!

In days before the match came to be used, the dry spongy threads were used as tinder to catch the sparks which flew from the flintstone when it was struck for fire. The spore dust was used to stanch the flow of blood.

MOREL (genus *Morchella*): Where a burn has occurred the year before (in orchards and coniferous forests) the morel may pop. A delicious, almost-extraterrestial being, the morel is a delightful edible. No matter how it is prepared it is a special taste thriller. The stalk end is a bit bulbous and practically impossible to clean, so discard it to the compost. Dry the rest thoroughly and cook in butter with a bit of lemon juice from 5-10 min-

utes. Sauteed, stuffed in squash blossoms, or with your favorite dish . . . wow!

SHAGYMANE (genus *Coprinus*): Inky caps are the favorite. They must be selected early toward maturity, or else, as the name implies, they will blacken and turn into an inky liquid by self-digesting. Expert mycophagists suggest taking a pan and butter into the field when collecting. Once I left some in the refrigerator and returned to find a mess. Baked, broiled or how about an omelet? Great! The colors on this mushroom as it matures are most amazingly expanding.

CHANTERELLE (genus *Cantherellus*): These are a European delicacy. As usual, the fresh, tender, young ones are best. Their taste is improved by cooking a long time at a very low temperature. Anyone for a chanterelle omelet?

There are many other edible species awaiting my discovery. As with the herbs I am content "to learn a few over periods of time." While in South America, near Cali, Colombia on the Ponce Rio, I gathered *psilocybin* that appeared from cow dung, a mushroom considered sacred and filled with vision. After the rains we gathered many, eating a few at a time. The world took on a new perspective, and the nature spirits danced. One morning we prepared *Hongos Rancheros Huevos*, that is scrambled eggs mixed with these mushrooms. Three days later (when I felt sure of my footing again) I wanted to eat more, but my body said, "Be patient, flight is considered sacred." So I waited.

Some authorities believe all mushrooms stimulate inner awareness. Certainly each time my friends and I forage for them we feel enlightened. It may be no more than our imaginations, but then nature has yet to be so fully defined as to say what really is so. Happy fungi make happy homes.

TEN

Meats, Fish and Fowl

Thomas Jefferson's revolutionary political thoughts are known to many, but they may not be aware that he also was a food revolutionary. "I have lived temperately, eating little animal food, and not as aliment so much as a condiment for the vegetables which constitute my principal diet."

It is not my intention to say, "That is the way, or this the diet to which you should adhere," for each has his own diet. I recognize the vegan's awareness and feel comfortable in that category. I used to be very strict about what I ate, but that is limiting. I recognize that the world's strongest animals, the gorilla and the elephant, are vegetable eaters. Vegetarianism seems to be the very old new way for many. Thus the lack of recipes of meat, fish, and poultry in this volume. But for those of you who are making a transition, I recognize your tastes and so include a few recipes for you. I have chosen only from foods that appeared on my family table while I was growing up.

I was fortunate to be of the land. I cannot believe that our meats and poultry are as chemicalized as they seem to be today, yet each day another article tells of the complete lack of care by food producers, all for the sake of profit.

It may be idealistic even in this humanitarian age when I say that I hope we can correct the mistakes before it's too late. There is nothing like the taste of wild game, or fish. As with our plant friends so it must be with our animal and mineral friends: let there be a reverence for what we eat.

Venison Steak

½ inch young venison steaks (one for
  each person)
garlic to taste
1 tablespoon butter
2 tablespoons cooking oil

Simply saute together all the above till crisp and brown outside and rare and juicy inside. About 3 to 5 minutes a side for rare or 5 to 7 minutes for medium. Serve garnished with your favorite green. Parsley and chives are favorites of mine. Some like a mustard sauce.

Brook Trout
(Rainbow, Golden, or Brown Trout)

1 trout per person   ¼ cup ghee
seasoned flour   chopped parsley
(whole wheat mixture   lemon wedges
  with salt and pepper)

Clean and wash the trout. Cut off the fins*, leaving the head and tail. Coat with flour mixture, and saute in half the ghee till golden brown on each side. Add the remaining ghee to the leftover dripping. Let this brown and cover the fish. Serve hot with parsley and lemon wedges.

*In the Orient shark's fin is used extensively. The idea is that the shark eats only protein and all of this is stored in the fin, which makes the fin a good protein source. The trout feeds off insects during the good weather, and in winter, from the bottom of the river or lake. The choice of taking the fins off or leaving them on is up to you. Even the eyeballs are thought to be medicine for the eyes and are considered a delicacy. My cousin Emerson likes them with catsup. Each to his own ritual.

Poached Salmon in Wine
(Harry Johnson)

1 salmon
1 bottle white cooking wine or mead
2 tablespoons butter
salt and pepper to taste
parsley and lemon
garlic

Immerse the salmon in wine in a pan for about 20 minutes. Before placing in oven, add a few bits of chopped garlic. Bake for 15 minutes at 350°F. Remove from the oven and drain off and save liquid. Cover salmon with parsley, garlic, salt, and sliced wedges of lemon. Serve. The leftover liquid may be used for soup or dressing base or eaten right along with the fish.

Lentinus SP.

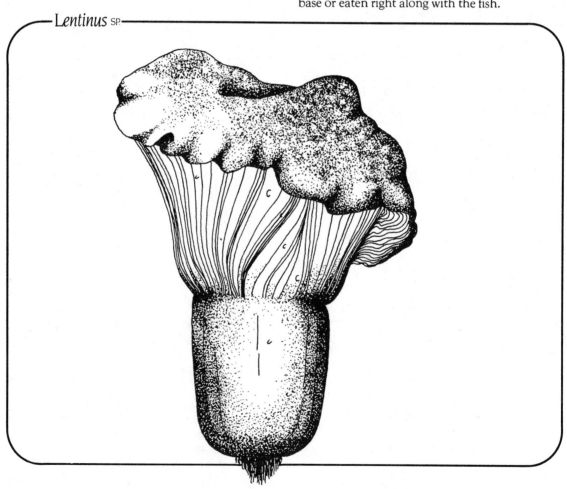

Antennaria margaritacum

Life Everlasting

This recipe is the hunters ideal. The juices run red and free when the duck is carved.

Roasted Wild Duck

1 duck per person or 1 duck for 2 people
butter
chopped onion and garlic
cored and sliced apple
spices

Draw, pluck and singe the duck. At room temperature, dry the bird inside and out and rub with butter. Place onion, garlic, and apple in cavities. Preheat oven to 500°F, then reduce to 350°F before roasting. Place duck on a rack in the roasting pan and roast uncovered for 20 minutes. The drippings can be degreased (skimmed of fat) and mixed with cultured sour cream to make a sauce. Dash with parsley and spices of your choice (paprika is nice). Serve hot.

Since hunting is still enjoyed by many, we who no longer eat meat, usually ask those hunters we know for the feathers of wild game. These are used to make headbands, stringed instrument picks, and so forth: reverent use of products normally discarded, yet valued for their beauty.

Growing up in California I ate many types of fish (snapper, clam, oyster, bass), fowl (pheasant, quail, dove), and meat (cattle, boar, bear). Each has a place in history.

Each was used by native Americans in accordance with the laws of nature. Today, however, many hunt with no knowledge or awareness of the life they will share. Many animals are slaughtered (as in meat packing and poultry packing plants) and as plants, if ripped off, are thought to release hormones from fear, animals, when slaughtered, may release substances that are carried over to those who eat them and cause many disorders. These are only thoughts of spirit. Yet many species are becoming rare because of lack of awareness. Think before hunting meat: Do I need this? Is there an alternative? I believe that in the coming years nature will provide for the reverent. Your diet will be your pathfinder, and awareness of nature your guide.

Before refrigeration and injections of preservatives, keeping meat fresh was a tricky thing. Herbs, such as sage, rosemary, oregano, thyme, and the other aromatics, were used extensively to mask the foul taste and smell of spoiling meat.

Lamb, for example, was often covered by bergamot mint (lamb's mint). Garlic was always added to the cooking pot to help rid the meat of adverse forms of bacteria. There is an easier way—fresh whenever possible—and an even easier way—turn toward our herbal friends.

ELEVEN

Brews and Other Yeastly Waters

Home again sippin' the long-awaited brew,
Smokin' my homegrown—thinkin' of you.

Many of us never think of brews as recipes. But they are, and I for one cannot imagine a book of recipes using the products of nature without a section on fermented spirits.

Many of the old cookbooks devoted a great deal of space just to the art of brewing. In fact, had I not become involved with so many yeasts when I was growing up, I would probably have been a vintner rather than a plant person. Yet here I am still preparing, but along more natural lines than others in the present day. Bulk process seems to take away the spirit even though the same alcoholic content may remain. One who prefers home brews to the store-bought kind may have as well developed a palate as a connoisseur of vintage wines. Have you tried vintage dandelion wine?

There is root beer, beer, mead, and cider. Metheglin is an old fashioned beverage, usually fermented, made of water and honey; mead is a spiced variety; hippocras is a cordial made of spiced wine; and hydromel is a fermented liquor made of honey in water. (In pharmacology this word is used for a laxative containing honey and water.) Early settlers made wide use of mead, hydromel, metheglin, and hip-

pocras because of the large amounts of wild honey prevalent at that time. Until our domestic vineyards and distillers were established, hippocras was more widely used near sea towns because, of course, imported wines were more readily available there. Sadly, when the spirits required a stronger drink, grains and distilling became popular, causing the old brews to go by the wayside. They appear now and again and interest is again rising. "For thee I wish a happy brew, your root brew or your stew."

There are many root beers on the market. This one has influenced my fantasy more than any other and led me to a variety of such beers. It is simple to make.

Blood Beer

2 ounces ginger
2 ounces sassafras root bark
2 ounces wild cherry bark
4 ounces burdock root
1 ounce cream of tartar (graperock)
1½ pounds turbinado sugar (or ¾ pound raw honey)
½ ounce orange peel
approximately ½ yeast cake (dependent on the amount of alcohol wanted and fermenting time)

141

Place the herbs in 2 gallons of boiling water for 10 minutes. Strain. Add the sugar or honey and the orange peel. Heat slightly to dissolve the sugar. Pour in a stone crock and add the cream of tartar. When lukewarm add some yeast. In a few days this will be ready to be drunk or bottled for future use. Caution: store in a cool place. If the product becomes too warm, the result may be on the walls—and raw beer has an odor all its own.

BEER

I have found, as I am sure the early settlers did, that bits of bread aid the yeast starters. If you are lucky, hops abound about your fence. The best hops thrive in good clear air and should be picked when the pollen is on the bud. Hop-flavored malt is available at brewing shops and wine arts shops.

> a 4 to 6 gallon pot
> a crock or vat that will hold 14 gallons
>   with measurements marked on the side
>   (preferably in gallons)
> 5 pounds honey (10 pounds sugar)
> water
> 2 3-pound cans of hop-flavored yeast
> 2 packages of yeast

In the pot, mix all but 2 cups of the sugar with 1 gallon water and bring to a slow boil. Stir constantly to dissolve the sugar completely. In another pot mix the malt with a gallon of water. When dissolved add this to the sugar water that is still cooking. Turn off and cool to about 80° F. Dissolve the yeast in a cup of cold water, add it to the crock or vat, and pour the malt sugar mixture over it. Do not add more water till fermentation has taken place. Set the crock in a moderately warm room (70-75°F) to ferment. When the first fermentation is completed in 2 to 3 days, fill the crock with 13 gallons of water and set it aside for a few more days. Depending on several factors, such as light and temperature, ripening should be completed within 3 to 7 days. When it stops fermenting, the color of your beer will have

changed from light to dark brown and clear. You will notice a bit of life about the edges, which is to be expected and is certainly a good sign. When clear it is ready for the final processes. Dissolve the remaining 2 cups of sugar or 1 cup honey in another gallon of water and bring to a boil. With the mixture still hot, add it to your brew and stir to blend thoroughly. Let stand at room temperature for several weeks before drinking. Bottle if you like and store the bottles on their sides in a cool place.

Home brews placed in bottles should be turned a quarter turn every other day to keep the cork from drying. If you are fortunate and have a bottle topper for beer then storage is of less concern. Yet a cool storage area for the bottles is important. As mentioned earlier, these bottles have a tendency to blow off yeast and tops when warm.

Hops Beer

A simple and good beer is made by putting 2 ounces of freshly gathered flowers (with pollen) in two quarts of water for seventeen minutes. Strain this and add one pound of loaf sugar, well dissolved. Add four more quarts of cold water and two tablespoons of fresh barm (the yeast formed on brewing liquors).

Before we continue I would like to interject:

A CAUTION

Please be aware, dear folk, as you read and prepare these recipes that I am in no way responsible for *your* results. I have tested the recipes and they work well when all goes according to plan. However, perfection is not one of man's dependable traits, so have patience and *please* don't call me asking about this or that variation. It is all up to you. I can only lay the groundwork. What I know is here. Your feelings and vibrations all affect the outcome.

So, let us put that behind and continue making our brews. There are several ways to prepare a mead. Essentially it is water and honey and whatever spices you want to add.

Rockin' Mead
(Tom Smith)

1 quart honey
2½ gallons rainwater (soft, preferably not the first rain)
1 lemon

Grate, peel, and juice the lemon to a fine consistency, trying not to lose the juices. Combine the lemon, water, and honey in a clean crock and mix thoroughly.

Set aside for 5 days, stirring the mixture each day. (Be sure your stirrer is clean of course.)

After 3 days siphon off the brew, bottle, cork, and store in cool place.

This mixture is ready now but letting it age will allow the ferments to grow, and the aging process will make the brew mellower.

Methaglin
(Buck Newby)

1 quart honey
6 quarts rainwater
1 teaspoon ginger powder
½ yeast cake

In a large pot mix the water and honey till well blended. Add the ginger and slowly bring to a boil. Continue to boil until the mixture is reduced one-third. Set aside till cool, then add the yeast.

Let this stand for 3 days, then draw off into bottles. To each bottle you may add a bit of lemon peel, possibly a cinnamon stick or two, and some raisins or bits of apple. Cork well and again place this in a dark, cool place for at least a couple of weeks before using.

A variation of this would be the following:

1 quart honey
2½ gallons water
1 lemon
3 pounds raisins, pineapple, plums, or other fruit
1 teaspoon nutmeg powder
4-7 cinnamon sticks in pieces
¼ teaspoons clove, powdered, or a couple of whole cloves

Grind the raisins to the finest possible mash. Mix the spices together with this (you could use a mortar and pestle if you prefer). Follow the above recipe for a spicier mead.

Hydromel

As mentioned, hydromel is a pharmaceutical laxative. This recipe has been handed down through the family and used when anyone was constipated. I realize this may sound like a claim but let me assure the medical profession that I am only sharing a historical fact. In the early days of California, as well as other states, hydromel was popular when one wanted a cleansing, felt sick, or wanted to have a good medicine. Should not all our food serve us this way?

15 pounds wild honey without the wax
6 gallons water
1 ounce hops
1½ yeast cakes or ½ pint wine yeast
optional: sassafras, fennel, clove, ginger

Place the honey and water in a fairly good sized pot, add the hops and bring this mixture to a very slow boil. Skim off the residue that forms on top. Cook about 1 hour, or as long as scum continues to appear. Remove from the heat and allow to cool slowly. Draw off (drain) into a clean barrel. Add the yeast and set the barrel in a warm place for 10 to 14 days. (Watch this mixture carefully for the weather may affect the fermentation process. If warm the fermentation will take less time; if cold, more.) Make sure that your barrel's hole is well sealed (bunged) or covered to protect from contaminants (bugs etc.). Residue will seep through the bung. Remove it daily or skim off carefully, adding a bit more honey and water every two days or so to keep the level up. When the fermentation stops there are three alternatives:

1. You may pound the bung into the barrel and let stand for 4 weeks before using the hydromel.

2. You may add the spices to the above process or to the next process:

3. You may strain the mixture through a cloth into another barrel, adding 1½ cakes yeast or ½ pint wine yeast, and let the whole process ferment again.

When the fermentation seems as though it has stopped, bung the barrel and leave 3 to 5 days to settle. Draw this off, cork well, and store in a cool dark place.

Sounds to me, as well as to others who have tried it, a much better medicine than many we use now: full of life and real ingredients. Granted wild honey is getting harder to find, but if you are working in the field with these natural products then you may sometimes find a wild hive. Clean it reverently. Take some of the honey, and place the bees in a new home. This is a very rewarding thing to do. Many of the beekeepers I have worked with swear that they never have stiff joints (arthritis and rheumatism) because the stings they get are helpful in some way: an old and persistent tale.

HIPPOCRAS

Hippocras—possibly named for Hippocrates because his school of therapeutics dealt with diet, medicinal waters, gymnastics, and fresh air—was an early favorite when wines could be procured to make the mixture.

> 1 gallon dry sauterne*
> ½ gallon chablis*
> 12 cinnamon sticks
> ½ quart milk or cream
> 2¼ pounds sugar (1 1/8 pounds honey)

or equivalent white variation, such as gooseberry wine.

> 2 tablespoons sliced ginger root
> 2 grated whole nutmegs
> ¼ tablespoon cloves
> (optional addition of coriander seed, cumin, fennel, dock, or plantain, not to exceed ½ teaspoon each)

Combine the wine, whole spices, and ½ pound of honey (or sugar). Stir this all together well and set aside for one or two days. Add the remaining honey and the milk. Stir well, strain, bottle, and cork.

The smell of apples and the vinegars derived therefrom are still my favorites. There is so much to be said of the biblical apple. Each time a new apple recipe appears on our table, associated memories flash by. Why did the Bible refer to this plant? The apple-a-day-keeps-the-doctor-away syndrome and so much more. The Apple! And its Cider!

First one must look for perfect apples, with no worms or rot (if that's at all possible with an organic apple). Gather toward the end of season, wash and take to the press. Turn the apple press and begin your work.

Simply Sweet Cider

Whatever amount of apples you desire.

As the apples are pressed, strain the pulp through linen or cheesecloth directly into the crock or barrel, which should be clean and freshly scalded. Let this stand for 3 to 4 days if the weather is cool; if it's still warm, 1 to 2 days. For the next 4 to 6 weeks turn a couple of times a week. Between the fourth and sixth week, draw off the cider into bottles or jugs, trying not to disrupt the sediment on the bottom of the crock or barrel. Cork well and place in a dark, cool spot. Continue to turn the bottles every now and again.

This is ready at the time of bottling. Eventually sweet cider will begin to turn harder. By this I mean the alcohol is getting stronger, because the apple's natural sugar is "growing." If you would like to help mother nature along,

Dock

open the top cork of the barrel or bottle and let the air in. Within a few days the cider will start to ferment and become "hard cider." If you left your sweet cider in the barrel to turn, now is a good time to bottle the brew. If left in the bottles, it will eventually turn again into the mother, and that's when we make mother cider vinegar.

Mother Cider Vinegar

2 quarts of hard cider
1 cup molasses (for a mellower version use honey that's dark such as oak honey)
½ cup yeast

Mix this together well, bottle, and set aside in a warm spot overnight. The next day pour it into a stone crock and set aside for a week. Make sure you draw off carefully leaving the sediment. Store in a cool place.

There are so many wine books that tell what grapes are best for what and how to do it, that I will deal with the more unusual varietals here, dandelion and blackberry. Over time, these seem to be the monks' favorites.

Dandelion Wine

2 quarts fresh dandelion petals
2 quarts boiling water
1 orange
1 lemon
1 pound honey (2 pounds sugar)
a piece of whole ginger
½ teaspoon brewer's yeast

Clean and dry the petals and place them in a pan of boiling water. Cover with a clean cloth and leave for 3 days, stirring frequently. Strain this into another clean pan and add the lemon and orange that have been thinly sliced, rind and all. To this add the honey (or sugar) and ginger. Boil for half an hour. Return to original pan and let cool. When lukewarm, spread the brewer's yeast on a piece of toast and add it to the wine. Leave for a couple of days. Pour into

a crock or cask (barrel) and keep bunged for 2 months. Then bottle and let set for another 2 months in a cool dark place, turning the bottles occasionally for a year. Wonderful during the winter.

Since fruits and berries seem to grow everywhere throughout the Americas, there is seldom a shortage. Even if the only wines we had were blackberry, raspberry, thimbleberry, gooseberry, strawberry or one of the many other native berries, we would not lack for spirits.

Berry Wine

Like the apple, gather only the freshest and most perfect berries.

For each gallon of berries:
1 gallon water, boiling
1½ to 2 pounds honey (3-4 pounds sugar)

Measure the berries into a fairly large crock. For each gallon of berries pour in 1 gallon of boiling water. Let this mixture cool and then mash together. Cover and let stand 4 to 5 days. Strain well. For each gallon of strained liquid, add 2 pounds honey (4 pounds sugar). Allow this to set 12 days or until the fermentation has stopped. When this occurs cover as tightly as possible and let stand for 6 months. Siphon off and then bottle, cork, and store in a cool dark place. Be sure to turn the bottles. After 2 months imbibe this great spirit.

Certainly there are many more such brews, but I am sure these will lead the kitchen explorer to conjure up new and probably better variations. There is just one more that we keep in the refrigerator or root cellar, because it's nice and it's another way to use the grape (when turned to raisin).

Raisin Glug

¾ pounds seedless raisins, chopped
5 quarts of boiling water

1¼ pounds honey (2½ pounds sugar)
juice of 1 lemon
another lemon thinly sliced
a touch of cinnamon

Combine the raisins, honey (or sugar), lemon juice, and lemon slices in a storage crock and pour the boiling water over the mixture. Stir until completely mixed and set in a warm dark place. Stir the mixture a couple of times a day for a week. Strain well, bottle, cork, and store in a cool, dry, dark place. This will be ready in a couple of weeks. Once we left some of this by mistake for over a year, drank a bit, and, whew, was it ever strong.

I hope you, as a new alchemist, may discover the joy of brewing and watching things grow. The longer you work with the airs—yeasts—the more you will appreciate the wonders of nature. There is no set way to do anything really. But by following these simple guidelines, you can be pleasantly brewing and tasting before the year is out.

This herbal brew was concocted by a close friend who was inspired by a walk we shared. He went out to the coast and picked the plants needed. Silently he prepared and then one afternoon said thanks. Here is the recipe in his own words.

This is an herbal brew—light and refreshing. It needs only a week's patience. Gather 1 pound of fresh leaves—stinging nettle (use gloves), betony, and dandelion in equal quantities. Heat 3 gallons of water with 1 ounce of wild and 2 ounces cultivated ginger root. When the water boils add the leaves and turn off the heat. Steep 10 to 15 minutes and add 3 pounds of honey. When the brew has cooled to 100°, remove 2 cups of it and blend in 2 packages dry active yeast, or 1 cube of compressed yeast. When the water is just about at room temperature, return this to the brew and cover the crock. Ferment for 24 to 36 hours. A good place would be in an oven with the door half open. Siphon the brew into jars with tight lids and leave in peace for 4 to 7 days. Enjoy.

TWELVE

Other Extracts

All the natural and beautiful instincts of the human mind and heart by which the life on earth can be enriched and beautified, are endangered by the hasty pursuit of false values. There can be no civilization without composure; and by composing itself, man becomes susceptible to the Universal Mind. The perfect sage is heaven-moved; that is, he is moved by Eternal Reason. The ignorant man functions on the surface and thinks in terms of extent. The wise man strives for penetration and depth rather than area. Penetration is possible only to those who attain tranquility. The faculties required for perception of depth are too sensitive to operate while the mind is possessed by tensions.

LAO TZU 600 B.C.
Chinese philosopher

I realize that to make our own alcohol, food, drugs, or cosmetics, we must abide by present standards of the law. Yet some very good stills continue to brew, the results of which are sometimes a bit devilish. Know your source for everything. The following pages will share some of the practices that early man evolved by refining natural processes. When we discussed extracts like infusions, decoctions, soups, and such, we were trying to share the validity and existence of a ritual preparation. The spirits are a rewarding bunch when cooked with reverence.

Before there was a drugstore on every corner of every city of the country, there were those in each household who concocted the potions that still abound today.

Solutions are preparations in which the substance is entirely dissolved in the menstruum (usually water). Examples of such mixtures are waters, infusions, decoctions, some spirits, vinegar, and honeys. A remedy made with honey in the past was often called a confection or conserve, because these were simples rendered into a soft mass (such as rose hip conserve) that made them more pleasant to taste.

The term *extract* used in the older books on preparations were of this type. There were others that have lost popularity due to modern technology and a declining appreciation for what nature can really do for us.

The contents of this chapter are recognized to be controversial. However, I am including it for the historical information of the alchemist (if I may use that word) and for those who like to work according to the laws of nature. It certainly is not meant to take the physicians' or pharmacists' role in our society, nor is it complete. But it would be hard to overlook the extracts called syrups, liniments, ointments, plasters, fluid extracts and tinctures.

Simple syrup is a concentrated solution of water and sugar. Honey is far preferable to sugar, but modern preparations cannot afford to use honey; the expense would be phenomenal. The pleasant idea formulated in this work is that the natural consumer takes his life into his own hands within nature.

Remember hearing of horse liniments? Or when gramps was out too much in the garden, and grandma used "her liniment." These are simply preparations contained or produced in oil (olive, corn, soy, avocado, coconut, etc.) and intended for use externally by friction or simple massage. The most common ones are wintergreen or mustard seed that has been crushed and placed in oil for several days and then strained and bottled. Olive and coconut oils seem to be the favorites because they have demulcent and nutritive properties when absorbed by the skin. They feel good and taste good. Olive tastes best, but be aware of what is in the oil, because both mustard or wintergreen have a tendency to be awfully strong in the mouth and eyes.

One liniment that I enjoy after sitting at a typewriter or chopping wood is made from:

> 1 ounce mustard seed, crushed or powdered
> 1 ounce mandrake root (angelica or dandelion root may be substituted)
> 1 ounce cayenne pepper powder
> ½ gallon spring water
> 1 cup oil

Boil the herbs in water until about 1 quart remains. Add 1 cup of your favorite oil. Simmer 10 minutes. Strain and bottle. Because oil and water don't mix, be sure to shake this before using. Enjoy in small amounts and relax.

Other herbs that make pleasant liniment are peppermint, pennyroyal, sage, wormwood, wood betony, woodruff, spikenard, and goldenrod. Horseradish root in oil is another good one.

An oldie, but one we seldom see, was offered when I was traveling through the South. It consisted of coal oil and salt. Since I was in West Virginia the natural products seemed suitable enough. The lady who told me about this liniment said she had a lame back and it helped a great deal.

Not too long after I got the coal oil liniment, I came across a recipe in a book totally unrelated to herbs. I copied the recipe down and have been able to procure the products, but it takes some doing. Whenever possible I try to share the idea that fancy, far away botanicals are nice, but in nature, where you are is what you have. Because we are so mobile these products are readily available. The large amounts imply that this recipe was produced and shared with friends or else used by an herbalist for his patients.

Melt together:

> 5 pounds rosin
> ¼ pound pine pitch
> ¼ pound beeswax
> ¼ pound mutton tallow

Stir in:

> 1 ounce balsam of fir
> 1 ounce oil of oregano
> 1 ounce oil of cedar
> 1 ounce Venice turpentine
> ½ ounce oil of wormwood

When this is thoroughly mixed, pour into a large pan of cold water and work like wax till cold. This may be applied by hand but seems to work better if applied with a sheepskin.

Another liniment was offered that had been based on a recipe originally developed by myself.

Denni McCarthy Balm

½ cup apricot kernel, almond, or olive oil
2 tablespoons menthol crystals
1½ ounces camphor (liquid)
1½ tablespoons eucalyptus oil
1 tablespoon peppermint oil
½ teaspoon lavender oil
¼ teaspoon clove oil
½-1 ounce beeswax

Gently heat the ingredients in a double boiler until the wax is just melted. Put a spoonful in the freezer to check consistency. Pour into sterilized containers. Good for aching muscles. Keep from eyes, nose, mouth, etc.

This formula brings us to the plasters (*emplastra*), preparations spread on muslin, linen, silk, or sheepskin. The mustard plaster is the most familiar. If you have a quince tree available, the following is suggested for general soreness.

1 handful quince seeds or fruit (hardwood) seeds
1 handful mustard greens
½ handful plantain seed

Crush these together adding just enough water to hold the mass together. Apply on the cloth to the sore area.

Mud is a nice plaster though one does not use it on a cloth. Going to the hot springs (Calistoga, Hot Creek, Stewart Springs, Pitt River, and so forth) I've encountered many of the different colored and textured muds. These oozed earthy excretions are liberally applied to the body, allowed to dry, then washed off. The sheer joy feeling like a salamander slithering along a mud bank is therapeutic in itself. One need not consult a physician for this type of therapy unless you are allergic to earth. In South America and the Orient muds play an integral part in healing rites. Oftentimes people travel hundreds or even thousands of miles just for a particular type of mud. Antonio Baca, a Quechua Indian educated in botany, took me and several others on a walk of Inca plants. During this time he mentioned muds (clays) for healing.

RED for blood disorders
BLUE for watery discharge and water conditions of the body
GREY for old sores, internal and external
GREEN for wounds, scrapes and burns

Once this past summer, Bob Gumpertz and I were backpacking in the Trinity Alps when we happened on the fork of two creeks. An eddy had formed causing an area to be filled with muds from high above us, virgin and clear. We looked at each other, remembered our past muddy experiences, and soon we were knee deep and covering ourselves with the earthy ooze.

For those of you who might not have experienced this, there are several commercial muds presently on the market. Some of the hot springs have warm mud, and that is a real treat, especially if your legs are tired from packing in the mountains. If you can graduate from one pond to another, hot, cool, hot, cool, it is quite invigorating.

Ointments are those gooey substances we all know, usually intended for external use and using a lard-like base. Many of these unguents or salves appear on the market today, and their popularity in many cases I am sure is due to the labeling. The labels are adorned with lovely flowers, meadows, birds, and colors and exotic names like "Seal salve," "Fern River Salve," "Traditional Medicinals," and so forth. These are not as popular yet as the present petroleum

Cannabis indica & sativa

Marijuana

base salves, but they are available and growing in popularity.

One of the pleasures of working with the products of nature is recalling the stories of gathering. Once when Carter and I were on a walk we discovered a bunch of pine pitch and decided to make an ointment. Molly had been dyeing some wool, and, unknown to her, I scraped a bit of fat off the top of the dye pot. We used that with our usual gathering of plants, Oregon grape root, wild ginger, rose hips, and comfrey to make an ointment of the stars.

C-R-Star Salve

4 ounces Oregon grape root
4 ounces wild ginger root
4 ounces rose hips (cleaned of seed and inner hair)
8 ounces comfrey root
⅛ pound beeswax
2 pounds base fat (lanolin, coconut oil, lard, etc.)

Chop and grind all the herbs together.

In a double boiler bring the base to a gentle boil and add the herbs. Reduce heat and simmer at least 20 minutes— the longer the better, up to 6 hours. Strain the herbs, add the beeswax and return to the heat for another 10 minutes.

When the beeswax is totally incorporated into the mixture, strain well, and whip the ointment with a spoon or wire whisk. Pour into sterile jars and seal.

Several ideas have developed over the years as I have made these salves. The base should be of a lard-like consistency. The base will set up and then you will have a cream. This is not like oils that require the addition of great amounts of beeswax for the oil to become clean and of hard consistency. For those folks who prefer not to have animal fat or lanolin in their preparation, coconut oil is a fine substitute, as are

many of the vegetable fats. For that matter, when nothing else is available, Crisco can be used. Although there are preservatives in this product, when you heat it to a slow boil, a majority of the preservatives evaporate, leaving you with the base, which is vegetable fat. The fat from sheeps' wool (lanolin) is a wonderfully appealing base. Theatrical cold cream also works well.

Recently I observed a placenta mixed into beeswax with the mother's favorite herbs. Why not? After all, if the mother does not use it, the hospital will sell it to a pharmaceutical company, which in turn uses it for cosmetics or medicinal purposes.

The amount of time the herbs and base should be cooked varies according to your vibrations, but 20 minutes is the minimum. If you are using large quantities, they can be simmered up to 6 hours. This seems to be an individual decision depending on the environment, stimuli, and weather.

The herbs that you incorporate are your choice. Since these ointments are for external purposes, any green leafy vegetable (herbal) matter is fine. Belladonna for instance (long considered poisonous internally) is made into ointments, plasters, and liniments that have properties (according to *Materia Medica* 1870) for relieving the pain of muscular rheumatism. Many Indian healers mention that a plant that may be poisonous if taken internally can often help clean a poisoned area externally—an interesting idea for our pathologists to work with. Throughout nature one often finds these particular traits, but I do not recommend that you go out and experiment until you feel confident with a particular herb.

Beeswax also has reputed medicinal claims. Placed in the ointment (salve or unguent) beeswax helps it to set. When oils, such as olive and avocado, are used, beeswax is a must; otherwise your work will become a runny mess. The remarkable properties of beeswax can be traced all the way back to ancient Egypt where quantities of wax were used for sacrificial offerings. Uncovered wall paintings in Pompeii show wax colors as bright as the day of the great volcanic burial. Beeswax is still a major ingredient in the colors of oil paint. Ancient Persians buried their dead after first immersing them in wax.

Beeswax plays an integral part in many pharmaceutical salves (some being cold cream, *unguentum leniens*, spermaceti ointment, and *unguentum cetacei*). In Russia the formulary for the pharmacist requires that all plasters, creams, and ointments be prepared with beeswax. Beeswax can also be used as a substitute for chewing gum (in addition to spruce sap). Nature does seem to provide for her children.

Three of my favorite ointments or unguents follow. They each have their own use; before you blend you should have a reason.

Rose Water Ointment

3½ troy ounces oil of sweet almond
1 troy ounce spermaceti
120 grains white wax
2 fluid ounces rose water

Melt together in a double boiler (water bath) the oil, spermaceti, and wax. Gradually add the rose water, stirring constantly till cool. (This formula is called cold cream.)

Elm Ointment

Slippery elm ointment feels good. One lady of elder experience presented me with a simple recipe from this shaved bark.

Gather and dry the slippery elm bark. Take ¼ ounce of chopped bark and 1 ounce of simple base and melt together. Strain through flannel and stir until it sets. This was used for children's skin problems.

This massage cream recipe came from a woman called "Tara-Earth Mother" by her friends.

Tara Cream-Earth Massage

Pine gum—22 grains
menthol—15 grains
wintergreen oil—36 drops
mustard oil—4 drops
peppermint oil—7 drops
sesame oil—5 drams
beeswax—1 ounce
lanolin—½ ounce

Mix together and store in a clean container.

In the Orient I observed the practice of placing ginseng root in rice wine. Although there are several types, ginseng liquor is as popular as angostura bitters, which is really a fluid extract. Ginseng root is left in the alcohol, while angostura bark is removed. Until recently, fluid extracts and tinctures were quite popular. Today they are becoming rare because of the phenomenal amount of work and cost required for mass extraction. For those who like to work with the herbs, these forms of cooking are ideal. Another extract I found in Korea was ginseng root in honey. This was allowed to soak for 7 days. Then the honey was used. Once I observed vegetables kept in honey and I was told:

> Honey, being antibacterial, is a good preservative because it won't go bad. We keep these vegetables in honey, the honey used absorbs some of the properties of the vegetable. When we want—six months later maybe—we take out the greens and eat them. The honey can be used over and over. Be sure your herbs (or vegetables) have been washed, though extract dirt certainly won't hurt you.

I have tried this. The honey will change its flavor subtly but pleasantly. Try plantain, comfrey, everlasting, or watercress.

During stressful times one finds oneself about the ole jug of pure grain or corn likker, sometimes containing roots, said by the user to be of great strength and tonic value.

The next two extracts, fluid extracts and tinctures, are probably the most acclaimed versions of food preparation.

The following formulas define accord elder medical practice:

FLUID EXTRACTS

Fluid extracts (extracta Fluida) are liquid preparations of uniform strength, 1 cc of which represent l gm (about 1 minim to the grain) of the crude drug, prepared chiefly with alcohol and glycerin.

Essentials of Materia Medica & Therapeutics *by Henry Harris M.D., 1891.*

Fluid Extracts are permanent and concentrated solutions of vegetable drugs, of uniformly definite strength if the crude drugs are so, a cubic centimeter in each case representing the medicinal powers of one gramme of the drug, or approximately a minim of the finished preparation representing the active constituents of a grain of the drug. They are usually and officially directed to be prepared by percolation and partial evaporation, the menstrua employed being chiefly alcohol, diluted alcohol, and alcohol and water in various proportions.

Materia Medica Pharmacy & Therapeutics *by Potter, 1908.*

TINCTURES

For Tincturae Herbarum Recentium or Tinctures of fresh herbs, the Pharmacopoeia prescribes a general formula, according to which, when not otherwise directed, they are to be prepared by macerating 50 grammes of the fresh herb, bruised or crushed, in 100 cubic centimeters of alcohol, for fourteen days, then expressing the liquid and filtering.

Tinctures are alcoholic solutions of medicinal substances, and with one official exception, Tincture of Iodine, are made of nonvolatile bodies. They are prepared by percolation, maceration, solution, or dilution; the menstrua employed being chiefly alcohol, diluted alcohol, and alcohol and water in various proportions.

Essentials of Materia Medica & Therapeutics *by Henry Morris M.D., 1891.*

Tinctura, or tinctures are alcoholic solutions, usually of nonvolatile substances. Alcohol, diluted alcohol, or alcohol and water, (though this not being employed often) is generally used as a solvent, but occasionally the aromatic spirits of ammonia is employed, the product being an ammoniated tincture.

Materia Medica Pharmacy & Therapeutics *by Potter, 1908.*

As each year goes by less and less is heard of these preparations. They were indicated by our elders (and still are in many parts of the country) as being good for stressful situations, such as cold weather or an argument, or for general toning. But, as with anything, one should use sparingly. If one does not want the alcohol to remain it can be eliminated by evaporation, which yields a rosin or concentrate.

Use alcohol for its preservative quality and potency for extracting. Each alcohol extract is used according to its strength. Thus water extracts certain properties more gently, though not as thoroughly as alcohol. Moreover, water does not preserve as alcohol does, but only holds in suspension.

Fluid extracts use alcohol that is no more than 49% in strength. The tinctures use alcohol that is 50% or more. Examples are:

Bourbon
Whisky
Gin
Vodka   (40%-45%)
Tequila
Brandy
Rum   (70.5%)
Everclear   (80%)
Ammonia   (Pure)
Ethyl Alcohol   (Pure)
Ether

The last two are included only for comparison, as at present they are still prescription items. Yet in studying our past medicines one will see they play an important role.

Many people ask, "Why would you want to preserve, and extract in this manner if alcohol is not good for you?" My answer is: When you have a root or product of nature, such as a rare herb, and you want to extract as much of its vital properties as possible, then alcohol is the menstruum usually employed. Some roots are rare and can be procured at only one or two times during the year. Water is not as strong as alcohol in extracting the salts and properties of the plant parts and for preserving your essence of extraction, something very much akin to granddad's roots in corn liquor. Whether to use alcohol for extraction would depend on the roots being extracted, your final product, and your intended use.

While in Bogota, Columbia, I spent time with Padre Hinjio, a Jesuit priest who is well-known for his work with plants and their related energies. One room was filled with wines and root brews. Another room held undug artifacts for preparations, garden tools, skull parts, and bone and wood carvings. Another room and hallway were filled with many types of ferns.

These ferns are supposed to take the positive ions and change them to negative ions, allowing the bodies between them to become balanced in charge, thus expanding the psyche as well as the ability to listen to nature. There was a room for writing, charting results, making observations, possible conclusions, and letters between the silent scholars of nature. Another room contained seeds for future work. In the days we spent together we exchanged plant ideas about adaptation, soil amending, the use of manure that was aged and free of modern chemicals, pruning of fruit trees, recycling of waste, and the use of a water hyacinth to clean water. Hinjio mentioned amatin, a by-product of the hyacinth extracted by the water that aids in purification. "We have so much to learn of our interaction with nature," he would say. The time we spent together made my commitment deeper to do all I could for the caretaking of life on this earth. He passed on several tonics to me. I tried them all, and each had its own power.

This first tonic is used for shortness of breath—to increase breath and inner light.

Maidenhair fern, tender young shoots or
    leaf—5 ounces
Licorice root peeled—2 ounces
Boiling water—5 pints

Let stand 6 hrs., then add:

Loaf sugar—13 pounds
or Honey—7½ pounds
Orange water—1 pint

This next one was in a large earth crock, kept with a skeleton used for anatomical observation.

4 ounces Peruvian bark
4 ounces wild cherry bark
1 dram cinnamon
2 drams cloves

2 ounces cherries pitted
4 quarts wine

(The wine was flower, unspecified.) This tonic was eight months old. Still very young, he said.

An appetite enhancer for those who have lost theirs, he said, was water and honey (about a quart in equal amounts) that had fermented for several days mixed with the following:

2 grams shavegrass
2 grams anise seed
4 grams red rose leaves
8 grams white skin of lemon (inner layer
   next to the fruit)
1 gram strawberry leaves

When I came back to the United States and tried this, although the water and honey were different because soil and energy conditions were different, the taste was similar. It tasted good. I ate as usual, but maybe there had been an incantation placed on Hinjio's work, or perhaps I have much more meditation to do to accomplish the same product.

This one, which he also gave me, I was able to do well. It is simple and was a different surprise taste when I made it. It felt good and refreshing.

4 ounces wine
1 dram ground cloves
1 dram grated nutmeg
¼ ounce cinnamon
¼ ounce anise seed

Mix and let stand for several days. Strain and add a drop or two of lemon oil. [Use as a gargle. Hinjio explained that if the second stomach (the mouth being first) was as foul, swallow a bit every now and again.]

Once while driving across the United States I stopped in Dodge City, Oklahoma. I went into a liquor store for some beer and saw a product called Everclear. Later, when I was teaching alternative lifestyles, I mentioned this product and some local Oklahomans gave me more, but I didn't realize what I really had brought home. I just liked the label. It waited till I had gathered some *Prunella vulgaris*, or self-heal. I wanted to make an extract but because the Everclear was so strong (190 proof, or 80% alcohol), I knew I would end up with a tincture. I thought a moment and realized I could dilute the extract (with one pint of water) to make a fluid extract.

one pint Everclear
one handful dried and powdered *Prunella*
   root (approximately 1½ cups)

Mix. Let stand for 14 days, shaking every other day. Strain and use in whatever way suits you.

A bottle of this on a pack trip tucked away in your corner pocket will help under stressful situations. Also use to sterilize your knife or place on a minor cut—a general cleansing product.

Each state has its own liquor law so be aware to be safe and in accordance with the law. This stuff isn't good to fool around with to drink as it's so strong. Once we were passing this around a campfire, and the bottle slipped. A flash of light from the alcohol igniting sobered us very quickly. Incredible spirit.

The *Prunella vulgaris*, or self-heal or heal-all has a long reputation with the American Indian. It is not given as much credit as it should be, but then it's only one more herb to get in touch with. This one—a sparkling purple-blue flower without much fragrance—may be prized for its delicate beauty alone. It tastes slightly bitter, yet bears a beaming light by the wayside of our travels.

Brewing and extracting can be fun. But be careful. In time you will become familiar and comfortable with the various herbs and

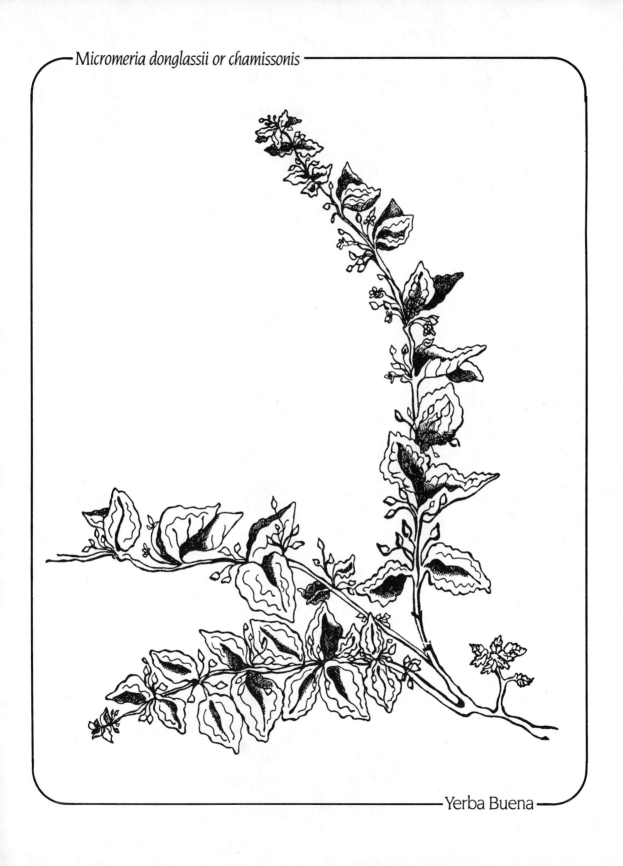

Micromeria donglassii or chamissonis

Yerba Buena

Verbascum thapsus

Mullein

preparations. This is a beginning for your own medicine chest.

The finishing approach to these ways of nature is similar to that of a meadow bedding down for winter. Going to the place of hibernation. To pass the winter in a resting state without vegetation, as do the spores and winter buds, etc., of various plants. This is what completes The Star Herbal. Now we move to THE RED-WOOD REMEDY.

We are all at the place where we have the final choice for the energy that results from our action with Nature. This is evident in Holistic Medicine, the reinstatement of the Absolute Reality of Ritual, and the divinity of sacrament, and its essential parts. This is the truth-thought that abounds from here to the ends of the Universe. Much like the garden is filled with dirt and its components, so is the universe within our body composed of such elemental parts. I have seen through the eyes of a tree and its Remedy is becoming most potent.

Our elders are passing and we become as they, the crystals of the ritual, and the crystals of past, as now till future. Ever gaining the knowledge that our elders sought. Few are genuine trackers of the Earth signs. The Great Spirit who walks amidst all things proclaims our need for better medicine. The time is right. The Earth, as our bodies, screams for attention. We have the capability to manifest light or dark, so why not light?! It's brilliant and filled with the greatness of the Universe. 'Tis a joyous place, this reverence of Absolute Truth in all things.

Remember the ole adage, IF LOST RELAX. Our fear also must relax if we are to become of this Light, with Nature and her products.

There is a way to overcome stress. Disaster transmutes to peace when we become aware of the earthly wonders. Lost is only disoriented molecular frequencies. And the list goes on: Shelter. Water. Star Orienting. Fire. Edible Plants. Equipment. Hunting the sign of Life Force. First Aid. Becoming familiar with the general habitats of nature. Desert. Tundra. Tropics. Savannas. Climbing. Signaling and such. Once again man has got to use not abuse, projecting Hope.

Take heed before Mother Nature rocks and slides us to oblivion to correct what Homeopathically is the Tao of Nature. We have overpotentized the planet. We have stripped Nature of her biochemic Salts or Wisdom, and for this there is the reverse to original medicine occurring. More directly, by strip mining and chemical contamination alone we are on the destructive path. This has been known for a long time. Now with NewClear information, the Atomic Age has accelerated this time and space of our existence.

We are beginning to spin too quickly and for this we are manifesting a poisonous effect about the planet. It would be as the salts of the earth that hold her together in relation to our own imbalance of vitamins that bind us. When we take the intelligence from the earth, we are causing the collapse that is being felt.

Life is too short not to become involved in some form of ritual or daily sacrament. A daily exercise possibly! One of a vital state discipline for upholding the light and eternal remedy that Mother Nature requires. Now it is our time to take hold of this Earth, hug graciously and prepare to make most holy the space we inhabit.

This may sound bizarre at first yet when prayer or mental calm reverberates, with good diet, proper rest and recreation, walks with nature, a bit of thermo/hydro therapeutic or chromotherapeutic laying on of the hands, then we begin to realize our potential within the scheme of Mother Nature. Add these together and we have the feelings that become reality when our ancestors in Tribe and Ritual ceremony were here on this planet with Nature.

What we may consider hard times is but a glimmer of what conditions used to exist but a few hundred years ago.

Today more than ever before we need to interact with Nature in a more harmonious fashion.

Today . . . we need the knowledge to create peace with this Tao of Nature. This knowledge is here, called Light and Its Remedy.

May the sweet smell of flowers and the dewy morning drops of glittered light be about you as you select your meal. In light, in spirit. In spirit within nature. Then will your preparation be full and life-giving, a completed step toward well-being.

Explanation of Medical Properties and Abbreviations

Abo—Abortifacient: An agent that induces or causes premature expulsion of a fetus.

Aci—Acidulous: Substances that possess a sour taste.

Acr—Acrid: An agent having a hot, biting taste or causing heat and irritation when applied to the skin.

Adj—Adjuvant: An herb added to a mixture to aid the effect of the principle ingredient. Synergist.

Ale—Alexipharmic: Preventing the bad effects of poisoning inwardly.

Alt—Alterative: Producing a salutary change without perceptible evacuation.

Ana—Analgesic: An agent which relieves or diminishes pain.

Ana—Anaphrodesiac: An agent which reduces sexual desire or potency.

Ane—Anesthetic: An agent that deadens sensation.

Ano—Anodyne: An agent that soothes or relieves pain.

Ant—Anthelmintic: An agent that destroys or expels intestinal worms.

A-bio—Antibiotic: An agent that destroys or arrests the growth of micro- organisms.

A-Coa—Anticoagulant: An agent that prevents clotting in a liquid, as in blood.

A-eme—Antiemetic: A remedy for vomiting.

A-hyd—Antihydrotic: An agent which reduces or suppresses perspiration.

A-hys—Antihysteric: A remedy for hysteria.

A-lit—Antilithic: An agent which reduces or suppresses urinary calculi (stones) and acts to dissolve those already present.

A-per—Antiperiodic: An agent which counteracts periodic or intermittent diseases.

A-phl—Antiphlogistic: An agent which reduces inflammation.

A-pyr—Antipyretic: An agent which prevents or reduces fever.

A-scr—Antiscrofulous: Counteracting scrofula.

A-sco—Antiscorbutic: A source of vitamin C for curing or preventing scurvy.

A-sep—Antiseptic: An agent for destroying or inhibiting pathogenic or putrefactive bacteria.

A-spa—Antispasmodic: An agent that relieves or checks spasms or cramps.

A-syp—Antisyphilitic: Opposed to or curing venereal diseases.

A-tus—Antitussive: An agent that relieves coughing.

A-ven—Antivenomous: Used against bites of venomous insects or snakes.

Ape—Aperient: An agent that acts as a mild stimulant for the bowels.

Aph—Aphrodesiac: An agent for arousing or increasing sexual desire or potency.

App – Appetizer: An agent that excites the appetite.

Aro – Aromatic: A substance having an agreeable odor and stimulating qualities.

Ast – Astringent: An agent that contracts organic tissue, reducing secretions.

Bal – Balsam: 1) A soothing or healing agent. 2) A resinous substance obtained from the exudations of various trees and used in medicinal preparations.

Bit – Bitter: Having a tonic effect.

Bit Ton – Bitter Tonic: Used for temporary loss of appetite. Stimulates the flow of saliva and gastric juices, assists digestion.

Cal – Calmative: An agent that has a mild sedative or tranquilizing effect.

Car – Cardiac: An agent that stimulates or otherwise affects the heart.

Car – Carminative: An agent for expelling gas from the intestines.

Cat – Cathartic: Increasing evacuations from the bowels.

Cau – Caustic: The property of burning or disorganizing animal substances.

Cho – Cholagogue: An agent for increasing the flow of bile into the intestines.

Coa – Coagulant: An agent that induces clotting in a liquid, as in blood.

Con – Condiment: Improving the flavor of food, as salt, pepper.

Cor – Cordial: A warm stomachic: exciting the heart.

Cos – Cosmetic: Used for improving the complexion or skin.

C-irr – Counterirritant: Causing irritation in one part to relieve pain in another part.

Dem – Demulcent: Soothing, mucilaginous, relieving inflammation.

Deo – Deobstruent: Removing obstruction; aperient in a general sense.

Dep – Depressant: An agent which lessens nervous or functional activity, the opposite of stimulant.

Dep – Depurative: Purifying the blood.

Des – Dessicative: Drying the moisture of wounds and ulcers.

Det – Detergent: Cleansing of wounds, boils or ulcers.

Dia – Diaphoretic: Producing insensible perspiration.

Dig – Digestive: An agent that promotes or aids digestion.

Dis – Disinfectant: An agent that cleanses infection by destroying or inhibiting the activity of disease producing micro-organisms.

Diu – Diuretic: Increasing the secretion and flow of urine.

D-ter – Detersive: Detergent.

Eme – Emetic: Producing or causing vomiting.

Emm – Emmenagogue: Promoting menstruation.

Emo – Emollient: Softening to inflamed parts; soothing.

Esc – Esculent: Eatable as a food.

Eup – Euphoriant: An agent that induces an abnormal sense of vigor and buoyancy.

Exa – Exanthematous: Relating to skin diseases or eruptions.

Exc – Excitant: Producing excitement; stimulant.

Exp – Expectorant: A medicine capable of facilitating expectoration.

Feb – Febrifuge: Abating or driving away fever.

F-com – Female Complaints: Ailments peculiar to women, as dysmennorhoea, amenorrhoea, etc.

Foe – Foetid: Bad smelling, disgusting, nauseous, stinking.

For – Forage: Used as food for domestic cattle, sheep or horses.

Gal – Galactigogue: An agent that encourages or increases the secretion of milk.

Hal – Hallucinogen: An agent that induces hallucinations.

Hem – Hemostatic: An agent that stops bleeding.

Hep – Hepatic: Related to disease of the liver.

Hyd – Hydragogue: A purgative that produces abundant watery discharge.

Hyp – Hypnotic: An agent that promotes or produces sleep.

Ins – Insecticide: A substance that destroys insects.

Irr – Irritant; An agent that causes inflammation or abnormal sensitivity in living tissue.

Lax – Laxative: A medicine that acts gently on the bowels without gripping.

Muc – Mucilaginous: Gummy, glutinous, viscid, demulcent.

Nar – Narcotic: A drug which relieves pain and induces sleep when used in medicinal doses, in large doses produces convulsions, coma or death.

Nau – Nauseant: an agent that produces an inclination to vomit.

Nep – Nephritic: An agent applicable to diseases of the kidney.

Ner – Nervine: Allaying nervous excitement, acting on the nervous system.

Nut – Nutritious: Having the quality of nourishing or sustaining life.

Opt – Opthalmicum: A remedy for diseases of the eye.

Orn – Ornamental: Cultivated for ornament.

Oxy – Oxytocic: An agent that stimulates contraction of the uterine muscle and facilitates childbirth.

Pec – Pectoral: A remedy for pulmonary or other chest diseases.

Per – Perfume: A plant or substance used for its fragrance.

Poi – Poisonous: Producing death if taken in improper doses.

Pun – Pungent: Biting, hot, acrid; prickly to the taste.

Pur – Purgative: A medicine that physics more powerfully than a cathartic.

Ref – Refrigerant: Cooling.

Res – Restorative: An agent that restores consciousness or normal physiological activity.

Rub – Rubifacient: Producing or causing redness of the skin.

Sac – Saccharine: Containing sugar; sweetish.

Sad – Salad: Fresh herbs eaten as condiments or as food.

Sal – Saline: Containing or having the properties of a salt.

Sap – Saponaceous: Soapy, making a lather with water.

Sed – Sedative: Directly depressing to the vital forces.

Sia – Sialagogue: Provoking the secretion of saliva.

Spe – Specific: An agent which cures or alleviates a particular condition or disease.

Sti – Stimulant: Exciting or inducing organic action of the animal economy.

Sto – Stomachic: Strengthening and giving tone to the stomach; tonic.

Sty – Styptic: Externally astringent; arresting hemorrhage or bleeding.

Sud – Sudorific: An agent that promotes or increases perspiration.

Tae – Taeniacide: A substance that kills tapeworms.

Ton – Tonic: An agent that strengthens or invigorates organs or the entire organism.

Vas – Vascoconstrictor: An agent that narrows the blood vessels, thus raising blood pressure.

Vas – Vasodilator: An agent that widens the blood vessels, thus lowering blood pressure.

Ver – Vermicide: An agent that destroys intestinal worms.

Ver – Vermifuge: Anthelmintic; expelling worms.

Ves – Vesicant: An agent that produces blisters.

Vul – Vulnerary: A healing substance to apply on wounds.

Cardrius

Thistle

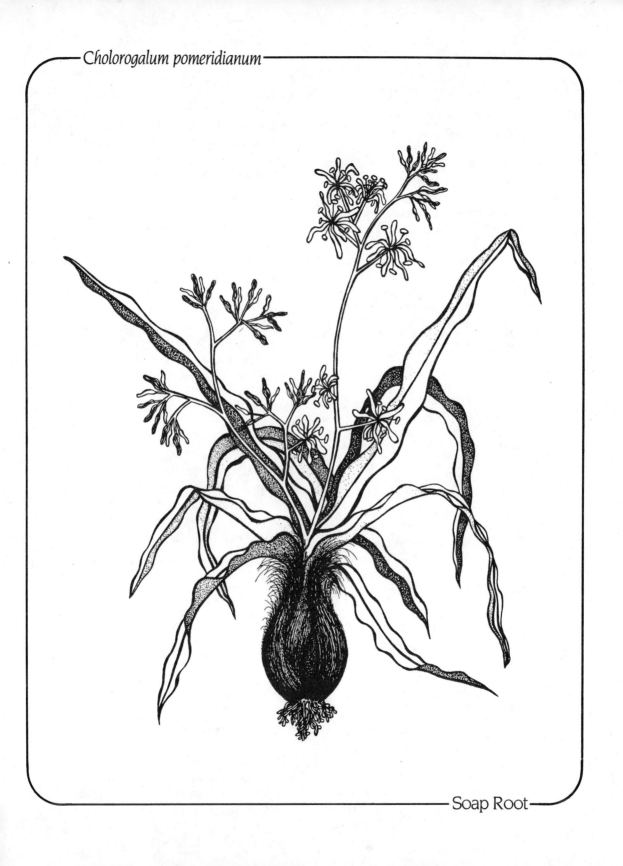

Chlorogalum pomeridianum

Soap Root

UTENSILS AND MEASUREMENTS

Utensils can be simple—one pan, a spoon and a knife—or they may be elaborate. One can, if desired, fabricate copper retorts and assemble stills with joints luted with clay after designs by alchemists of yore.

The following utensils were chosen largely on the basis of safety, economy, ease of cleaning and simplicity. This is so they may be all cleared away by the time another meal approaches or preparation beckons.

The physician has to be skilled in nature and must strive to know what Man is in relation to food, drink, occupation, and which effect each of these has on the other.

Hippocrates

A few of the basics include:

WOODEN SPOONS AND BOWLS: Wood carved from local hardwood (all fruit trees) is the best vibratory interactor for our preparations.

CHOPPING BOARD AND BREADBOARD: Use one only for cutting; the other for kneading and shaping the dough. One should never cut on the dough board that is always kept "flavored" by flour which increases the blending frequency and maintains the aged wood.

KNIVES: Always keep them sharp. Use one for fruits and one for vegetables. There should be one for chopping harder materials and another for foraging, such as a sturdy pocket knife.

CAST IRON PAN: One good heavy pan is all that is necessary. This can be a skillet, but a deeper pan is more versatile. This type of pot is good for cooking soups, grains, and breads. It is the old "all-in- one" kettle on the hearth. Keep well oiled as oxidation causes rust.

When man developed skills to cast different metals, a certain basic sense of earthen material was left behind—modern implementation brought such wonders as aluminum and forks, when in the past mother earth provided us with clay and fingers. How about comfrey, cabbage or grape leaves for a plate with a fennel stalk as fork?

MIXING BOWLS: The best are made of earthenware, china, or stainless steel. When possible use local fired material.

VARIOUS SIZE POTS: A teapot, soup pot and casserole are also useful. What about a melting pot? A cauldron possibly? Earthenware, heat-resistant glass or copper are great. Copper is probably the best conductor of heat; no matter what is cooked, nothing sticks or burns. Much has been said about cooking with aluminum. It is best to avoid using it because it oxidizes, causing impurities in the foods.

BAKING TINS: Stainless steel is best. They never need washing. Simply wipe them clean and oil them. You'll notice after each use the flavor becomes better.

PRESSURE COOKER: This pot retains many essential nutrients and elements that normally evaporate in a standard pot, unless you have one with a lid so heavy that it requires several people to lift it off and on.

A few of the extras that one might find about the table are:

SOUP LADLE: How about using a cup to pour, or simply pouring? The latter is a bit homier though sometimes messier.

A FLAT SPATULA: There are numerous uses that no other utensil can handle as well. Wood is superior to metal.

POT HOLDERS: For the prevention of burns.

PORCELAIN GRATER: A good tool for ginger, garlic, cheeses, and veggies—saves the tips of fingers.

A GRAIN MILL: In olden days this used to be as important an item as the stove (and still is in some countries). Freshly ground flour makes anything prepared a delight to taste.

WEIGHTS AND MEASURES

1 pound	454.6 grams
1 ounce	28.35 grams
16 ounces (dry)	1 pound
4 pecks	1 bushel
8 quarts (dry)	1 peck
4 quarts (liquid)	1 gallon
2 quarts	½ gallon
2 pints	1 quart
4 cups (32 fluid ounces)	1 quart
2 cups (16 fluid ounces)	1 pint
1 cup (8 fluid ounces)	16 tablespoons
¾ cup (6 fluid ounces)	12 tablespoons
⅔ cup	10 ⅓ tablespoons
½ cup (4 fluid ounces)	8 tablespoons
⅓ cup	5 ⅓ tablespoons
¼ cup (2 fluid ounces)	4 tablespoons
⅛ cup (1 fluid ounce)	2 tablespoons
3 teaspoons (½ fluid ounce)	1 tablespoon
60 drops	1 teaspoon
a dash, a bit, a touch	less than ⅛ teaspoon

SIMPLIFIED COMPARISONS

dram	60 grains for weight and 60 minims (drops) for liquid
1 ounce	8 drams for weight or liquid
1 cup	8 fluid ounces
1 pound	16 ounces (approximately 3½ cups for 1 pound whole wheat flour)
1 pint	16 fluid ounces
1 quart	2 pints liquid
1 gallon	4 quarts

APOTHECARIES' WEIGHT OR TROY WEIGHT

(used to dispense solids)

In apothecaries' weight the pound is divided into ounces, drams, scruples, and grains, as follows:

> 20 grains (gr) = 1 scruple (   )
> 60 grains or 3 scruples = 1 dram (   )
> 480 grains or 24 scruples or 8 drams = 1 ounce (   )
> 5760 grains or 288 scruples or 96 drams or 12 ounces = 1 pound (lb)

The grain (gr), dram (   ) and ounce (   ) should alone be used in writing your recipe.

WINE MEASURE OR APOTHECARIES' MEASURE

(employed in dispensing liquids)

In the wine measure, the gallon is divided into pints, fluid ounces, fluidrams and minims, thus:

> 60 minims (   ) = 1 fluidram (ƒ)
> 480 minims or 8 fluidrams = 1 fluid ounce (ƒ   )
> 7680 minims or 128 fluidrams or 16 fluid ounces = 1 pint (O)
> 61440 minims or 1024 fluidrams or 128 fluid ounces or 8 pints = 1 gallon (C)

The minim (   ), fluidram (ƒ   ), fluid ounce (ƒ   ) and the pint (O) are rarely used.

SEED PROCUREMENT STORES, RETAIL AND WHOLESALE

The following list contains but a few of the numerous outlets for botanicals, natural products, and tools of nature. It is always a good idea to compare catalogs and try a few items. Certain recipes require certain spices, and you will find each outlet has its specialty. The following system of identification of each name and address has been used for your convenience.

COMPANIES

if the company sells medicinal plants – M
if the company sells rare plants – R
if the company sells culinary plants – C
if the company sells ornamental plants – O
if the company sells native plants – N
if the company sells vegetable plants – V
if the company sells herb seed – H

STORES

r – retail   h – health items
w – wholesale   t – tools
b – botanicals

BRITISH COLUMBIA

Golden Bough Herbs
1913 Yew St.
Vancouver, B.C. v6k 3g3
Tel. 733-2724
(C-M-r-w-b)

Cactus and Succulent
 Information Exchange
5512 Clinton St.
Burnaby 1 B.C. Canada
(r-resource)

CALIFORNIA

Health Research
Mokelumne Hill, CA 95245
(Resource-Books)

The Lhasha Karnak
 Herb Co.
2513 Telegraph Ave.
Berkeley, CA 94704
(H-r-w)

Nature's Herb Co.
281 Ellis St.
San Francisco, CA 94101
(H-r-w)

New Age Creations
219 Carl St.
San Francisco, CA 94117
(b-H-r-w)

The Whole Herb Company
 dba Star Herb Co.
250 E. Blithedale
Mill Valley, CA 94141
(H-r-w-quality oils)

Star & Crescent Herb Co.
1021 R St.
Sacramento, CA
Tel (916) 442-1181
(H-r-w-b)

Tree Frog Nursery
1305 Fulton Road
Santa Rosa, CA 95401
Tel (707) 545-2426
(r-w-M-N)

COLORADO

Nutri-Books
Box 5793
Denver, CO 80217
(W-books)

CONNECTICUT

Caprilands Herb Farm
Silver Street
North Coventry, CT 06238
Tel (203) 742-7244
(C-O-M)

Comstock, Ferre & Co.
263 Main St.
Wethersfield, CT 06109
Tel (203) 529-3319
(M-C)

The Chas. C. Hart Seed Co.
Main and Hart Streets
Wethersfield, CT 06109
Tel (203) 529-2537
(V-M-C-O-R)

MARYLAND
Laurel Brook Foods
P.O. Box 47
Bel Air, MD 21014

MASSACHUSETTS.
Erewhon
33 Farnsworth
Boston, MA 02110
(h-r-w-resource)

Herb Society of America
Horticultural Hall
300 Massachusetts Ave.
Boston, MA 02115
(resource)

MICHIGAN
Vaughn's Seed Company
125 N. Pork St.
Ard, MI 48866
Tel (517) 831-2241
(V)

Orchid Gardens
Route 3, Box 224
Grand Rapids, MI 55744
(N-R-ferns-shrubs)

NEW YORK
Kiehl Pharmacy
109 Third Ave.
New York, NY 10003
(H-r-w-quality essences)

NORTH CAROLINA
Gardens of the Blue Ridge
Edw. P. Robbins, Manager
Estate of E.C. Robbins,
   Nurseryman
Ashford, McDowell
   County, NC 28603
(N-R-O)

The Three Laurels
Route 3, Box 15
Marshall, NC 28753
(N-O-C-M)

OREGON
Nichols Garden Nursery
1190 N. Pacific Highway
Albany, OR 97321
(M-R-N-b)

PENNSYLVANIA
W. Atlee Burpee Co.
Hunting Park Ave.
   at 18th St.
Philadelphia, PA
Tel (215) 228-8800
(H-C-W)

Rodale Press
Organic Gardening and
   Prevention Magazine
Emmaus, PA 18049
(resource)

SOUTH CAROLINA
Geo. W. Park Seed Co. Inc.
P.O. Box 31
Greenwood, SC 29647
(V-C-R-O)

TEXAS
Sweethardt Herbs
Box 12602
Austin, TX 78711

STUDY OF HEALING

Hippocrates Health Institute
25 Exeter St.
Boston, MA

Live food and grass therapy for chronic ailments—study subsistence, survival diet, new age disciplines. A complete home study course. Naturana. Send 32¢ in stamps for free literature. Will help you set up chartered branches.

Holistic Life University
1627 10th Avenue
San Francisco, CA 94122

Anyone who would like to become a holistic health counselor or educator. Offering a two-year A.A. or B.A. program thru New College of California Independent Study Program.

Arctostaphylos glauca

Manzanita

Medical Emergency Education

Civil Defense Director of every local community. The U.S. Public Health Service and office of civil defense sponsors a 16-hour medical self-help training course that covers the basic Red Cross first aid and deals with such emergency situations as childbirth, water purification, food storage, garbage disposal, and heart attack.

Holistic Health & Nutrition Institute

150 Shoreline Hwy #31
Mill Valley CA 94941

A nonprofit organization pioneering in the field of health. Offering medical services, nutritional services, psychological services, acupuncture, podiatry, spiritual consultation, and such adjunct services as herbs, homeopathy, and physical fitness.

A Few Manufacturers and Distributors of Preparedness Products

Containers

American Barrel & Cooperage Co., Inc.
49 South 5th West
Salt Lake City, UT 84101
  50 gal. drums with covers and locking rims.

Kerr Glass Manufacturing Corp.
P.O. Box 67
Sand Springs, OK 73063
  Bottles, lids, rims for home canning.

Equipment

Smithfield Implement Co., Inc.
99 North Main
Smithfield, UT 84335
  Mills, juicers, mixers, water distillers, pressure cookers, stoves, etc.

Foods for Storage

Chico-San
126 Humbolt Ave.
Chico, CA 95926
  Organically-grown foods; rice, wheat, beans, sesame seeds, etc. No chemicals or preservatives.

Generators

Cannon, S. Gilbert
359 East 1700 South
Bountiful, UT 84010
  Kits or assembled hand-operated generators for emergency use of radio equipment.

Water Distillers

Loft Enterprises Inc.
278 Mayfield St.
Pittsburgh, PA 15214
  Electric water distillers

Botanical List of Plants

(Common Name, Genus, Species, Family,
Plant Part Used, Usage, other
Common Names)
For list of abbreviations and explanations see page 163.

AGAR-AGAR: *Gracilaria lichenoides (Gracilariaceae)* Plant. Nut., Muc. Ceylon Moss, Jaffna Moss

AGRIMONY: *Agrimonia eupatoria (Rosaceae)* Plant. Ast.*, Sto., Ton. Church Steeples, Cockletop, Cockleburr.

ALDER: *Alnus glutinosa (Betulaceae)* Park & leaves: Alt., Bit., Ton., Ast. Nut Fruit: Ton. Inner Bark: Eme. European Alder, Black Alder, owler, Smooth Alder.

ALFALFA: *Medicago sativa (Leguminoseae)* Leaf: Ton. Seed: Yellow dye, Nut. Lucerne, Buffalo Herb.

ALLSPICE: *Eugenia pimenta (Myrtaceae)* Fruit (unripe). Aro., Cat., Sto., Sti. Clove Pepper. Jamaica Pepper.

ALMOND: *Prunus amygdalus* or *Amygalus dulcis (Rosaceae)* Fruit: Ton. Kernel: Eme., Emo., Dem. Greek Nuts, Jordan Almonds, Hunza Almonds.

ALOE: *Aloe vera (Liliaceae)* Gum. Sti., Cat., Emm., Ant., Sto. Bombay Aloes, Turkey Aloes, Mocha Aloes, Zanzibar Aloes, Shining Aloes, Spiked Aloes, Cape Aloes.

ALTHEA: *Althea officinalis (Malvaceae)* Root & Leaves. Muc., Dem., Diu. Marsh Mallow, Mortification Root, Sweat Weed, Wymote, Malva, Mallow, Cheeseweed.

ALUM: *Geranium maculatum (Geraniaceae)* Root. A powerful Ast., Sty., A-sep., Ton. Spotted Geranium, Dovefoot, Alum Root, American Kino Root, Crowfoot.

AMARANTH: *Amaranthus hypochondriacus (Amarantaceae)* Leaves: Ast., Det. Seed: Ton., Sad. Lovely-Bleeding, Red Cockscomb, Pilewort, Spleen Amaranth.

ANGELICA: *Angelica officinalis (Umbelliferae)* Root & Seed. Aro., Sti., Res., Ton., Car. Master Wort, Purple Angelica, Alexanders, Archangel, Holy Root, Eurona, Garden Angelica.

ANISE: *Pimpinella anisum (Umbellifera)* Seed. Ar., Car., Ton., Sti., Sto.

ARNICA: *Arnica montana (Compositae)* Plant. Nar., St., Diu., Vul., Poi. Wolfsbane, Mountain Tobacco, Mountain Arnica, Leopardsbane.

ARROW ROOT: *Maranta arundinacea (Podostemonaceae)* Yields Arrow Root Starch. Arrow Plant.

BALM OF GILEAD: *Populus candicans (Salicales)* Bark. Sti., Ton., Diu., A-sco., Buds., Vul., Bal. Balsom Poplar, American Balm of Gilead.

BALMONY: *Chelone glabra (Scrophulariaceae)* Leaves. Bit., Tom., Cat., Ant. Snakehead,

175

Turtle Bloom, Salt Rheum Weed, Bitter Herb.

BARBERRY: *Berberis vulgaris (Berberaceae)* Root & Bark: Bit., Ast., Ton., Hep. Berries: Aci., Ref. Rocky Mountain Grape, Pepperidge Bush, Sowberry, Jaundice Berry.

BASIL: *Ocimum basilicum (Labiatae)* Herb. Aro., Sti., Ner., Con. Sweet Basil, Common Basil.

BAY LAUREL: *Laurus nobilis (Lauraceae)* Leaves & Fruit. Aro., Fra., Ast., Sto., Car. Bay Tree, Laurel Leaves, Indian Bay, Bay Leaves, European Bay Laurel, Laurel Berries, Sweet Bay, Bay Berries.

BAYBERRY: *Myrica cerifera (Myriaceae)* Bark: Ast., Ton., Sti. Leaves: Aro., Sti. Waxberry, Bay Berry Bush, American Vegetable Tallow Tree, Tallow Shrub, American Vegetable Wax, Myrtle Candle Berry, Vegetable Tallow.

BEARBERRY: *Arctostaphylos uva-ursi (Ericaceae)* Leaves. Diu., Ast., Ton. Bearberry, Upland Cranberry, Mountain Box, Bear's Grape, Kinnikinnick.

BENZOIN: *Styrax benzoin (Symplocaceae)* Gum Benzoin. Acr., Irr., Sti., Pec., Err. Benzoin Laurel. Benjamin Tree.

BETH ROOT: *Trillium pendulum (Liliaceae)* Root. Ast., Ton., A-sep., Emm., Exp., Dia., Alt., F-com. Trillium, Milk Ipecac, Three Leaved Nightshade, Lamb's Quarter, Snake Bite.

BISTORT: *Polygonum bistorta (Polygonaceae)* Root., Ast., Diu., Alt., Sad. Patience Dock, Snake Weed, Dragonwort.

BITTERSWEET: *Solanum dulcamara (Solanaceae)* Root and Stem. Nar., Dep., Deo., Ano., Res., Eme. Woody Nightshade, Wolf Grape, Felonwort.

BLACKBERRY: *Rubus villosus (Rosaceae)* Leaves: Ast. Bark: Ast. Fruit: Edi., Diu., Ast. Bramble.

BLACK HAW: *Viburnum prunifolium (Caprifoliaceae)* Leaves. As Tea. Bark. Ton., Ast., Diu., Alt., Opt. Sloe, Sweet Viburnum.

BLACK COHOSH: *Cimicifuga racemosa (Ranunculaceae)* Root. Alt., Ner., Exp., Emm. Rattle Root, Black Snake Root, Bugwort, Squaw Root, Bug Gane, Richweed.

BLADDERWRACK: *Fucus versiculosus.* Yields kelp when weed is burned in open air. Sea Wrack, Bladder Fucus, Seaweed, Sea Oak, Kelpware, Black Tany.

BLESSED THISTLE: *Centaurea benedicta (Compositae)* Plant. Ton., Dia., Bit., Feb. Holy Thistle, Bitter Thistle, Cursed or Spotted Thistle, Spotted or Blessed Cardus.

BLOOD ROOT: *Sanguinaria canadensis (Papaveraceae)* Root. Eme., Ton., Sed., Feb., Sti., Diu., Emm. Red Puccoon, Tetterwort, Sanguinaria, Indian Plant, Pauson, Indian Red Paint Root.

BLUEBERRY: *Vaccinium frondosum (Vacciniaceae)* Leaf. Fruit. A-sco., Diu., Sac. Whortleberry, Bilberry, Blue Tangle.

BLUE COHOSH: *Caulophyllum thalictroides (Berberaceae)* Root. Sti., Emm., Sud. Blue or Yellow Ginseng, Papoose Root, Squaw Root, Blue Berry.

BONESET: *Eupatorium perfoliatum (Compositae)* Herb. Ton., Ape., Dia., Eme., Feb. Indian Sage, Fever Wort, Ague Weed, Tedral.

BORAGE: *Borago officinalis (Boraginaceae)* Plant. Cor., Pec., Ape. Burrage, Bugloss.

BUCHU: *Barosma crenata (Rutaceae)* Leaves. Sti., Diu., Dia., Ton. Bookoo, Bucku.

BUCKTHORN: *Rhamnus crocea* Bark. Ton., Aft., Lax.

BURDOCK: *Articum lappa (Compositae)* Root: Alt., Diu., Dep. Leaves: Mat. Seed: Diu., Alt. Clotbur, Bardana, Burr Seed, Hardock, Turkey Burr Seed, Hurr Burr, Beggars' Buttons, Lappa, Thorny Burr.

BURNET: *Sanguisorba officinalis (Rosaceae)* Plant. Ast., Ton.

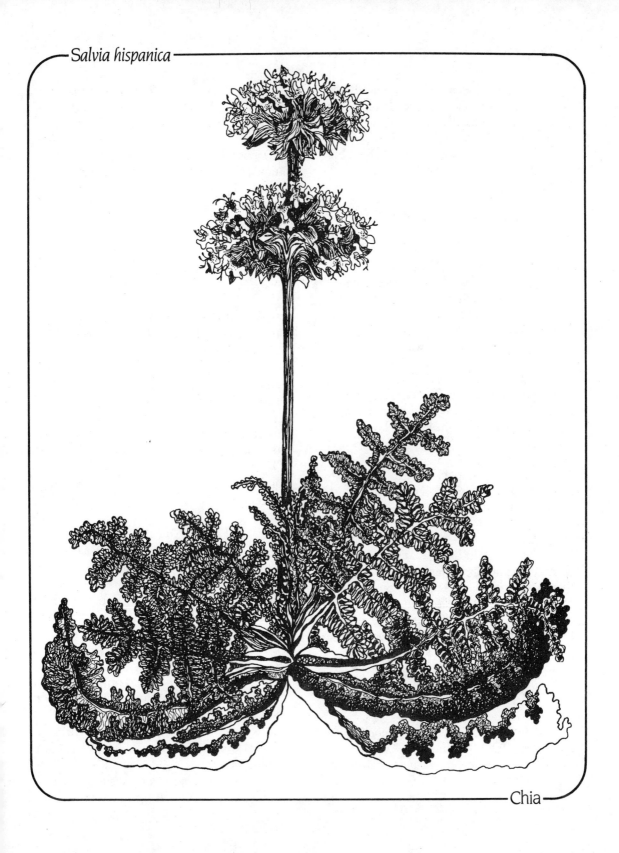

Salvia hispanica

Chia

CALAMUS: *Acorus calamus (Lemnaceae)* Root. Aro., Car., Ton., Vul. Sweet Flag, Sweet Myrtuel, Sea Sedge, Sweet Cane.

CALENDULA: *Calendula officinalis (Compositae)* Flowers & Leaves: Vul., Dis., Sti. Garden Marigold, Mary Bud, Pot Marigold.

CAPSICUM: *Capsicum annum (Solanaceae)* Fruit. Pun., Sti., Ton., Sia., Alt. Cayenne, Red, African or Bird Pepper, Cayenne Pods or Pepper.

CARAWAY: *Carum carui (Umbellifrae)* Seed. Car., Aro., Fra., Sto. German: Kummel.

CARDAMOM: *Elettaria cardamomum (Elettaria)* Seed. Aro., Sti., Car., Con. Malabar Cardamom.

CAROB: *Ceratonia siliqua.* Powder. Sac., Edi., Nut., Cat. St. John's Bread, Algaroba Bean, Husks of the Ancients, Locust Bean, Sweet Pod, Bean Tree. French: Carou.

CASCARA BARK: *Rhamnus purschiana (Rhamnaceae)* Bark. Bitter, Ton. Jujube Tree, Fruit Pulp, Chittam Bark, Sacred Bark, Persiana Bark.

CASCARILLA BARK: *Croton eluteria (Euphorbiaceae)* Bark. Bit., Aro., Ton., Car., Sto. Sweet woorbark.

CATNIP: *Nepeta cataria (Labiatae)* Leaves. Aro., Dia., Car., A-spa., Aro. Catmint, Nep, Catrup, Field Balm, Cat's Wort.

CELERY: *Apium graveolens. (Umbelliferae)* Root and seed. Diu., Acr., Poi. Smallage.

CENTAURY HERB: *Sabbatia angularis (Gentianales)* Plant. A-Bil., Ton., Bit., Ver., Emm., Feb. Bitter Bloom, Wild Succory, Rose Pink, Eyebright, Bitter Clover.

CHAMOMILE: *Matricaria chamomilla (Compositae)* Flowers. Ton., Emm., Sto., Car., Nep., Ver. Wild Chamomile, German Chamomile.

CHERVIL: *Anthriscus cerefolium (Umbelliferae)* Plant. Deo., Diu., Emm., Lit.

CHESTNUT: *Castana americana. (Fagaceae)* Bark. Ast., Ton. Leaves Ast. American Chestnut.

CHIA: *Salvia hispanica. (Labiatae)* Seed. Opt., Muc.

CHICORY: *Cichorium intybus (Compositae)* Root. Ape., Deo., Bit. Succory, Wild Chicory, Blue Eyes.

CHICKWEED: *Stellaria media (Caryophyllaceae)* Plant. Dem., Muc., Dis., Alt. Starwort, Stickwort, Adder's Mouth, Satin Flower.

CINNAMON: *Cinnamomum zeylanicum (Lauraceae)* Bark. Aro., Cor., Sto., Car., Sti., Ast. True Ceylon Cinnamon, Saigon Cassia, Saigon Cinnamon.

CLEAVERS: *Galium aparine (Rubiaceae)* Herb. Diu., Ape., Ref. Goose Grass, Catch Straw, Bedstraw, Savoyan, Milk Sweet, Poor Robin, Gravel Grass, Clabbergrass, Cheese Rennet Herb.

CLOVES: *Caryophyllus aromaticus (Caryophyllales)* Buds. Aro., Sti., Irr., A-Eme. Mother Cloves.

CLUB MOSS: *Lycopodium clavatum.* Pollen used to treat diaper rash in infants. Cycopodium, Staghorn, Vegetable Sulphur, Wolf Claw, Lycopodial Moss.

COLA NUTS: *Cola acuminata (Sterculiaceae)* Nuts. Sti., Ner., Caffein. Goora Nut. Kola Nut.

COLOMBO ROOT: *Cocculus palmatus (Menispermaceae)* Root. Ton., Feb., A-Eme. Calamba Root. Calumbo. Colomba.

COLTSFOOT: *Tussilago farfara (Compositae)* Plant. Emo., Dem., Ton., Exp., Pec. British Tobacco, Bullsfoot, Foalsfoot, Horse Hoof, Butterbur, Flower Velure Root.

COMFREY: *Symphytum officinalis (Boraginaceae)* Root. Dem., Ast., Muc., Pec., Vul., F-com., Led., Nut., Dem., Ton. Knit Bone, Healing Herb, Gum Plant, Slippery Root, Nip Bone.

CORIANDER: *Coriandrum sativum (Umbelliferae)* Seed. Aro., Pun., Car., Cor., Sto. Coliander.

CORNSILK: *Zea mays or Stigmata maydis (Gramineae)* Fruit. A product for dyeing silk. Sea Mays, Indian Corn, Maize, Turkey Corn.

COWSLIP: *Mertensia virginica (Boraginaceae)* Plant. Muc., Dem., American Lungwort. Lungwort. Virginia Cowslip.

CUMIN: *Cuminum cyminum (Umbelliferae)* Seed. Aro., Sti., Car., Veterinary. Cumin Plant, Sweet Cumin.

CUBEB BERRIES: *Piper cubeba (Piperaceae)* Unripe Fruit. Sti., Diu., A-Syp., Pur., Aro. Java Pepper. Tailed Pepper. Cubebs.

DAMIANA: *Turnera aphrodisiaca (Turneraceae)* Leaves and Tops. Ton., Lax.

DANDELION: *Taraxicum dens-leonis (Compositae)* Root: Sto., Ton., Diu., Ape., Dep., Hep. Leaf: Bit., Ton. Lion's Tooth, Wild Endive, Cankerwort, Blowball, Swine Snout, Priest's Crown.

DEER TONGUE: *Liatrus odoratissima (Compositae)* Leaves. Aro., Per., Ton., Sti., Dia., Wild Vanilla. Hound's Tongue.

DILL: *Anethum graveolens (Umbelliferae)* Seed. Aro., Sti., Car., Sto. Garden Dilly, Dill Seed.

DOCK: *Rumex* Spp. See Yellow Dock.

DULSE: *Rhodymenia palmata.* Leaf. Ton. Dillisk, Water Leaf.

ECHINACEA: *Echinacea angustifolium (Compositae)* Root. Dia., Sia., Alt., A-syp. Purple Coneflower, Wild Niggerhead, Black Sampson.

ELDER: *Sambucus nigra (Caprifloiaceae)* Bark: Cat. Flower/Fruit: Diu., Exp., Dep. Sambucus, Boor Tree, Bountry, Ellanwood, Ellhorn American, Sweet or Black Berries.

ELECAMPANE: *Inula helenium (Compositae)* Root. Diu., Exp., Emo., Ton., Dia. Horse Heal, Scabwort.

EYEBRIGHT: *Euphrasia officinalis (Scrophulariaceae)* Leaves. Ton., Ast., Opt.

FENNEL: *Foeniculum officinale (Umbelliferae)* Root & Seed. A-spa., Aro., Car., Diu., Exp., Sti., Sto. Wild Fennel, Bastard Anise, Sweet Fennel.

FENUGREEK: *Trigonella foenum-graecum (Papi-lionaceae)* Seed. Exp., Muc., Res. in poultices.

FEVERFEW: *Pyrethrum parthenium (Compositae)* Herb. Car., Emm., Pur., Sti., Ton. Feather Few, Febrifuge Plant.

FIVE FINGER: *Potentilla canadensis (Rosaceae)* Plant. Ton., Ast. In Night Sweats. Cinquefoil. Finger Leaf.

FLAXWEED: *Linum usitatissimum (Linaceae)* Seed. Dem., Emo., Muc., Pec., Pur. Linseed, Winterlien, Flax Seed, Common Flax.

FLEABANE: *Erigeron heterophyllum. (Compositae)* Plant. Diu., Ast., Ton., Dia.

FRANKINCENSE: *Boswellia serrata (Burseraceae)* Resin. Fra., Aro., Bit., Ast. Indian Olibanum. Indian Incense.

FUMATORY: *Fumaria officinalis (Fumariaceae)* Leaves. Sal., Bit., Ton., Alt., Diu., Lax. Earth Smoke.

GARLIC: *Allium sativum (Liliaceae)* Bulb. Sti., Diu., Ant., Emo., Mat.

GENTIAN: *Gentiana lutea (Gentianaceae)* Root. Ant., A-bil., Bit., Eme., Sto., Ton. Bitterroot, Bitterwort, Yellow Gentian, Gentian Root.

GINGER ROOT: *Asarum canadense (Aristolochiaseae)* Root. Aro., Car., Dia., Exp., Sti. Canada Snakeroot, False Coltsfoot, Indian Ginger, Wild Ginger, Broadleaved Asarabacca, Southern Snakeroot.

GINSENG: *Panax quinquefolia (Araliaceae)* Root. Dem. Sri, Sang, Seng, Ninsin, American Ginseng, Red Berry, Five Finger Root.

GOLDENROD: *Solidago odora (Compositae)* Leaves & Oil. Ast., Cor., Dia., Diu., Sti. Sweet Goldenrod, Wound Weed, Sweetscented Goldenrod.

GOLDEN SEAL: *Hydrastis canadensis (Ranunculaceae)* Rootstock. Alt., A-sep., Ast., Det., Diu., Lax., Opt., Ton. Eye Root, Eye Balm, Turmeric Jaundice Root, Yellow Paint Root.

GRINDELIA: *Grindelia robusta (Compositae)*

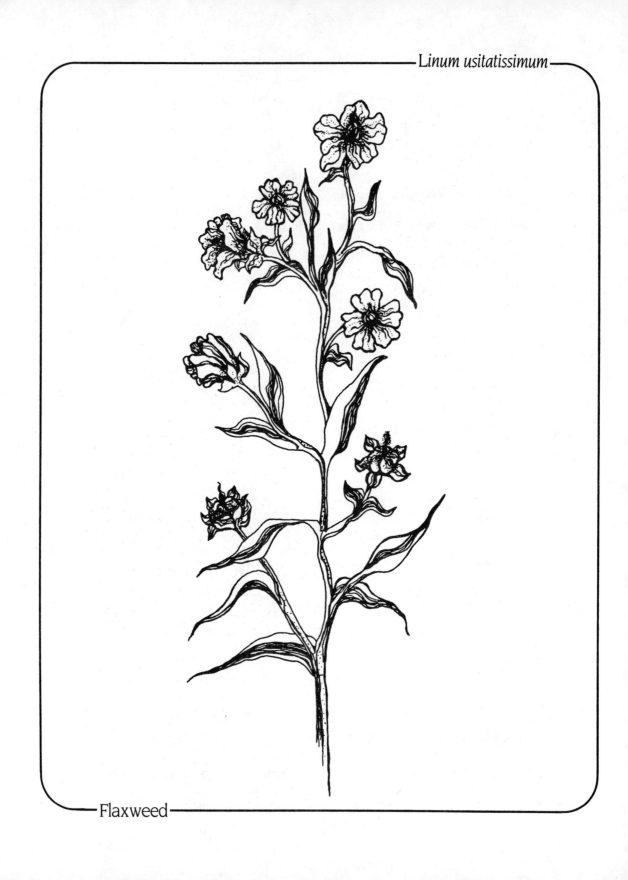

Linum usitatissimum

Flaxweed

Althaea rosea

Holly Hock

Plant. In asthma, Dem., Vul. Gumplant, Gumweed, Tarweed.

GROUND IVY: *Nepeta glechoma (Labiatae)* Leaves & Flowering Herb. Cep., Diu., Pec., Sti., Ton. Gillrun, Hedge Maids, Robin Run Away, Alehoop, Cat's Foot, Gill-go-over- the-ground.

GUARANA: *Paullinia sorbilis. (Sapindaceae)* Extract. Ast., Sti. In Sick Headache.

GUM ARABIC: *Acacia vera (Mimosaceae)* Egyptian Thorn. Cape Gum.

HAWTHORN: *Crataegus oxyacanthus (Rosaceae)* Fruit. Ast., Cardiac Sed. English Hawthorne, Quickset, Thorn Apple Tree, May Apple, Haws.

HENNA: *Lawsonia inermis (Lythraceae)* Root. Ast. Juice. Powder. Dye. Alcanna. Egyptian Privet.

HIBISCUS: *Hibiscus rosa-sinensis (Malvaceae)* Flowers. Ast., Ton. Flower of the Hour, Venice Mallow.

HICKORY: *Carya alba (Juglandaceae)* Bark. Cat., Acr. Shagbark. Ackroot.

HOLLYHOCK: *Althaea rosea (Malvaceae)* Flowers. Dem., Diu., Emo. Althae Rose, Large Malva Flower.

HOPS: *Humulus lupulus (Moraceae)* Flowers. Bit., Ner., Ton., Ano., Hyp., Diu., Feb.

HOREHOUND: *Marrubium vulgare (Labiatae)* Herb. Bit., Aro., Ton., Exp., Dia., Pec. White Hoarhound.

HORSEMINT: *Monarda punctata (Labiatae)* Herb. Sti., Car., Sud., Diu., Emm., Origanum. American Horsemint:

HORSERADISH: *Cochlearia armoracia (Cruciferae)* Root. Sti., Ton., Diu., Abo.

HORSETAIL: *Equisetum hyemale (Equisetaceae)* Plant. Diu., Ast., Ton. Horsepipe, Shave Grass, Polishing Rush, Pewter Wort, Horsetail.

HUCKLEBERRY:: *Vaccinium myrtillus (Vacciniaceae)* Fruit. Es., A-sco., A-sep. Whorleberry, Whinberry, Wineberry, Dyeberry, Bilberry, Hockelberry.

HYSSOP: *Hyssopus officinalis (Labiatae)* Herb. Aro., Sti., Sud., Pec.

IRISH MOSS: *(Chondrus crispus) (Gigartinales)* Plant. Nut., Muc., Dem., Pec., Carrageen. Pearl Moss.

JUNIPER: *Juniperus communis (Pinaceae)* Bark & Leaves: Aro. Berries: Diu. Juniper Berries, Bush and Bark.

KELP (ATLANTIC): *Laminaria saccharina.* Plant. Sac., Ed., Sal. Devil's Apron.

KELP (PACIFIC): *Fucus versiculosus.* Used in obesity. Sea Wrack, Bladder Fucus, Seaweed, Sea Oak, Bladderwrack, Kelp (the weed burned in air), Kelpware, Black Tany.

LABRADOR: *Ledum latifolium. (Ericaceae)* Leaves. Pec., Ton., As Tea. Continental Tea.

LADIES' MANTLE: *Alchemilla vulgaris (Rosaceae)* Plant. Ast. in hemorrhage.

LADIES' SLIPPER: *Cypripedium pubescens (Orchidaceae)* Root. Ton., Sti., Ner., Dia., Aspa., Nar. Indian Shoe, Slipper Root, Venus Cup, American Valerian, Nerve Root, Umble, Moccae Plant, Male Nervine, Yellow Moccasin Flower, Umbil Root, Monkey Flower, Noah's Ark, Venus Shoe, Bleeding Heart, Yellows, Aphrodite's Shoe.

LAMBS' QUARTERS:: *Chenopodium album (Chenopodiaceae)* Leaves. A-sco.

LAVENDER: *Lavandula vera (Labiatae)* Plant: Fra., Aro., Sti. Oil: Fra., Per. Garden, Spike, or Common Lavender, Lavers.

LEEK: *Allium porrum (Ciliaceae)* Bulb & Leaves. Ant., Diu., Emo., Mat., Sti. Leek.

LEMON: *Citrus limonum (Rutaceae)* Fruit. Aci., Ast., A-sco., Ref. Peel, Oil of Lemon, Rind.

LEMON BALM: *Melissa officinalis (Labiatae)* Herb & Flower. Aro., Cep., Dia., Emm. Blue Balm, Sweet Balm, Citronelle, Cure All, Bee Balm Dropsy Plants, Balm Min.

LEMON GRASS: *Andropogon citratum.* Oil: Per.,

Fra., Aro., Sti. Leaf: Ton., Sti. Verbena Grass.

LEMON PEEL: *Citrus limonum (Rutaceae)* Fruit: Aci., Ref., A-sco. Peel: Oil of Lemon.

LENTILS: *Ervum lens (Papilionaceae)* Seed. Adi., Ast., Nut. Till Seed.

LETTUCE: *Lactuca sativa (Compositae)* Leaves: Sed. Juice: Ano., Hyp. Common Garden Lettuce.

LICORICE: *Glycyrrhiza glabra (Papilionaceae)* Root & Extract. Dem., Pec., Sac. Sweet Wood, Liquorice, Italian Juice Root, Sweet Liquorice, Spanish Juice Root, Common Licorice Root.

LIFE EVERLASTING: *Antennaria margaritacum (Compositae)* Plant. Ast., Dia., Pec., Feb. Pearl Everlasting, Cud Weed, Cotton Weed, Silver Leaf.

LINDEN: *Tilia americana (Tiliaceae)* Bark. Emo., Muc., Vul. Flower. Cep., Sti.

LOBELIA: *Lobelia inflata (Lobeliaceae)* Plant. Eme., Exp., Nev., Dia., Diu., A-spa. Wild Tobacco, Emetic Weed, Eyebright, Poke-weed, Asthma Weed, Gag Root, Vomit Wort.

MACE: *Myristica moschata (Myristicaceae)* Kernels of Fruit. Aro., Sti., Sto., Con.

MAIDENHAIR: *Adiantum pedatum (Polypodiaceae)* Plant. Exp., Ref., Muc.,Ton. Five Finger Fern, Maiden Fern, Rock Fern.

MANDRAKE: *Podophyllum peltatum (Berberidaceae)* Root. Alt., Cat., Dia., Eme., Emm., Res., Ver. May Apple, Hog Apple, Indiana Apple, Raccoonberry, Wild Lemon, American Mandrake, Yellow Berry, Duck's Foot, Ground Lemon.

MANZANITA: *Arctostaphylos glauca (Ericaceae)* Leaves. Ast., A-syp. California Manzanita, Red Bark, Scrub Weed.

MARIGOLD: *Calendula officinalis (Compositae)* Flowers and leaves. Vul, Dis., Stil. Calendula. Marybud.

MARIJUANA: *Cannabis indica & sativa (Cannabinaceae)* Leaf. Ano., Ton., A-spa., A-syp., Ano., Ner., Sud. Hemp, Bhang, Gunjah, Charas, Indian Hemp, Hempweed.

MARJORAM: *Origanum majorana (Labiatae)* Plant. Aro., Cep., Con., Emm., Ton. Sweet Marjoram, Knotted Majoram, Joy of the Mountain.

MARSH MALLOW: *Althaea officinalis (Malvaceae)* Root and Leaves. Muc., Dem., Diu. Althaea, Mortification Root. Sweat Weed.

MASTERWORT: *Heracleum lanatum (Umbelliferae)* Root and Seed. Sti., Car., Nar., A-spa.

MEXICAN DAMIANA: *Turnera aphrodisiaca (Turneraceae)* Leaves. Lax., Sti., Ton. Damiana.

MINT: *Mentha crispa (Labiatae)* Leaves. Aro., Car., Sti., Sto. Garden Mint, Common Curled Mint.

MISTLETOE: *Viscum flavescens (Loranthaceae)* Leaves. A-spa., Eme., Nar., Ner. Birdlime, Mistletoe, Golden Bough.

MOTHERWORT: *Leonrus cardiaca (Labiatae)* Lion's Ear, Throwwort.

MUGWORT: *Artemisia vulgaris* or *japonica (Compositae)* Herb. A-epi., Emm. Felon Herb, Moxa.

MULLEIN: *Verbascum thapsus (Scrophulariaceae)* Plant. Diu., Dem., Ano., A-spa., Vul. White Mullein, Verbasum Flowers, Woolen Blanket Herb, Flannel Flower, Cow's Lure, Vet Leaf, Bullock's Lungwort, Shepherd's Club, Hare's Beard, Hig Taper.

MUSTARD: (BLACK & YELLOW) *Sinapis nigra & alba (Cruciferae)* Seed. Acr., Con., Lax., Pun., Sti. Nigra: Black or Red Mustard. Alba: Yellow or White Mustard. Kedlock.

MYRRH: *Myrospermum pubescens (Umbelliferae)* Seed. Aro., Sti.

NASTURTIUM: *Tropaeolum majus (Tropaeolaceae)* Leaf. Flower. Seed. Juice used in itch. A-sep., A-aco., Exp., Sad. Indian Cress.

NETTLE: *Urtica capitata* or *dioica (Urticaceae)* Plant. Diu., Ast., Ton., Pec. Great Nettle, Stinging Nettle, Common Nettle.

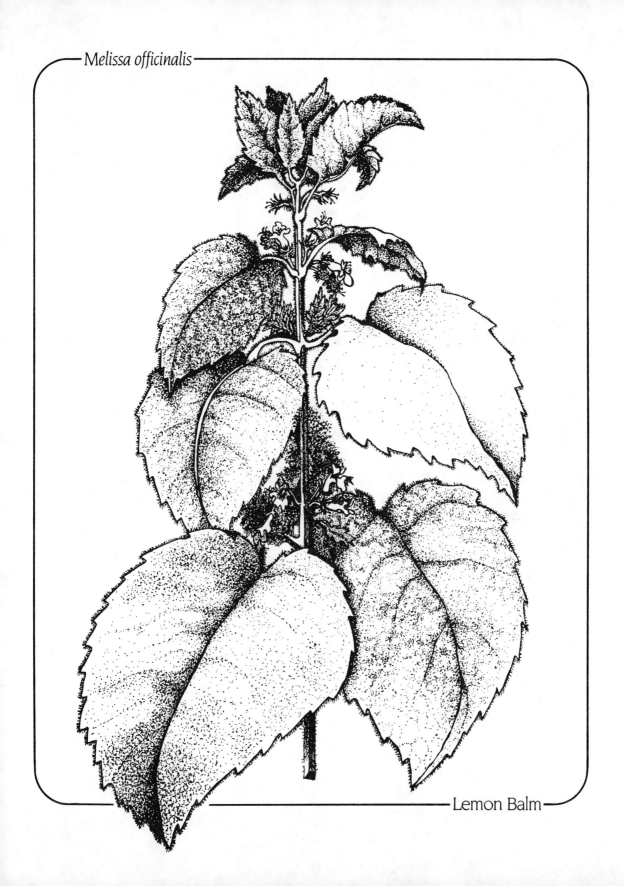

Melissa officinalis

Lemon Balm

NUTMEG: *Myristica moschata. (Myristicaceae)* Kernels of fruit. Aro., Sti., Sto., Con., Mace.

OAT: *Avena sativa* Grain & Straw. A-spa., Ner., Sti. Oatstraw, Wild Oats.

OATSTRAW: *Avena sativa (Gramineae)* Groats.

OAK: *Quercus alba (Fagaceae)* Bark. Ast., Ton., A-sep. White Oak.

OKRA: *Abelmoschus esculentus.* Pods (or Capsules). Dem., Edi., Muc., Sal. Ochra, Bendee, Combo Leaves, Amber Seed.

OLIVE: *Olea europaea (Oleaceae)* Bark & Leaves: Feb. Fruit: Yields Olive Oil. Dem., Nut., Ton.

ONION: *Allium cepa (Liliaceae)* Bulb. Ant., A-sep., A-spa., Car., Diu., Exp., Sto., Ton. Cepa. Common Onion, Pentateuch.

ORANGE: *Citrus aurantium (Rutaceae)* Fruit: Edi., Nut., Rep. Flowers: Fra., Per. Common Sweet Orange, Sweet Orange, Forbidden Fruit, Golden Apple.

OREGANO: *Origanum vulgare (Labiatae)* Herb. Aro., Emm., Pun., Sti., Ton. Origanum, Winter Marjoram, Winter Sweet, Mountain Mint.

PARSLEY: *Petroselinum sativum (Umbelliferae)* Root: Ape., Diu., Nep., Seed: Feb. Juice: A-per. Garden Parsley, Parsley Breakstone, Rock Parsley, March.

PASSION FLOWER: *Passiflora coerulea (Passifloraceae)* Plant & Flowers. Diu. Orn.

PEACH: *Amygdalus persica (Rosaceae)* Leaves. Sed., Bit., Aro., Lax., Poi.

PENNYROYAL: (American) *Hedeoma pulegioides (Labiatae)* Herb. Sti., Dia., Emm., Cer., Sud. Squaw Mint, Thickweed, Hedeoma, Stinking Balm, American Pennyroyal, Tickweed.

PEPPER (WHITE): *Piper album.* Black pepper deprived of its husk or skin.

PEPPERMINT: *Mentha piperita (Labiatae)* Herb: Aro., A-spa., Emm. Oil: Sti., Emm.

PERIWINKLE: *Vinca minor* or *Vinca major (Apocynaceae)* V. minor: Plant. Ast., Bit., Ton.

V. major: Plant. Ast., Dis., Ton. Small periwinkle.

PIPSISSEWA: *Chimaphila umbellata (Heath)* Plant. Alt., Ast., Dia., Diu., Ton. Princes Pine, Rheumatism Weed, King's Cure, Ground Holly, Noble Pine, Pine Tulip.

PLANTAIN: *Plantago lanceolata (Plantaginaceae)* Plant. Alt., Ast., Dem., Exp., Vul. Indian Buckwheat, Buckhorn, Headsman, Ribgrass, Ribwort, Ripplegrass, Snake Plantain, Solder's Herb.

POKE ROOT: *Phytolacca decandra (Phytolaccaceae)* Root. Alt., A-sco., A-syp., Dep., D., Res. Red Ink Plant (the berries), Red Weed, Ink Berry, Pigeon Berry, Garget, Coakum Scoke, Virginia Poke, American Nightshade, Cancer Jalap.

POPPY: *Papaver somniferum (Papaveraceae)* Seed. Bud. Yields Opium. Nar., Ano., Sti., Hyp.

PSYLLIUM: *Plantago psyllium (Plantaginaceae)* Seed. Dem., Det., Muc., Pur. Branching Plantain, Fleawort, Flea Seed.

QUASSIA: *Simarouba excelsa (Simarubnaceae)* Wood. A Bitter Tonic. Feb. Bitterwood, Lofty Quassia, Bitter Ash.

QUEEN OF THE MEADOW: *Spirea ulmaria* or *Eupatorium purpureum (Corymbiferae)* Leaves: Ast., Div. Flowers: A-spa. Gravel Root, Joe-Pye Weed, Kidney Root, Purple Boneset, Trumpet Weed.

RADISH: *Raphanus sativus (Cruciferae)* Root. A-spa., Cho., Diu. Common Radish, Garden Radish, Red Root.

RASPBERRY: *Rubus idaeus (Rosaceae)* Leaves: Ast., Eme., Par., Sti., Ton. Fruit: Esc., Lax., Ton. Hind Berry, Garden Berry, Wild Red or American Raspberry.

RED CLOVER: *Trifolium pratense (Leguminosae)* Flower. Dep., Det. Purple Clover, Trefoil, Cleaver Grass, Cow Grass, Marl Grass.

REST HARROW: *Ononis spinosa (Papilionaceae)* Root. Diu., Det., Ape. Cammock, Pretty Whin.

RHUBARB: *Rheum palmatum* or *Theum hybridum* (*Polygonaceae*) R. *palmatum*: Root. R. hybridum: Stalk. Ast., Lax. As appetizer: Pur., Ton. Garden Rhubarb, Pie Plant, Turkey Rhubarb, Chica Rhubarb.

ROSEBUDS: *Rosa canina* (*Rosaceae*) Fruit used in conserve. Ton. Hip Rose, Brier Rose, Wild Brier, Hip Tree, Hip Seed, Dog Rose.

ROSEMARY: *Rosmarinus officinalis* (*Labiatae*) Leaves & Flowers: Aro., Bit., Emm., Cep., Sti. Garden Rosemary, Rosemary Plant, Ros Marinus (Dew of the Sea).

RUE: *Ruta graveolens* (*Rutaceae*) Herb. Act., Aro., Bit., Emm., Pun., Ton. Garden Rue, Herb of Grace, Rue, Common Rue.

SAFFLOWER: *Carthamus tinctorius* (*Compositae*) Flower: Dia., Diu., Sud. Seed: Aro., Cat., Div. Dyer's Saffron.

SAFFRON (Spanish): *Crocus sativus* (*Iradaceae*) Flowers. Car., Dia., Exa., Emm. Cake Saffron, Spanish Saffron, Autumnal Crocus, Hay Saffron.

SAGE: *Salvia officinalis* (*Labiatae*) Leaves. A-aph., Aro., Ast., Exp., Ton., Sud. Garden or Wild Sage.

ST. BENEDICT THISTLE: *Cnicus benedictus* (*Compositae*) Herb. Dia., Diu., Eme., Ton. Blessed Thistle, Spotted Thistle, Cardin, Holy Thistle.

SAINT JOHNS' BREAD: *Ceratonia siliqua* (*caesalpiniaceae*) Powder. Sac., Edi., Nut., Cat. Algaroba Bean. Carob Tree. Honey Bread.

ST. JOHN'S WORT: *Hypericum perforatum* (*Hypericaceae*) Herb. A-spa., Ast., Exp., Ner., Vul. Amber, Goatweed, Klamath Weed, Tipton Weed.

SALEP: *Orchis mascula* (*Orchidaicea*) Root. Yields Salep.

SANDALWOOD: *Santalum album* (*Santalaceae*) Wood. Fragrant. Per., Sti., Sud. White Sandal Wood, White Saunders.

SANICLE: *Sanicula marilandica* (*Umbelliferae*) Root. Ner., Ano., A-per., Ast. Black Sanicle, Black Snakeroot.

SARSAPARILLA: *Smilax officinalis* (*Araliaceae*) Root. Alt., A-syp., Dem., Diu. Red Sarsparilla, Small Spikenard, Spignet, Quay, Quill, Jamaica, Honduras or Guayaquil Sarsparilla.

SASSAFRAS: *Sassafras officinale* (*Lauraceae*) Bark. Alt., Aro., Dia., Diu., Sti. Saxifrax, Saloop, Ague Tree, Cinnamon Wood.

SAVORY: *Satureja hortensis* (*Labiatae*) Herb. Aph., Aro., Car., Con., Emm., Sti. Summer Savory.

SCOTCH BROOM: *Cytisus scoparius* (*Papilionaceae*) Tops: Diu., Cat. Seeds: Eme., Cat. Common Broom, Irish Broom, Broom Flowers.

SCULLCAP: *Scutellaria lateriflora* (*Labiatae*) Plant. A-spa., Diu., Ner., Ton. Blue Scullcap, Mad Dog Weed, Hoodwort, Hooded Willow Herb, Side Flowering Scull Cap, Blue Pimpernel, Mad Weed, Helmut Flower, American Scull Cap.

SENNA: *Cassia autifolia* (*Caesalpiniaceae*) Leaves. A valuable cathartic.

SHEEP SORREL: *Rumex acetosella* (*Polygonaceae*) Leaves. Aci., Ref., Diu., A-Sco. Root. Ast. Common Sorrel, Garden Sorrel.

SHEPHERD'S PURSE: *Capsella bursa pastoris* (*Cruciferae*) Herb. Acr., Ast., Det. Mother's Heart, Picklooker, Shepherd's Sprout, Case Wort, Cocowort, Pick Purse, Toywort, Poor Man's Pharmacetly, St. James Weed.

SLIPPERY ELM: *Ulmus fulva* (*Elm*) Bark. Dem., Diu., Emo., Exp., Lem., Muc., Nut. Red Elm, Indian Elm, Sweet Elm, American Elm, British Tea (the leaves), Slipweed.

SNAKE ROOT: *Polygala senega* (*Polygalaceae*) Root. Dia., Diu., Emm., Exp., Sia., Sti. Senega Snake Root, Senega, Seneca or Neka Root, Snake Root, Milkwort, Mountain Flax.

SOAP BARK: *Quillaya saponaria* (*Rosaceae*) Bark. Sap., Feb. In Coryza, Soap Tree Bark, Quillai Bark, China Bark.

SOAPWORT: *Saponaria officinalis* (*Caryophyl-*

Rhus toxicodendron

Poison Oak

laceae) Plant. Rootstock. Cho., Ton, Alt., Dia., Exp., Pur. Dog, Cloves, Bruisewort, Soaproot.

SORREL: *Rumex acetosella* or *acetosa*. Leaves: Aci., A-spa., Diu., Ref. Root: Ast. Common Sorrel, Field Sorrel, Red Top Sorrel.

SPEARMINT: *Mentha viridis*. Herb: Aro., A-spa., Car., Diu., Sti. Oil: Sti.

SPIKENARD: *Aralia racemosa (Araliaceae)* Bark. Root. Bal., Alt., Dia. Indiana or American Spikenard, Pretty Morrel, Like of Man, Spignet, Old Man's Root.

STAR ANISE: *Illicum anisatum (Magnoliaceae)* Seeds. Car., Sti., Sto., Aro.

STRAWBERRY: *Fragaria vesca (Rosaceae)* Leaves: Ast., Diu., Ton., Ref. Fruit: Diu. Mountain Strawberry, Pine Apple Strawberry, Wild Strawberries, Red Pops.

SUNFLOWER: *Helianthus annuus (Compositae)* Leaves & Seeds: Diu., Exp., Pec. Garden Sunflower, Sunflower, Comb Flower, Wild Flower, English Moxa (the pith prepared.)

SYCAMORE MAPLE: *Acer pseudo-platanus (Aceraceae)* Bark. Ast., Vul.

TANSY: *Tanacetum vulgare (Compositae)* Herb. Aro., Dia., Emm., Ton., Vul., Ver. Hindheel, Double Tansy, Flowered Tansy.

TARRAGON: *Artemisia dracunculus (Compositae)* Leaf & Oil: Used as a condiment in foods. Variety of artemisia absinthium.

THYME: *Thymus vulgaris (Labiatae)* Herb. A-spa., Car., Emm., Res., Ton. Garden or Common Thyme, Mother of Thyme, Serpyllum.

UVA URSI: *Arctostaphylos uva ursi (Ericaceae)* Leaves. Ast., Diu., Nep., Ton. Wild or Mountain Cranberry, Bearberry, Bear's Grape, Upland Cranberry, Universe Mountain Box, Kinnikinnick, Meal Berry, Sagackhomi, Rapper Dandies (the fruit.)

VALERIAN: *Valeriana officinalis (Valerianaceae)* Root. Ano., Aro., A- sap., Ner., Sti., Ton. Great Wild Valerian; English, German, Vermont, or American Valerian; Capon's Tail.

VERVAIN: *Verbena officinalis (Verbenaceae)* Plant. Eme., Feb., Rub., Vul. European Vervain, Enchanter's Herb, Pigeon Grass, Holy Herb, Juno's Tears, Weed Vervain (analogous to verbena hastata.)

VIOLET: *Viola tricolor (Violaceae)* Plant. Dis., Lax., Muc., Pec., Vul. Heartsease, Johnny Jumper, Garden Violet, Pansy.

WALNUT: *Juglans nigra (Juglanaceae)* Bark: Ast. Juice: Her. Fruit Rind: A-syp. Oil: A-syp. Black Walnut, English Walnut, European Walnut, Rigia, Jupiter's Nuts, Maderia Nut, French Nut or Walnut.

WATERCRESS: *Nasturtium officinale (Cruciferae)* Plant. A-sco., Dep., Diu., Emm., Exp., Sad., Sti., Sto. Scurvy Grass, Tall Water Nasturtium.

WHITE OAK: *Quercus alba (Fagaceae)* Quercus: Acorn-fruit of oak, Acorn coffee. Bark: A-sep., Ast., Ton. Nuts: Roasted. Tanner's Bark.

WHITE PINE: *Pinus palustris (Pinaceae)* Yields from gum, turpentine & tar, thus resin & pitch.

WHITE POPLAR: *Populus tremuloides (Salicaceae)* Bark. A-per., Feb., Sto., Ton. American Poplar or Aspen, Quiver Leaf, Aspen, Quaking Aspen, Trembling Tree, Poplar, Aspen Poplar, Abele Tree.

WHITE WILLOW: *Salix alba (Salicaceae)* Bark: A-per., Bit., Feb. Leaves: Ast. Willow, Willow Bark, Salacin Willow, Withe, Withy.

WILD CHERRY: *Prunus virginiana (Rosaceae)* Bark. Bit., Ton., Sti., Sed., Pec., Poi. Wild Black Cherry, Black Cherry, Black Choke, Rum or Cabinet Cherry, Choke Cherry.

WILD LETTUCE: *Lactuca elongata*. Leaf & Juice: Ano., Diu., Hyp., Nar., Sed. Wild Onion Lettuce, Snake Weed or Bite, Trumpet Weed, Wild Opium Lettuce.

WILD YAM: *Dioscorea villosa (Dioscoreaceae)* Root. A-spa., Dia. Colic Root, China

Root, Rheumatism Root, Devil's Bones, Yam.

WITCH HAZEL: *Hamamelis virginica (Hamamelidaceae)* Bark & Leaf. A-phi., Ast., Com., Ton. Spotted or Striped Alder, Snapping Hazel Nut, Winter Bloom, Tobacco Wood.

WINTERGREEN: *Gaultheria procumbens (Ericaceae)* Leaves. Aro., Ast., Diu., Sti. Canada Tea, Tea, Box, Orpartridge Berry, Mountain or Redberry Tea, Hillberry or Ground Berry, Ivory Plum, Red Pollom, Checker or Chicker Berry, Wax Cluster Berry, Spring Wintergreen.

WOOD BETONY: *Pedicularis canadensis (Labiatae)* Plant, Ton., Sed., Ast. Eme. Wood Betony, Betony Lousewort, Red Rattle.

WOODRUFF: *Asperula odorata (Rubiaceae)* Leaf. Diu., Ton. Wood Root.

WORMWOOD: *Artemisia absinthium (Compositae)* Plant. Ant., Aro., A-sep., Bit., Feb., Ton. Absinthium.

WOUNDWORT: *Prunella vulgaris (Labiatae)* Herb. A-spa., Ast., Bit., Ton., Diu., Sty., Ver., Vul. All Heal, Selfheal, Blue Curls, Carpenter's Herb, Sicklewort.

YARROW: *Achillea millefolium (Compositae)* Plant. Alt., Ast., Diu., Ton., Vul. Milfoil, Noble Yarrow, Ladies' Mantle, Nosebleed, Thousand Leaf, Millfolium.

YELLOW DOCK: *Rumex crispus (Polygonaceae)* Root. Alt., A-sco., Ast., Dep., Ton. Sour Dock, Narrow Dock, Curled Dock, Rumex, Garden Patience.

YERBA BUENA: *Micromeria donglassii* or *chamissonis (Labiatae)* Leaves. A-feb., Car., Ton. Good Herb, Redwood Mint.

YERBA SANTA: *Eriodyction glutinosum californicum (Hydrophyllaceae)* Used to allay thirst. Exp., Ton. Mountain Balm, Bear's Weed, Tar Weed, Gum Bush, Consumptive Weed.

Yerba Mansa

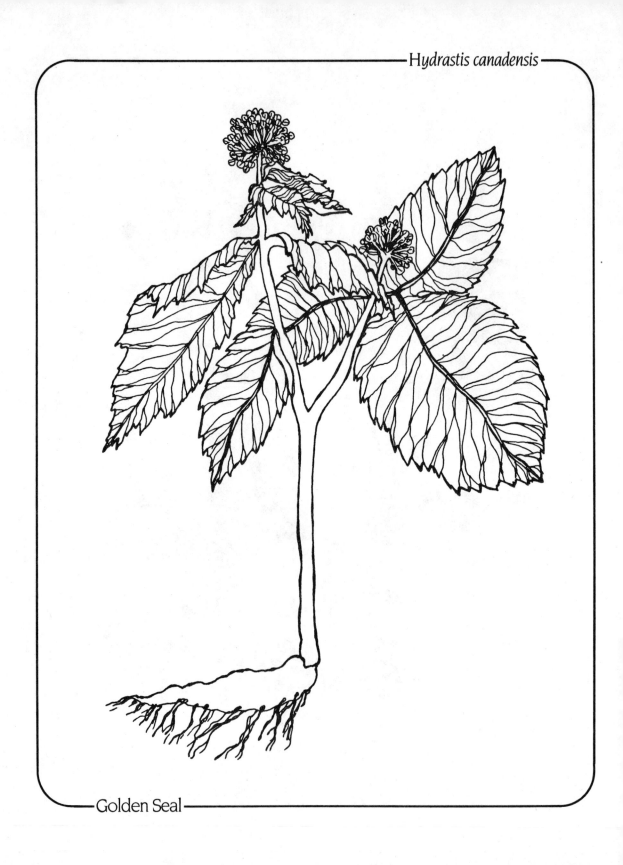

Golden Seal

Bibliography

Coleman, Bonnie. *A Background Gourmet Garden*. Auberry: Homestead Press, 1974.

Culpeper, Nicholas. *Culpeper's Complete Herbal*. London: Wehman Bros.

Gibbons, Euell. *Stalking the Good Life*. New York: David McKay Company, Inc., 1971. *Stalking The Healthful Herbs*. New York: David McKay Company, Inc., 1966. *Stalking the Wild Asparagus*. New York: David McKay Company, Inc., 1962.

Hutchens, Alma R. *Indian Herbology of North America*. India: The Homoeopathy Press, 1969.

Hurd, Frank J. and Rosalie. *Ten Talents*. Tennessee: The College Press, 1968.

Grieve, Maud. *A Modern Herbal*. Third Printing. New York & London: Hafner Publishing Co., 1967.

Kirk, Donald. *Wild Edible Plants of the Western United States*. Healdsburg, California: Naturegraph Publishers, 1970.

Kloss, Jethro A. *Back To Eden*. New York: Beneficial Books, Benedict Lust Publications, 1971.

Kulvinskas, Viktoras. *Survival Into the 21st Century*. Connecticut: Omangod Press, 1975.

Lappe, Frances Moore. *Diet for a Small Planet*. New York: Ballantine Books, Inc., 1971.

Meyer, Joseph E. *The Herbalist*. Revised & Enlarged Edition by Clarence Meyer. No Publisher. 1960.

Muenscher, Walter Conrad. *Poisonous Plants of the United States*. New York: Collier Books, 1975.

Munz, Philip A. *A California Flora*. Fourth Edition. Berkeley, California: University of California Press, 1968.

Olsen, Larry Dean. *Outdoor Survival Skills*. Utah: Brigham Young University Press, 1967.

Rose, Jeanne. *Herbs & Things: Jeanne Rose's Herbal*. New York: Grosset & Dunlap, 1972.

Watt, Bernice K. and Merrill, Annabel L. *Composition of Foods. Agricultural Handbook No. 8*. Washington, D.C.: United States Department of Agriculture, 1963.

Index

Abelmoschus esculentus. See Okra
Abies canadensis. See Pine pitch
Abies nigra, 37
Acacia vera (Gum arabic), 183
Acer pseudo-platanus (Sycamore maple), 191
Acetylsalicylic acid, 4
Aches, chamomile for, 58
Achillea millefolium. See Yarrow
Aconus calamus (Calamus), 178
Adder's tongue, 5
Adiantum pedatum. See Maidenhair
Agar-agar *(Gracilaria lichenoides),* 35, 175; in recipes, 38, 126, 1
Agaricus sp., *130*
Agaricus bisporus, 129, 131
Agaricus campestris, 129, 131-32
Agrimony *(Agrimonia eupatoria),* 4, 55, 175
Air freshener, goldenrod as, 64
Alchemilla vulgaris (Ladies mantle), 183
Alchemists, cooks as, 94, 120
Alcohol, in extracts and tinctures, 156-57
Alcoholism, 72
Al dente, 76
Alder *(Alnus glutinosa),* 55, 175
Alfalfa *(Medicago sativa)* 8, 9, 10, 29, 175; in Green Drink, 42; juniper berries with, 64; kelp and, 78; sprouts, 29; tea, 29
Alkanet, 13
Allantoin, in comfrey, 32
Allergies, capsicum for, 86
Allium cepa. See Onion
Allium porrum. See Leek
Allium sativum. See Garlic
Allspice *(Eugenia pimenta),* 175

Almonds *(Prunus amygdalus; Amygalus dulcis),* 55, 117, 175
Almond butter, 117
Almond milk, 55
Almond oil, in massage cream, 154
Alnus glutinosa (Alder), 55, 175
Aloe *(Aloe vera),* 55, 175
Althaea rosea (Hollyhock), *181,* 183
Althaea officinalis (Marsh mallow), 184
Althea *(Althea officinalis),* 175
Altitude sickness, hawthorn for, 64
Alum *(Heuchera americana),* *54,* 55, 175
Amaranth *(Amaranthus hypochondriacus),* 55, 56, 175
Amatin, 157
American mandrake. *See* Mandrake
American scullcap. *See* Scullcap
Amygalus dulcis. See Almond
Andropogon citratum (Lemon grass), 183-84
Anethum graveolens (Dill), 13, 179
Angelica *(Angelica officinalis),* 175; as poison antidote, 26, 63; as tea, 63
Angostura Bitters, 154
Anise *(Pimpinella anisum),* 13, 18, 72, 175; in tonics, 158
Antennaria margaritacum. See Life everlasting
Anthriscus cerefolium Chervil), 178
Antibacterial, honey as, 36
Antidotes, for plant poisoning, 26
Antiviral, capsicum as, 86, 87
Ant repellant, tansy as, 72
Apium graveolens (Celery), 178
Appetite, increasing, 58, 64, 65, 158
Apple(s): cider, 144, 147; drying, 23; vinegar, 147
Apple Mint Pie, 126

Apricot Banana Curry, 113
Apricots, crying, 23
Aralia racemosa. See Spikenard
Arctostaphylos glauca. See Manzanita
Arctostaphylos uva-ursi. See Bearberry
Arnica montana, 55, 175
Arnica Salve, 55
Arrow root *(Maranta arundinacea),* 175
Artemisia absinthum. See Wormwood
Artemisia dracunculus (Tarragon), 191
Artemisia vulgaris; A. japonica. See Mugwort
Arthritis, 58, 144. *See also* Joints, herbs for
Articum lappa. See Burdock
Asarum canadense. See Ginger root
Asparagus Pie, 124-25
Asperula odorata. See Woodruff
Aspirin, 4
Assyrian midwives, 106
Asthma, sage for, 71
Astringents: alum, 55; amaranth, 55; redwood, 71
Atrope belladonna. See Belladonna
Aura, gathering herbs and, 18
Autumn crocus, 2
Avena sativa. See Oats
Avocadoes, in Guacamole, 93

Balm, Denni McCarthy, 151
Balm of Gilead *(Populus candicans),* 175
Balmony *(Chelone glabra),* 175-76
Balms. *See* Salves
Balsam of fir, in liniment, 150
Bamboo shoots, 125
Barberry *(Berberis vulgaris),* 55, 176
Barks, gathering, 17

Barley: cooking, 104; peas and, 4
Barley Burger, Herbal, 96, 107
Barley Root Soup, 79
Barley Soup, Scotch, 77
Barm, 142
Barosma crenata (Buchu), 176
Basil (*Ocimum basilicum*), 13, 99, 176
Baths: foot, 55, 86–87; herbal tea, 51; noble pine, 65; nettles for, 52
Bayberry (*Myrica cerifera*), 176
Bay laurel (*Laurus nobilis*), 21, 55, 176
Bay leaf. *See* Bay laurel
Beans, 25, 113, 115–16; cooking, 113, 115; Indian Garbanzos, 116; leftover, over rice, 106-7; in salad, 113; Soy, 115-16; storing, 23
Bearberry (*Arctostaphylos uva-ursi*) 55, 176
Bee balm (*Monarda*), 55, 57, 58
Bee Pollen and Wheat Grass Juice, 36
Beer, 142; essence of spruce in, 37; hawthorn, 64; hops, 142; hops infusion vs., 64
Beeswax: in liniments, 150, 151; in massage cream, 154; in salves, 153-54
Beet Soup with Yogurt, 77-78
Beets, drying, 23
Belladonna (*Atrope belladonna*), as poison, 26, 55; for salves, 153
Benzoin (*Styrax benzoin*), 176
Berberis vulgaris (Barberry), 55, 176
Bergamot mint, lamb and, 140
Berries, drying, 23
Berry Wine, 147
Beth root (*Trillium pendulum*), 176
Betony, in smoking mix, 61 *See also* Wood betony
Beverages: Bee Pollen and Wheat Grass Juice, 36; fermented; *see* Brews; Milk, fermented; of Pythagoras, 4; sassafras as flavoring for, 71; Vodfrey, 35; Wild Green Drink, 42-43. *See also* Coffee; Teas
Bistort (*Polygonum bistorta*), 176
Bites, 72; poisonous, 58. *See also* Stings
Bitters, Angostura, 154
Bittersweet (*Solanum dulcamara*), 176
Bitter tonic, wormwood as, 72
Blackberries (*Rubus villosus*), 58, 72, 176; drying, 23
Black cohosh (*Cimicifuga racemosa*), 58, 176
Black haw (*Viburnum prunifolium*), 176
Black mustard. *See* Mustard
Bladder upsets, club moss for, 61
Bladderwrack (*Fucus versiculosus*), 176
Blanching, for nuts, 117
Bleeding: after childbirth, 106; stopping, 71, 134. *See also* Hemorrhages

Blessed thistle (*Centaurea benedicta*), 58, 68, 176
Blisters, 4, 36
Blood, sassafrass for, 71
Blood Beer, 141-42
Blood cleanser, red clover as, 71
Blood disorders, plasters for, 151
Blood purifiers: arnica, 55; burdock, 58; golden seal, 64; hyssop, 64; mustard, 38; quick grass, 68; spikenard, 71; woodruff, 72
Blood rejuvenator, burnet as, 58
Bloodroot (*Sanguinaria canadensis*), 58, 176
Blueberry (*Vaccinium frondosum*), 176
Blue cohosh (*Caulophyllum thalictroides*), 176
Blues, wintertime, hyssop for, 64
Body powder, polypody for, 68
Boils, slippery elm for, 71
Boletus sp., 132, *133*
Boneset (*Eupatorium perfoliatnum*), 176. *See also* Borage; Comfrey
Borage (*Borago officinalis*), 5, 13, *155*, 176; tea, 58
Boraginaceae, 13
Borago officinalis. See Borage
Borsch, 77-78
Boswellia serrata (Frankincense), 18, 179
Bowel disorders, slippery elm for, 71
Bowel worms, 72
Botanical list of plants, 175-92
Bracken fern, toxicity of, 26
Brake rock fern. *See* Polypody
Brazil nuts, 117
Breads, 119-24; amaranth in, 55; basic recipe, 120, 122; buried, 123-24; Dog, 124; Earth, 124; honey, 36; Indian Buckwheat, 43; Indian Cattail Cakes, 125; kneading, 119, 120, 122; lamb's quarters seeds on, 65; Pita, 122; Sourdough, 123; soy-cornmeal, 124
Breath, shortness of, 58, 157
Breath freshener, okra seeds as, 68
Breathing, feverfew for, 61
Brews, 141-48; Beer, 142; Berry Wine, 147; Blood Beer, 141-42; Cider, 144, 147; Dandelion Wine, 147; Herbal, 148; Hippocras, 141, 144; Hops Beer, 142; Hydromel, 141, 143-44; Mead, 141, 143; Methaglin, 141, 143; Raisin Glug, 147-48; Rockin' Mead, 143; Root Beer, 141-42
Bronchitis, capsicum for, 86
Brook Trout, 137-38
Broom, 58. *See also* Scotch broom
Brownies, Carob Nut, 128
Brown Rice, 111; and Herbal Greens, 111

Bruises, 61, 64, 71
Brujo, 4
Brunella, 68. See also *Prunella vulgaris*
Buchu (*Barosma crenata*), 176
Buckthorn (*Rhamnus crocea*), 176
Buckwheat: groats, 104, 106; sprouts, 29. *See also* Indian buckwheat
Bug repellants, 21, 72
Burdock (*Articum lappa*), 58, 176; in coffee, 52; for sluggishness, 71-72; in soup, 79
Burger, Herbal Barley, 107; sauce for, 96
Burnet (*Sanquisorba officinalis*), 58, 176
Burns, remedies for: aloe vera, 55; burdock, 58, clay, 151; elderberry salve, 61; grindelia, 64; slippery elm, 71
Buttercup (*Ranunculus*), 26, 55

Cabbage: fermented, 113; planting, 14
Cakes: Indian Cattail, 125; mustard seed, 38, 125
Calamus (*Acorus calamus*), 178
Calendula (*Calendula officinalis*), 13, 58, 178. *See also* Marigold
Calming herbs. *See* Nervousness; Relaxing herbs
Calvatia sp. (Puffballs), 134
Camphor, in liniment, 151
Cannabis indica; C. sativa. See Marijuana
Cantherellus sp. (Chanterelle), 134
Capsella bursa pastoris. See Shepherd's purse
Capsicum (*Capsicum annuum*), 84, 86-87, *91*
Caraway (*Carum carui*), 13, 178
Cardamom (*Elettaria cardamomum*), 178
Cardrius (Thistle), 166
Carob (*Ceratonia siliqua*), 126, 178; in Teleport Fudge, 126. *See also* St. John's bread
Carob Nut Brownies, 128
Carpenter's herb, 68. *See also Prunella vulgaris*
Carrageen, 38
Carrots, 13; drying, 23; wild, hemlock vs., 26
Carrot Pie, 125
Carthamus tinctorius (Safflower), 188
Carum carui (Caraway), 13, 178
Carver, Jonathan, 107
Carya alba (Hickory), 183
Caryophyllus aromaticus. See Cloves
Cascara bark (*Rhamnus purschiana*), 58, 178
Cascarilla bark (*Croton eluteria*), 178
Cashews, 117
Cassia autifolia (Senna), 188
Castana americana. See Chestnuts

Cathartic, hermodactyl as, 2
Catnip (*Nepeta cataria*), 178
Cattail (*Typha latifolia*), 43, *44*, 125; Cakes, Indian, 125
Caulking, cattail for, 43
Caulophyllum thalictroides (Blue cohosh), 176
Cayenne. *See* Capsicum
Cedar, oil of, in liniment, 150
Celery (*Apium graveolens*), 178
Centaurea benedicta. See Blessed thistle
Centaury herb (*Sabbatia angularis*), 178
Ceratonia siliqua. See Carob; St. John's bread
Chafing, club moss for, 61
Chamomile (*Matricaria chamomilla*), 5, 58, 59, 178; with hops, 64; for morning sickness, 71; in sleep pillow, 65; in smoking mix, 61; tea, 58; with yarrow, 65
Champignons a la Mingus, 132
Chaney, Dr. G. 29
Chanterelle (*Cantherellus* sp.), 134
Chaparral, for herb picker, 18
Chard, in Green Drink, 42
Cheeseweed. *See* Malva
Cheesy Tofu Dressing, 115-16
Chelone glabra (Balmony), 175-76
Chenopodium album. See Lamb's quarters
Cherries: drying, 24; in tonic, 158
Chervil (*Anthriscus cerefolium*), 13, 178
Chestnuts (*Castana americana*), 117, 178
Chewing gum, 37, 68, 154
Chia (*Salvia hispanica*), *177*, 178
Chickweed (*Stellaria media*), 6, 58, 61, 178; in Green Drink, 42
Chicory (*Cichorium intybus*), 13, 31-32, *33*, 68, 178; coffee, 28, 31, 32, 52; flowers, pickled, 32
Children: capsicum for, 86-87; laxative for, 71; nervousness in, 58; stomach ache in, 68
Chilean clover, 29
Chills, St. Hohn's wort for, 71
Chimaphila umbellata. See Pipsissewa
Chlorophyll, 37, 38
Cholorogalum pomeridianum (Soap root), 71, *167*
Chommos, 89
Chondrus crispus (Irish moss), 183
Chrysanthemums, 13
Chutney, Gooseberry, 98
Cichorium intybus. See Chicory
Cider, 144, 147
Cider Vinegar, 147
Cimicifuga racemosa. See Black cohosh
Cinnamon (*Cinnamomum zeylanicum*), 157, 158, 178

Circulation, gentian for, 61
Circulatory disorders, dandelion for, 31
Citric acid, 93
Citrus aurantium. See Orange
Citrus limonum. See Lemon; Lemon peel
Clarified butter, 98
Clay plasters, 151
Cleansing: horsetail for, 64; saps for, 18; wintergreen leaves for, 72. *See also* Skin cleansers
Cleavers (*Galium aparine*), 178
Clove oil, in liniment, 151
Cloves (*Caryophyllus aromaticus*), 178; in tonics, 157, 158
Club moss (*Lycopodium clavatum*), 61, 178
Cnicus benedictus (St. Benedict thistle), 188
Coal oil liniment, 150
Cocculus palmatus (Colombo root), 178
Cochlearia armoracia. See Horseradish
Coffee: dandelion, 28, 31, 52; chicory root, 28, 31, 32, 52; comfrey, 33
Cola nuts (*Cola acuminata*), 178
Colchicum (Meadow-saffron), 2, 26
Cold cream, in salves, 153, 154
Colds, herbs for, 55, 61, 86
Cold Yogurt and Cucumber Soup, 77
Colombo root (*Cocculus palmatus*), 178
Coltsfoot (*Tussilago farfara*), 61, 178
Comfrey (*Symphytum officinale*), 5, 32, 35, *34*, 178; digging, 17; in flu tea, 71; in Green Drink, 42; growing, 32, 35; for morning sickness, 71; in salve, 153; in Vodfrey, 35; in Wild Green Goo, 35
Common sorrel, 61. *See also* Sorrel
Compositae, 13
Composting, 11, 13; comfrey for, 35; urine in, 49
Concentrate, 156
Confections, 149
Congestion, herbs for, 65, 71, 72, 86
Conium maculatum. See Hemlock
Conserve(s), 149; Rose Hip, 42
Cookies: Carob Nut Brownies, 128; Cosmic Honey Bars; Italian Sesame, 125-26; Peanut Butter, 128
Coprinus sp. (Shagymane), 134
Coriander (*Coriandrum sativum*), 4, 13, 178; harvesting, 18
Corn, yellow or white, 104
Cornmeal, 104, 124
Cornsilk (*Zea mays*; *Stigmata maydis*), 178-79
Cornstarch, substitute for, 43
Cosmic Honey Bars, 126
Coughs, herbs for, 61, 71, 72
Cowslip (*Mertensia virginica*), 179
Cradle padding, cattail for, 43

Cramps, herbs for, 58, 68; stomach, 71
Cranberry preserves, 36
Crataegus oxyacanthus (Hawthorn), 183
Cress, 28
Cress, 28
Crisco, for salves, 153
Crocus sativus (Saffron), 188
Croton eluteria (Cascarilla bark); 178
C-R-Star Salve, 153
Cruciferae, 13
Cubeb berries (*Piper cubeba*), 179
Cucumber seeds, in beverage, 4
Cucumber and Yogurt Soup, 77
Cumin (*Cuminum cyminum*), 13, 179
Curried Rice, 112
Curry, 111-13; Apricot Banana, 113; Davood's, 112-13
Curry Powder Mixtures, 112
Cuts, herbs for, 61, 64, 68
Cypripedium pubescens. See Ladies' slipper
Cytisus scoparius. See Scotch broom

Daffodil flowers, 4
Daisy, 13
Damiana (*Turnera aphrodisiaca*), 179, Mexican, 184
Dandelion (*Taraxicum dens-leonis*), 16, 29, 31, 179; coffee, 28, 31, 52; gathering, 17; in Green Drink, 42; salads, 31, 84; for sluggishness, 71-72; sprouts, 29; in Wild Green Goo, 35
Dandelion Wine, 31, 147
Datura stramonium (Jimson weed), *182*
Davood's Curry, *112-13*
Deadly nightshade (*Atrope belladonna*). *See* Belladonna
Debility, herbs for: barberry, 55; blessed thistle, 58; gentian, 61; sarsaparilla, 71
Decoctions, 51
Decongestant, capsicum as, 86. *See also* Congestion
Deer Dew Meadow Salad, 84
Deer Tongue (*Liatrus odoratissima*), 179
Demulcent tea, flaxweed as, 61
Dendrobium, 4
Denni McCarthy Balm, 151
Desert tea, 61
Dew water, 46
Diabetics, almond tea for, 55
Diaper rash, club moss for, 178
Diapers, cattail for, 43
Diarrhea, bloodroot for, 58
Digestion, herbs for, 55, 64, 71
Dill (*Anethum graveolens*), 13, 179
Dilution, 156
Dioscorea villosa (Wild yam), 191
Disinfectant, honey as, 36
Distilled water, 46

Diuretics: nettles, 46; quake grass blend, 68

Dock (*Rumex crispus*), 146; in Green Drink, 42. *See also* Yellow dock

Doctrine of signatures, 4, 5, 7

Dog Bread, 124

Dog grass, 68

Dogwood, Virginia, 72

Dong Kwai. *See* Angelica

Dream pillows, 65

Dressing, Cheesy Tofu, 115-16. *See also* Salad dressings

Dried Scaly Lentinus, 134

Drought, 8, 13

Drying: foods, 21, 23-24; herbs, 18, 20-21

Duck, Roasted Wild, 140

Dulse (*Rhodymenia palmata*), 179. *See also* Seaweeds

Dusty miller, 13

Dyeing: alum for, 55; cornsilk for, 178-79

Dysentery, burdock for, 58

Ear drops, ground ivy for, 64

Ear infections, capsicum for, 86

Earth Bread, 124

"Earth Massage," 154

Earthy Sea Soup, 78

Echinacea (*Echinacea angustifolium*), 179

Eglantine (*Rosa eglantaria*), 42

Elder (*Sambucus nigra*), 179

Elderberry, 26, 61

Elecampane (*Inula helenium*), 60, 61, 68, 179

Elettaria cardamomum (Cardamom), 178

Elm Ointment, 154

Emetic, lobelia as, 65

Emollients: aloe vera, 55; okra, 68; slippery elm, 71

Enema, witch hazel as, 72

Energy, increasing, desert tea for, 61

Ephedra, 61

Ephedrine, 61

Equisetum hyemale. See Horsetail

Ergot, poisoning by, 106

Erigeron heterophyllum (Fleabane), 179

Eriodyction glutinosum californicum. See Yerba santa

Ervum lens. See Lentils

Eucalyptus oil, in liniment, 151

Eugenia pimenta (Allspice), 175

Eupatorium purpureum. See Queen of the meadow

Euphrasia officinalis. See Eyebright

Everclear, 158

Evil, expelling, mugwort for, 65

Extracts, 149-58; fluid, 154, 156-58

Eyebright (*Euphrasia officinalis*), 61, 179

Eyes, herbs for: chamomile, 5; coltsfoot, 61; eyebright, 61. *See also* Eye wash herbs

Eyewash herbs: eyebright, 61; golden seal, 64; huckleberry, 64

Faircheeses. *See* Malva

Fantasy Mayonnaise, 94-95

Farrell, Michael, 89

Fatigue, scullcap for, 55

Fats, for salves, 153

Feebleness, wormwood for, 72

Feet, herbs for: alder, 55; coltsfoot, 61

Fennel (*Foeniculum officinale*), 13, 61, 62, 179; in bread, 2; in cough formula, 72; harvesting, 18; in stomach remedy, 68

Fenugreek (*Trigonella foenum-graecum*), 29, 61, 179

Fermented cabbage, 113

Fermented milk, 77

Fermented spirits. *See* Brews

Ferns, 157; Bracken, 26; Brake rock; *see* Polypody

Fever, herbs for: alum, 55; bee balm, 55; desert tea, 61; fenugreek, 61; Virginia dogwood, 72

Feverfew (*Pyrethrum parthenium*), 61, 179

Fir, balsam of, in liniment, 150

Fireash, as snail repellent, 13

Fish, 137-38; Brook Trout, 137-38; Goldenrod Sauce for, 96; Poached Salmon in Wine, 138

Five finger (*Potentilla canadensis*), 179

Flatulence, peppermint for, 4

Flavorings: fennel, 61; sassafrass, 71; woodruff, 72

Flax sprouts, 29

Flaxweed (*Linum usitatissimum*), 61, 179, 180

Fleabane (*Erigeron heterophyllum*), 179

Fleas, bay leaf for, 55

Floor mats, cattail for, 43

Flour, plantain for, 43

Flower Power Flower Salad, 101

Flowers: drying, 20-21; gathering, 18

Fluid extracts, 154, 156-58

Flu, herbs for, 71, 86

Fly poison, flaxweed as, 61

Foeniculum officinale. See Fennel

Foods, drying, 21, 23-24

Foot baths: alder, 55; noble yarrow as, 65; capsicum, 86-87

Foraging, 13-14; awareness and, 84; survival recipe for, 25-26, 28; tools for, 13-14. *See also* Gathering herbs

Forget-me-not, 13

Fragaria vesca. See Strawberry leaf

Frankincense (*Boswellia serrata*), 18, 179

Fruitfly, repelling, 23

Fruits: drying, 21, 23-24; gathering, 20

Fruit Salad, 92

Fucus versiculosis. See Bladderwrack; Kelp

Fudge, Teleport, 126

Fumatory (*Fumaria officinalis*), 179

Fungi, 129-36, 138

Furniture stain, 71

Galium aparine (Cleavers), 178

Garbanzo(s): Indian, 116; sprouts, 29

Garden green salad, 96

Gargle, herbs for: agrimony, 55; alder, 55; alum, 55; angelica, 55; barberry, 55; fenugreek, 55; kelp tea, 64; pimpernel, 68; strawberry leaf, for gums, 71; witch hazel, 72

Garlic (*Allium sativum*), 74, 179; and lemon wash, 93; planting, 14; skin, as moisture retardant, 23; toxicity of, 26

Garlic Miso Soup, 76

Garlic oil, toxicity of, 26

Garlic Soup, 75, 76

Garlic Vinegar, 98

Garlic/Watercress Soup, 76

Gathering herbs, 14, 17-18, 20, 24, 28, *See also* Foraging

Gaultheria procumbens. See Wintergreen

Gentian (*Gentiana lutea*), 61, 179

George Jones' Sensuous Soup, 79

Geranium maculatum (Storksbill), 190

Gerard, *Herball*, on comfrey, 32

Ghee, 96, 98

Giddiness, coltsfoot for, 61

Gillenia trifoliata. See Meadow sweet

Ginger root (*Asarum canadense*), 5, 61, 102, 179; in salve, 153

Ginseng (*Panax quinquefolia*), 28, 50, 61, 64, 179; foraging for, 14, 17; in honey, 24, 154; "women's," 55

Glucose, 35

Glug, Raisin, 147-48

Glycyrrhiza glabra. See Licorice

Godu kola, 55

Goldenrod (*Solidago odora*), 5, 64, 179; liniment, 150

Goldenrod Sauce, 96

Golden seal (*Hydrastis canadensis*), 28, 64, 179, 194; gathering, 17

Goldy's Goldenrod Sauce, 96

Gooseberries, drying, 23

Gooseberry Chutney, 98

Gooseberry preserves, 36

Gourmet magazine, 112

Gracilaria lichenoides. See Agar-agar

Grains, 103-13; leftover, over beans,

106-07; storing, 23. *See also* Breads
Grapes: drying, 24; wild, 4
Greek Pilaf Salad, 87
Green Dressing, 90
Green Drink, 42-43; lamb's quarters in, 65
Green Goo, Wild, 35
Greens: drying, 24; Herbal, Brown Rice and, 111; Mixed Herb, 90
Green Soup, 80
Grindelia (*Grindelia robusta*), 64, 179, 183
Groats, 104, 106
Ground ivy (*Nepeta glechoma*), 64, 183
Growing herbs, 11, 13, 14
Guacamole, 93
Guacamole Nasturtiums, 93
Guarana (*Paullinia sorbilis*), 183
Gum. *See* Chewing gum
Gum arabic (*Acacia vera*), 183
Gumpertz, Bob, 58, 151

Hair, herbs for, 58, 61, 71
Hamamelis virginica. See Witch hazel
Hawaiian kahuna, 4
Hawthorn (*Crataegus oxyacanthus*), 64, 183
Headaches, herbs for: lavender, 65; rue, 71; violets, 4; woodruff, 72
Heal-all. *See* Prunella vulgaris
Healing, places to study, 171, 173
Heart, herbs for, 5, 72
Heart trefoil, 5
Helen Smith's Seed Soup, 79
Helianthus annuus. See Sunflower
Heliotrope, 13
Hebron, Neil, 112
Hedeoma pulegioides. See Pennyroyal
Hemlock (*Conium maculatum*), 27; as poison, 26, 55
Hemorrhages, herbs for, 71, 86; postpartum, 106
Henna (*Lawsonia inermis*), 183
Heracleum lanatum (Motherwort), 184
Herb, defined, 14
Herbal Barley Burger, 107; Tomato Sauce for, 96
Herbalist's Charter, vii
Herbal Greens, Brown Rice and, 111
Herbal tea baths, 51
Herb drying box, 20
Herb Greens, Mixed, 90
Herb picker, 18
Herb Salad with Green Dressing, 90
Herb salt, 84
Herb vinegars, 98
Herby Lentil Herb Soup, 76
Hermodactyl, 2

Herpes simplex, 86, 87
Herpes zoster, 86
Hibiscus (*Hibiscus rosa-sinensis*), 183
Hickory (*Carya alba*), 117, 183
Hills, Lawrence D., 35
Hinjio, Padre, 157
Hippocras, 141, 144
Hollyhock (*Althaea rosea*), *181*, 183
Honey, 2, 4, 35-36; as basic food, 24; in berry preserves, 36; in blister ointment, 36; for extracts, 154; as preservative, 154
Honey Bars, Cosmic, 126
Hongos Rancheros Huevos, 134
Hook-heal. *See Prunella vulgaris*
Hops (*Humulus lupulus*), 64, 142, 183
Hops Beer, 142
Horehound (*Marrubium vulgare*), 13, 64, 72, 183
Horsemint: (*Mentha sp.,*), *12*; (*Monarda punctata*), 183
Horseradish (*Cochlearia armoracia*), 183; liniment, 150
Horsetail (*Equisetum hyemale*), 64, 183
Huckleberry (*Vaccinium myrtillus*), 64, 183
Hummos, 89
Humulus lupus. See Hops
Humus producers, wild greens as, 38
Hydrastis canadensis. See Golden seal
Hydromel, 141, 143-44
Hypericum perforatum. See St. John's wort
Hyssop (*Hyssopus officinalis*), 63, 64, 183

Illicum anisatum(Star anise), 191
Indian buckwheat, 43. *See also* Plantain
Indian Buckwheat Bread, 43
Indian Cattail Cakes, 125
Indian Garbanzos, 116
Indian nuts, gathering, 116
Indigestion, burdock for, 58
Infants: chafing, 61; diaper rash, 178; diapers for, 43
Irish moss (*Chondrus crispus*), 183
Infusions, 51
Ink, recipe for, 71
Inky caps, 134
Insects, herbs to repel, 13, 21, 23, 72. *See also* Bites; Stings
Insomnia, valerian root for, 72
Insulation, cattail for, 43
Interferon, capsicum and, 86
Internal bleeding, herbs for, 71, 86
Intestines, herbs for, 5
Inula helenium. See Elecampane
Iron, in mugwort, 65
Italian Sesame Cookies, 125-26

Itching, herbs for: lobelia, 65; nasturtium, 184; soap root, 71

Jam, 36; Tomato, 89-90
Japanese rose (*Rosa rugosa*), 42
Jefferson, Thomas, 137
Jenny Nelson's Barley Root Soup, 79
Jerusalem Artichoke Soup, 79-80
Jimson weed (*Datura stramonium*), *182*
Johnson, Lilia, 123
Joints, herbs for: nettles, 46, 52; shepherd's purse, 71. *See also* Arthritis
Juglans nigra. See Walnuts
Juniper (*Juniperus communis*), 64, 183

Kahuna, Hawaiian, 4
Kasha, 104, 106
Kathy's Herb Salad with Green Dressing, 90
Katz, Richard, 115
Kelp, 64, 78; Atlantic (*Laminaria saccharina*), Bladderwrack, 176; 183; Pacific (*Fucus versiculosus*), 183
Kidney beans, 5. *See also* Beans
Kidneys, herbs for, 5; black cohosh, 58; club moss, 61; dandelion, 31; elderberry, 61
Kif, 128
Kim chi, 87, 125
Kingston, Wayne, 124
Kinnikinnik, 55
Kirsch, Felicity, 124
Kneading bread, 119, 120, 122
Knit bone. *See* Comfrey

Labiatae, 13
Labrador (*Ledum latifolium*), 183
Lactuca elongata (Wild lettuce), 191
Lactuca sativa. See Lettuce; Miner's lettuce
Ladies' mantle (*Alchemilla vulgaris*), 183
Ladies' slipper (*Cypripedium pubescens*), 64-65, 183
Lamb, bergamot mint and, 140
Lamb's-quarters (*Chenopodium album*), 65, 183; in Green Drink, 42
Laminaria saccharina. See Kelp
Laminariales (Sea rocket), *118*
Lanolin: in massage cream, 154; in salves, 153
Laurus nobilis. See Bay laurel
Lavender (*Lavandula vera*), 13, 65, 183; in smoking mix, 61; in vinegar, 71
Lavender oil, in liniment, 151
Lawsonia inermis (Henna), 183
Laxatives: cascara bark, 58; slippery elm, 71

Leaves: drying, 20; gathering, 18
Ledum latifolium (Labrador), 183
Leek *(Allium porrum)*, 183
Leek oil, toxicity of, 26
Leftover Rice Over Beans Over, 106-07
Lemon *(Citrus limonum)*, 183; and garlic wash, 93; peel, 184; skin, in tonic, 158
Lemon balm *(Melissa officinalis)*, 52, 55, 65, 183, *185*
Lemon grass *(Androgpgon citratum)*, 183-84
Lentil Herb Soup, 76
Lentils *(Ervum lens)*, 184; sprouts, 29
Lentinus sp., 132, 134, *138*
Leonrus cardiaca (Motherwort), 184
Lettuce *(Lactuca sativa)*, 184; wild *(Lactuca elongata)*, 191
Liatrus odoratissima (Deer tongue), 179
Licorice *(Glycyrrhiza glabra)*, 184; in cough formula, 72; substitute for, 61; in tonic, 157
Life everlasting *(Antennaria margaritacum)*, 28, 52, *139*, 184
Life Force, 8, 14
Linden *(Tilia americana)*, 184
Linen, 61
Liniments, 150-51
Linseed oil, from flaxweed, 61
Linum usitatissimum. See Flaxweed
Liqueurs, coloring for, 64
Liver, herbs for, 5; agrimony, 4; black cohosh, 58; dandelion, 31; elderberry, 61
Lobelia *(Lobelia inflata)*, 65, 184
Lovage, 13
LSD, 106
Lungs, herbs for, 5; bay leaf, 55; goldenrod, 64; sarsaparilla, 71; smoking mixture, 61; violets, 4; yerba santa, 72
Lycopodium clavatum (Club moss), 61, 178

Macadamias, 117
Mace *(Myristica moschata)*, 184
Maceration, 156
Ma huang, 61
Maidenhair *(Adiantum pedatum)*, 157, 184
Majoon, 128
Mallow *(Malva)*, 37-38, *39*; in chewing gum, 37; in diuretic blend, 68; in Green Drink, 42; juniper berries with, 64; polypody with, 68; in Wild Green Goo, 35
Malva. See Mallow
Malva Mellow-jello, 38
Mandrake *(Podophyllum peltatum)*, 55, 184; in liniment, 150

Manure, 11
Manzanilla, See Chamomile
Manzanita *(Arctostaphylos glauca)*, 65, *172*, 184
Maple syrup, gathering, 18
Maranta arundinacea (Arrow root), 175
Marigold *(Calendula officinalis)*, 58, 184. See also Calendula
Marijuana *(Cannabis indica; C. sativa)*, 65, *152*, 184
Marinated Dandelion Salad, 84
Marjoram *(Origanum majorana)*, 65, 184
Marrubium vulgare. See Horehound
Marshmallow *(Althaea officinalis)*, 184
Marshmallow. See Mallow
Marty's Salad, 92
Masa, 124
Massage cream, 154
Masterwort *(Heracleum lanatum)*, 184
Marticaria chamomilla. See Chamomile
Mayapple. See Mandrake
Mayonnaise, 94-95; Fantasy, 94-95
May Wine, 72
Mead, 141; Rockin', 143
Meadow-saffron: as cathartic, 2; as poison, 26, 55
Meadow sweet *(Gillenia trifoliata)*, 18, 186
Measurements, 169
Meats, 137, 140; *protecting from spoilage,* 140; *Roasted Wild Duck, 140; Venison Steak, 137*
Medical properties, explained, 163-65
Melissa officinalis. See Lemon balm
Menstrual cycle, herbs for, 68
Mentha crispa. See Mint
Mentha piperita. See Peppermint
Mentha viridis. See Spearmint
Menthol: in liniment, 151; in massage cream, 154
Menzies, Archibald, 46
Mertensia virginica (Cowslip), 179
Metheglin, 141, 143
Mexican damiana. See Damiana
Micromeria donglassii; M. chamissonis (Yerba buena), 72, *159*, 192
Milk, fermented, 77
Millet, cooking, 104
Minerals: in amaranth, 55; in honey, 36; in malva, 37
Miner's lettuce *(Lactuca sativa)*, 46, *48*; in Green Drink, 42
Miner's Lettuce Luncheon Salad, 84
Mint *(Mentha crispa)*, 13, 28, *53*, 65, 184; in Green Drink, 42; growing, 14; in iced tea, 52; sprouts, 29; in vinegar, 71
Mint Apple Pie, 126
Miso, 76
Mistletoe *(Viscum flavescens)*, 184

Mixed Herb Greens, 90
Molluscum contagiosium, capsicum for, 87
Monarda. See Bee balm
Monarda punctata. See Horsemint
Morchella sp. (Morel), 134, *136*
Mordant, alum as, 55
Morel *(Morchella* sp.), 134, *136*
Morning Mush with Mushrooms, 132
Morning sickness, 68, 71
Moroccan Majoon, 128
Mother Cider Vinegar, 147
Mother-in-law Salad, 92
Mother's milk, increasing, 58
Motherwort *(Leonrus cardiaca)*, 184
Mountain ash preserves, 36
Mouth, refreshing, fennel for, 61
Mucous membranes, capsicum for, 86
Mud plasters, 151
Mugwort *(Artemisia vulgaris; A. japonica)*, 5, 13, *22*, 65, 66, 184; to repel insects, 21; in tea, 52
Muir, John, ink recipe from, 71
Mullein *(Verbascum thapsus)*, 5, 65, *160*, 184
Munchin' Luncheon, 124
Mung sprouts, 29
Muscles, sore, tansy oil for, 72
Mushrooms, 129-36, *138*; basic recipes for, 131; Champignons a la Mingus, 132; drying, 24; fried, 132; Morning Mush with, 132; soup, 132; stewed, 131
Mustard, 13, 38, 184; black *(Sinapis nigra)*, 97; in plaster, 151; in Wild Green Goo, 35; yellow *(Sinapis alba)*, 40
Mustard Flower Salad, 38
Mustard Leaf Syrup, 38
Mustard oil, in massage cream, 154
Mustard plaster, 151
Mustard seed, in liniment, 150
Mustard Seed Cakes, 38, 125
Mutton tallow, in liniment, 150
Myddfai physicians, 31
Myrica cerifera (Bayberry), 176
Myristica moschata (Mace), 184. See also Nutmeg
Myrospermum pubescens. See Myrrh
Myrrh *(Myrospermum pubescens)*, 13, 18, 184

Nasturtium officinale. See Watercress
Nasturtiums *(Tropaeolum majus)*, 67, 184; flowers, 65; Guacamole, 93
Nature's Herb Co., 83
Nepeta cataria (Catnip), 178
Nepeta glechoma. See Ground ivy
Nervousness, herbs for, 65, 72; in

children, 58. *See also* Relaxing herbs
Nettle (*Urtica capitata; U. dioica*), 46, 47, 184; bath, 52; rash, 61, 71; in tea, 52
Noble pine, 65
Noble yarrow, 65. *See also* Yarrow
Nose, sores in, bloodroot for, 58
Nut butters, 117
Nutmeg (*Myristica moschata*), 187; in tonic, 158
Nuts, 117

Oak (*Quercus* sp.), 68; white (*Quercus alba*), 191
Oats (*Avena sativa*), 105, 187; cooking, 104
Ocimum basilicum. See Basil
Oils: for liniments, 150; for salves, 153
Oil and Vinegar Dressing, 96
Ointments, 151, 153-54; Elm, 154; calendula, 58; C-R-Star Salve, 153; Rose Water, 154
Okra (*Abelmoschus esculentus*), 68, 187
Olive (*Olea europaea*), 7, 187
Onion(s) (*Allium cepa*), 114, 187; drying, 24; skin, as moisture retardant, 23; toxocity of, 26; wild, 28
Ononis spinosa (Rest harrow), 187
Orange (*Citrus aurantium*), 187
Orange-mint, 13
Orange water, in tonic, 157
Orchid, Dendrobium, 4
Orchis mascula (Salep), 188
Oregano (*Origanum vulgare*), 187; in liniment, 150
Oregon grape root, 55, 153
Origanum majorana. See Marjoram
Origanum vulgare. See Oregano
Overexcitement, scullcap for, 55
Oxalic acid, 61
Oxalis weed, 61

Padre Hinjio, 157
Pan, 119
Panax quinquefolia. See Ginseng
Pancreas, infections of, 71
Papaver somniferum (Poppy), 4, 187
Parkinson, *Theatrum Botanicum*, on comfrey, 32
Parsley (*Petroselinum sativum*), 13, 187; in Green Drink, 42; hemlock vs., 26; with huniper berries, as diuretic, 64
Passion flower (*Passiflora coerulea*), 68, 187
Pasture rose (*Rosa carolina*), 42
Paullinia sorbilis (Guarana), 183
Peaches (*Amygdalus persica*), 187; drying, 24

Peanut Butter Cookies, 128
Peanuts, 117
Pears, drying, 24
Pecans, 117
Pedicularis canadensis. See Wood betony
Penicillin, 95
Pennyroyal (Gedeoma pulegioides), 68, 100, 187; in liniment, 150; to repel insects, 21, 23
Pepper, cayenne. *See* Capsicum
Pepper, white (*Piper album*), 187
Peppergrass, 13
Peppermint (*Mentha piperita*), 5, 13, 68, 187; in liniment, 150; for putrefaction/flatulence, 4
Peppermint oil: in liniment, 151; in massage cream, 151
Peppermint Stomach Essence, 68
Percolation, 156
Periwinkle (*Vinca minor; V. major*), 187
Perspiration, inducing: broom for, 58; elderberry for, 61
Peruvian bark, in tonic, 157
Petroselinum sativum. See Parsley
Pfardresher, Leslie, 96
Pickled Chicory Flowers, 32
Pickled Vegetables, 89
Pies: Apple Mint, 126; Asparagus, 124-25; Carrot, 125; Vegetable, 122-23
Pignolia, 116
Pillow stuffing, cattail for, 43
Pimpernil, 13, 68
Pimpinella anisum. See Anise
Pine: noble, 65; white (*Pinus palustris*), 191
Pineapple-mint, 13
Pine gum, in massage cream, 154
Pine nuts, 116
Pine pitch (*Abies canadensis*), 37; in blister ointment, 36; gathering, 18; in liniment, 150
Pinon, 116
Pinus palustris (White pine), 191
Piper album (White pepper), 187
Piper cubeba (Cubeb berries), 179
Pipsissewa (*Chimaphila umbellata*), 65, 187
Pita, 122
Plantago lanceolata. See Plantain
Plantago psyllium (Psyllium), 187
Plantain (*Plantago lanceolata*), 3, 4, 43, 45, 46, 187; in cakes, 125; gathering, 17; as grain, 1-2, 43, 106; as Indian buckwheat, 1-2; in plaster, 151; sprouts, 29
Plantain Seed Mush, 43
Plasters, 151
Pleurotes, 132

Plums, drying, 24
Poached Salmon in Wine, 138
Podhurst, Nathan and Emma, 83
Podophyllum peltatum. See Mandrake
Poisoning, antidotes for, 26; Angelica, 26, 55; hound's tongue, 5
Poison oak (*Rhus toxicondendron*), 189; elderberry salve for, 61; ladies' slipper, 64; plaintain, 46; quercus, 68
Poisonous bites, blessed thistle for, 58
Poke (*Phytolacca decandra*), 28, 187; gathering, 17
Polenta, 104
Pollen, cattail, 125
Polygala senega. See Snakeroot
Polygonum bistorta (Bistort), 176
Polypody (*Polypodium*), 68, 69
Poplar, white (*Populus tremuloides*), 191
Poppy (*Papaver somniferum*), 4, 187
Populus candicans (Balm of Gilead bud), 175
Populus tremuloides (White poplar), 191
Potato(es): Goldenrod Sauce for, 96; poison parts of, 26; wild, 28; Yogurt Salad, 90
Potentilla canadensis (Five finger), 179
Preparedness products, 173
Preserves, 36
Protein: in almond, 55; in amaranth, 55; in cattail pollen, 43; in grains, 103; in mustard buds, 38; in soybeans, 115-16
Prunella vulgaris (Self-heal; Woundwort), 68, 192; extract of, 158
Prunus amygdalus. See Almond
Prunus virginiana. See Wild cherry bark
Psiulocybin mushrooms, 134
Psyllium (*Plantago psyllium*), 187
Puffballs (*Calvatia* sp.), 134
Putrefaction, peppermint for, 4
Pyrethrum parthenium. See Feverfew
Pythagoras, 2, 4, 35

Quaccia, Lawrence, 131
Quassia (*Simarouba excelsa*), 187
Queen of the meadow (*Spirea ulmaria; Eupatorium purpureum*), 187
Quercus (Oak), 68
Quercus alba (White oak), 191
Quake grass, 68
Quillaya saponaria (Soap bark), 188
Quince: plaster, 151; preserves, 36

Radioactivity, soup for combating, 79
Radish (*Raphanus sativus*), 187; sprouts, 29
Rain water, 49
Raisin Glug, 147-48

Ranunculus (Buttercup), as poison, 26
Raphanus sativus. See Radish
Raspberry(ies) (*Rubus idaeus*): berries, drying, 23; leaves, 68, 71, 187
Rash, from nettles, 61, 71. *See also* Poison oak
Read, Hugh, 51
Red clover (
Read, Hugh, 51
Red clover (*Trifolium pratense*), 71, *145*, 187
Redwood, 71
Redwood Remedy, 161-62
Relaxing herbs: chamomile, 58; hops/chamomile, 64; okra seeds, 68; passion flower, 68. *See also* Nervousness
Rennet, alternative to, 46
Respiratory troubles, yew syrup for, 72
Rest harrow (*Ononis spinosa*), 187
Rhamnus crocea (Buckthorn), 176
Rhamnus purschiana. See Cascara bark
Rheumatism, 144
Rheum palmatum. See Rhubarb
Rhodymenia palmata (Dulse), 179
Rhubarb (*Rheum palmatum; Theum hybridum*), 1, 188; drying, 24; for sluggishness, 71-72
Rhus toxicodendron. See Poison oak
Rice, 107, 110-13; Brown, with Herbal Greens, 111; cooking, 110-11; Curried, 112; leftover, with beans, 106-07; Wild, 107, 110, 111
Roasted Wild Duck, 140
Roasting, for nuts, 117
Rockin' Mead, 143
Root beer, 141-42
Roots: drying, 20; gathering, 17
Roquefort Mayonnaise, 95
Rosa carolina (Pasture rose), 42
Rosa eglantaria (Sweetbriar rose; Eglantine), 42
Rosa rugosa (Japanese rose), 42
Rose (*Rosa* sp.), 38, 42; in tonic, 157; wild, *41*
Rosebuds (*Rosa canina*), 188; in sleep pillow, 65
Rose Hip Conserve, 42
Rose hips, 188; for Vitamin C., 42; in flu tea, 71; in salve, 153
Rosemary (*Rosmarinus officinalis*), 5, 13, 85, 188; for falling hair, 58; in sleep pillow, 65; in smoking mix, 61
Rose Petal Salad, 98, 101
Rose Vinegar, 42
Rose Water Ointment, 154
Rosicrucians, 42
Rosin, 156; in linimenty, 150
Rosin weed, 64
Rosmarinus officinalis. See Rosemary

Rubus villosus (Blackberry), 176
Rue (*Ruta graveolens*), 71, 188
Rumex acetosella; R. acetosa (Sorrel), *81*
Rumex crispus. See Dock; Yellow dock
"Russian asparagus," 43. *See also Cattail*
Ruta graveolens (Rue), 71, 188
Rye: cooking, 106; gathering, 106; wild (*Secale cereale*), *108*

Sabbatia angularis (Centuary herb), 178
Safflower (*Carthamus tinctorius*), 188
Saffron (*Crocus sativus*), 188
Sage (*Salvia officinalis*), 5, 13, 28, 70, 71, 188; in liniment, 150; in sleep pillow, 65; in vinegar, 71
Sage (*Salvia* sp.), 127
St. Benedict thistle (*Cnicus benedictus*), 188
St. John's bread (*Ceratonia siliqua*), 126, 188. *See also* Carob
St. John's wort (*Hypericum perforatum*), 5, 71, 188
Salad bowl, 83
Salad dressings: Fantasy Mayonnaise, 94-95; Green, 90; Gucacamole, 93; herb vinegar blend for, 71; ingredients for, 96; Mayonnaise, 94-95; Mother-in-law, 92; Oil and Vinegar, 96; Roquefort Mayonnaise, 95; Thousand Island, 95
Salads, 2, 83-84, 87-93, 98, 101; amaranth in, 55; bean, 113; burnet in, 58; cattail in, 43; chicory in, 31, 32; Chommos, 89; dandelion, 31, 84; Deer Dew Meadow, 84; dressings for; *see* Salad dressings; elecampane in, 61; fennel in, 61; Flower Power Flower, 101; Fruit, 92; garden green, 95-96; Hummos, 89; Kim chi, 87; lamb's quarters in, 65; Marty's 92; miner's lettuce in, 46; Miner's Lettuce Luncheon, 84; Mother-in-law, 92; mugwort in, 65; Mustard Flower, 38; mustard leaves in, 38; Pickled Vegetables, 89; plantain in, 46; Rose Petal, 98, 101; Sandy's, 90; Tabuli, 87; Yogurt Potato, 90
Salep (*Orchis mascula*), 188
Salicin, 4
Salix alba (White willow), 191
Salmon, Poached in Wine, 138
Salt, herb, 84
Salting, for nuts, 117
Salt supplement, kelp as, 64
Salves, 151, 153-54; Arnica, 55; burn, 58; C-R-Star, 153; mullein, 65
Salvia hispanica (Chia), *177, 178*
Salvia officinalis. See Sage
Salvia sp. *See* Sage

Sambucus nigra (Elder), 179. *See also* Elderberry
Sandalwood (*Santalum album*), 188
Sandy's Salad, 90
Sanguinaria canadensis. See Bloodroot
Sanicle (*Sanicula marilandica*), 188
Sanquisorba officinalis (Burnet), 58, 176
Santalum album (Sandalwood), 188
Sap, gathering, 18
Saponaria officinalis. See Soapwort
Sarsaparilla (*Smilax officinalis*), 28, 71, 188
Sassafras (*Sassafras officinale*), 28, 71, 188; in sleep pillow, 65
Satureja hortensis (Savory), 188
Sauces: Goldy's Goldenrod, 96; Tomato, 96
Sauerkraut, 113
Savory (*Satureja hortensis*), 188
Sciatica, rue for, 71
Scotch Barley Soup, 77
Scotch broom (*Cytisus scoparius*), 18, *19*, 188. *See also* Broom
Scrapes, plasters for, 151
Scratches, polypody for, 68
Scullcap (*Scutellaria lateriflora*), 55, 188
Scurvy: essence of spruce for, 37: oil of lemon for, 93; passion flower for, 68
Scurvy weed, 84. *See also* Miner's lettuce
Sea onion, 4
Sea rocket (*Laminariales*), *118*
Sea water, 46
Seaweed(s), 78-79; products, 8. *See also* Dulse
Seaweed-Burdock-Onion Soup, 79
Seaweed Soupreme, 78-79
Secale cereale (wild rye), *108*
Seed procurement stores, 170-71
Seeds: drying, 18; gathering, 13, 18; storing, 23. *See also* Sprouts
Seed Soup, 79
Self-heal. *See Prunella vulgaris*
Seng. *See* Ginseng
Senna (*Cassia autifolia*), 188
Sesame butter, 89
Sesame Cookies, Italian, 125-26
Sesame oil, in massage cream, 154
Sesame Tahini, 89
Shagymane (*Coprinus* sp.), 134
Shalfey. *See* Sage
Shaman, 4
Shavegrass, 64; in tonic, 158
Sheep sorrel. *See* Sorrel
Shepherd's purse (*Capsella bursa pastoris*), 71, 188
Shortness of breath: bee balm for, 55; tonic for, 157
Shurtleff, Bill, 115
Sicklwort, 68. *See also Prunella vulgaris*

Signatures, doctrine of, 4, 5, 7
Silica: in desert tea, 61; in horsetail, 64; in quick grass, 68
Simarouba excelsa (Quassia), 187
Simples, 4, 29-49
Simply Sweet Cider, 144, 147
Sinapis alba; S. nigra. See Mustard
Sinus infections, capsicum for, 86
Skin, eliminating impurities through, elderberry for, 61
Skin, herbs for: lamb's quarters, 65; lobelia, 65; pimpernel, 68; *St. John's wort*, 5; *sycamore*, 72; *woodruff*, 72
Skin cleansers: ladies' slipper, 64; *witch hazel*, 72
Skin disorders, herbs for: bloodroot, 58; *capsicum*, 86; *sarsaparilla*, 71
Sleep pillows, 65
Slippery elm (Ulmus fulva), 71, 188
Slippery Elm Food Beverage, 38
Slippery tongue. *See* Mallow
Sluggishness, tea for, 71-72
Smilax officinalis. See Sarsaparilla
Smoking herbs: bearberry, 55; broom, 58; ceremonial, 72; coltsfoot, 61; goldenrod, 64; marijuana, 65; marjoram, 65; mixture, 61; yerba santa, 72
Snail repellent, fireash as, 13
Snakebite, 5
Snakeroot (*Polygala senega*), 5, 28, 188
Snuff, lobelia as, 65
Soap, yucca roots for, 72
Soap bark (*Quillaya saponaria*), 188
Soap root (*Cholorogalum pomeridianum*), 71, 167
Soapwort, (*Saponaria officinalis*), 188, 191
Soil, improving. *See* Composting; Humus producers
Solanum dulcamara (Bittersweet), 176
Solar tea, 51
Solidago odora. See Goldenrod
Solomon's seal, 5
Solutions, 149, 156
Soma, *viii*
Sores: coltsfoot for, 61; internal and external, plasters for, 151; in nose, bloodroot for, 58
Sore throats: capsicum for, 86; Malva Mellow-jello for, 37-38
Sorrel (*Rumex acetosella; R. acetosa*), 81, 188, 191
Soups, 75-82; Barley Roots, 79; Borsch, 77-78; cattail in, 43; chicory in, 31, 32; Earthy Sea, 78; Garlic, 75; Garlic Miso, 76; Garlic/Watercress, 76; George Jones' Sensuous, 79; Green, 80; Helen Smith's Seed, 79; Herby Lentil Herb, 76; Jenny Nelson's Barley Root,

79; Jerusalem Artichoke, 79-80; miner's lettuce in, 46; mugwort in, 65; mushroom, 132; nettle in, 46; plantain in, 46; sage in, 71; Scotch Brley, 77; Seaweed-Burdock-Onion, 79; Seaweed Soupreme, 78-79; Seed, 79; suggestions for, 82; Thrower's Jerusalem Artichoke, 79-80; Weedy Wild, 80; Yogurt Beet, 77-78; Yogurt and Cucumber, 77
Sourdough Bread, 123
Sourdough Starter, Grandmother's, 123
Soya Milk, 115, 116
Soybeans, 115-16; sprouted, 29, 115
Soy-cornmeal bread, 124
Spearmint (*Mentha viridis*), 13, 191
Spermaceti ointment, 154
Spikenard (*Aralia racemosa*), 71, 191; liniment, 150
Spirea ulmaria. See Queen of the meadow
"Spirits," 92
Sprains, wormwood for, 72
Spring tonic, 46
Spring water, 49
Sprouting, 13, 29-30; altitude and, 21; beans, 113,; grains, 103
Sprouts, 29-30; alfalfa, 29; quack grass, 68; soybean, 29, 115
Spruce, essence of, for beer, 37
Spruce pitch, for chewing gum, 68
Spruce sap, for chewing gum, 37
Squash Blossoms, Stuffed, 98; with Morels, 134
Squaw mints. *See* Pennyroyal
Stain, redwood, 71
Star anise (*Illicum anisatum*), 191
Stellaria media. See Chickweed
Stigmata maydis (Cornsilk), 178-79
Stings, herbs for: plantain, 46; wormwood, 4. *See also* Bites
Stomach, herbs for, 5; bay leaves, 55; calendula, 58; ginger root, 61; yew twig, 72
Stomach, strengthening herbs for: American scullcap, 55; ginseng, 64
Stomach complaints, herbs for: blessed thistle, 58; for children, 68; huckleberry, 64; St. John's wort, 71; slippery elm, 71; tansy, 72; yarrow, 4
Stomach worms, wormwood for, 72
Storing: dried foods, 23; herbs, 21
Storksbill (*Geranium maculatum*), 190
Strawberry leaf (*Fragaria vesca*), 71-72, 191; with huckleberry, 64; in tonic, 157; with woodruff, 72
Strep throat, capsicum for, 86
Stress, ladies' slipper for, 65
Stuffed Squash Blossoms, 98; with Morels, 134

Styrax benzoin (Benzoin), 176
Succory, 32. *See also* Chicory
Sugar, 35-36
Sunflower (*Helianthus annuus*), 191; sprouts, 29
Sun infused tea, 51
Survival foraging recipe, 25-26, 28
Survivalists's tinder, 72
Survival preparedness products, 173
Survival soup, 78
Sweet bay. *See* Bay laurel
Sweetbriar rose (*Rosa eglantaria*), 42
Swellings, wormwood for, 72
Sycamore, 72
Sycamore maple (*Acer pseudo-platanus*), 191
Symphytum officinale. See Comfrey
Syphilis, spikenard for, 71
Syrups, 150; blackberry, 58

Tabuli, 87
Tahini, sesame, 89
Tanacetum vulgare. See Tansy
Tansy (*Tanacetum vulgare*), 72, 191; to repel insects, 13, 23, 72
Tap water, 46
Tara Cream-Earth Massage, 154
Taraxicum dens-leonis. See Dandelion
Tarragon (*Artemisia dracunculus*), 191
Tar weed, 64
Teas, 51-72; alfalfa, 29; for baths; *see* Baths; brewing, 51, 52; decoction, 51; iced, 52; infusion, 51; plantain, 46; solar, 51
Teleport Fudge, 126
Theum hybridum. See Rhubarb
Thirst, herbs for: barberry, 55; yerba santa, 72
Thistle (*Cardrius*), *i*, 166
Thousand Island Dressing, 95
Throat, herbs for: goldenrod, smoked, 64; horehound, 64. *See also* Sore throat
Thrower's Jerusalem Artichoke Soup, 79-80
Thyme (*Thymus vulgaris*), 13, 28, 88, 191; in woodruff tea blend, 72
Tilia americana (Linden), 184
Tinctures, 154, 156; Arnica montana, 55
Tinder: puffball threads as, 134; yucca as, 72
Tiredness, nettles for, 46
Tisanes, 52
Titus, Roy, 120
Tobacco. *See* Smoking herbs
Tofu Dressing, 115-16
Tomatoes, poison parts of, 26
Tomato Jam, 89-90

Tomato Sauce, 96
Tongue, herbs for, 5
Tonics, 157-58; bearberry, 55; black cohosh, 58; elecampane, 61; goldenrod, 64; manzanita, 65; quercus, 68; for shortness of breath, 157; strawberry leaf, 71
Tonics, bitter: noble yarrow, 65; wormwood, 72
Tonic, digestive, soap root/watercress as, 71
Tonics, kidney and liver: black cohosh, 58; elderberry wine, 61
Tonic, preventive, capsicum as, 86
Toothache, herbs for: pimpernel, 68; yarrow, 4
Tree beard, 61
Trifolium pratense. See Red clover
Trigonella foenum-graecum. See Fenugreek
Trillium pendulum (Beth root), 176
Triticum sp. (Wild wheat), *109*
Tropaeolum majus. See Nasturtiums
Trout, Brook, 137-38
Turner, *1568 Herball,* on comfrey, 32
Turpentine, Venice, in liniment, 150
Tussilago farfara (Coltsfoot), 61, 178
Turnera aphrodisiaca. See Damiana
Typha latifolia. See Cattail

Ulcers: comfrey for, 32; okra for, 68; peptic, preventive, 29; sarsaparilla for, 71
Ulmus fulva. See Slippery elm
Umbelliferae, 13
Unguentum cetacei; U. leniens. 154
Upper respiratory complaints, capsicum for, 86
Urine, 49; increasing flow of, 64
Urtica capitata; U. dioica. See Nettle
Utensils, 168
Uva ursi, 55, 191. *See also* Bearberry

Vaccinium frondosum (Blueberry), 176
Vaccinium myrtillus (Huckleberry), 64, 183
Valerian (*Valeriana officinalis*), 52, 72, 191
Vegetable Pie, 122-23
Vegetables: *al dente,* 76; drying, 21, 23-24
Venereal disease, sarsaparilla for, 71; spikenard for, 71
Venice turpentine, in liniment, 150
Venison Steak, 137

Verbascum thapsus. See Mullein
Verbena officinalis (Vervain), 191
Vervain (*Verbena officinalis*), 191
Viburnum prunifolium (Black haw), 176
Villoldo, Alberto, 31
Vinca minor; V. major (Periwinkle), 187
Vinegar: blackberry wine, 58; Garlic, 98; Herb, 98; herbal blend for, 71; Mother Cider, 147; Rose, 42
Viola tricolor, 5
Violets (*Viola tricolor*), 4, 68, 191
Viral illnesses, capsicum for, 86, 87
Virginia dogwood, 72
Viscum flavescens (Mistletoe), 184
Vitamin A: in capsicum, 86; in chicory, 31; in malva, 37; in mustard, 38
Vitamin B, in whole grains, 103
Vitamin C: in capsicum, 86; in chicory, 31; in mustard, 38; in rose hips, 4
Vitamin E, in mustard, 38
Vitamin U, 29
Vodfrey, 35
Voice, fading, Mustard Leaf Syrup for, 38

Walnuts (*Juglans nigra*), 5, 117, 191
"Warming," alder nuts in brandy for, 55
Warts, capsicum for, 86
Wasp stings, wormwood for, 4
Water, 46, 49; dew, 46; distilled, 46; for extracts, 156, 157; of life, 49; purifying, 157; rain, 49; recycling of, 49; sea, 46; spring, 49; tap, 46
Watercress (*Nasturtium officinale*), 13, 15, 191; in digestive tonic, 71; sprouts, 29
Water retention, herbs for. *See* Diuretics
Watery conditions, mud plasters for, 151
Weedy Wild Soup, 80
Weights and measures, 169
Wheat: as basic food, 25; cooking, 106; wild (*Triticum* sp.), *109*
Wheat grass juice, bee pollen and, 36
White corn, cooking, 104
White oak (*Quercus alba*), 191
White pine (*Pinus palustris*), 191
White poplar (*Populus tremuloides*), 191
White rice, 110, 111
White willow (*Salix alba*), 191
Whole wheat. *See* Wheat
Whild cherry bark (*Prunus virginiana*), 191; in tonic, 157
Wild Duck, Roasted, 140
Wild Green Drink, 42-43
Wild Green Goo, 35

Wild greens. *See* Greens
Wild lettuce (*Lactuca elongata*), 191
Wild oats (*Avena sativa*), 105
Wild rice, 107, 110, 111
Wild rose (*Rosa* sp.), *41. See also* Rose
Wild rye (*Secale cereale*), *108*
Wild wheat (*Triticum* sp.), *109*
Wild yam (*Dioscorea villosa*), 191-92
Willow, white (*Salix alba*), 191
Willow bark, for aches and pains, 4
Wine: Berry, 147; blackberry, 58; dandelion, 147; in tonics, 158
Wintergreen (*Gaultheria procumbens*), 72, 192; liniment, 150; in massage cream, 154
Witch hazel (*Hamamelis virginica*), 72, 192
"Women's ginseng," 55
Wood betony (*Pedicularis canadensis*), 192; liniment, 150. *See also* Betony
Woodruff (*Asperula odorata*), 72, 73, 192; liniment, 150
Worms, expelling, wormwood for, 4
Wormwood (*Artemisia absinthium*), 4, 13, 72, 192; in liniment, 150; in stomach remedy, 68; tea, 52; in vinegar, 71
Wounds, herbs for, 5; burnet, 58; cattail, 43; goldenrod, 64; golden seal, 64; nettles, 46; comfrey, 32; slippery elm, 71; soap root, 71; spikenard, 71; yarrow, 4
Wounds, mud plasters for, 151
Woundwort. *See Prunella vulgaris*

Yarrow (*Achillea millefolium*), 4, *121,* 192; in blister ointment, 36
Yellow corn, cooking, 104
Yellow dock (*Rumex crispus*), 28, 192; gathering, 17
Yellow mustard. *See* Mustard
Yerba buena (*Micromeria donglassii; M. chamissonis*), 72, *159,* 192
Yerba mansa, *193*
Yerba santa (*Eriodyction glutinosum californicum*), 72, 192
Yew, 72
Yogurt, 77
Yogurt Beet Soup, 77-78
Yogurt and Cucumber Soup, 77
Yogurt Potato Salad, 90
Yucca, 72; as grain, cooking, 106

Zea mays (Cornsilk), 178-79